Gertruda's Oath

Doubleday

NEW YORK LONDON TORONTO

SYDNEY AUCKLAND

Gertruda's Oath

A CHILD, A PROMISE, AND
A HEROIC ESCAPE
DURING WORLD WAR II

Ram Oren

Consultation by Michael Stolowitzky
Translation by Barbara Harshav

DD

DOUBLEDAY

Translation copyright © 2009 by Doubleday

Published in the United States by Doubleday Religion, an imprint of the Crown
Publishing Group, a division of Random House, Inc., New York.
www.crownpublishing.com

DOUBLEDAY and the DD colophon are registered
trademarks of Random House, Inc.

Originally published in Hebrew in Israel as *Shevu'ah* by Keshet Publishing,
Tel Aviv, in 2007. Copyright © 2007 by Keshet Publishing.

Library of Congress Cataloging-in-Publication Data
Oren, Ram.
[Shevu'ah. English]
Gertruda's oath : a child, a promise, and a heroic escape during
World War II / Ram Oren ; consultation by Michael Stolowitzky ; translation
by Barbara Harshav. — 1st ed.
p. cm.
Includes bibliographical references.
ISBN 978-0-385-52718-7 (alk. paper)
1. Stolovitski, Mikha'el, 1936– 2. Jews—Poland—Biography. 3. Babilinskah,
Gertrudah, 1902–1995. 4. Righteous Gentiles in the Holocaust—Biography.
5. Holocaust survivors—Biography. 6. Holocaust, Jewish (1939–1945)—Poland—
Biography. 7. Holocaust, Jewish (1939–1945)—Germany—Biography.
8. World War, 1939–1945—Jews—Rescue—Poland. I. Title.
DS134.72.S76O7413 2009
940.53'18092—dc22
[B]
2008054444

ISBN 978-0-385-52718-7

PRINTED IN THE UNITED STATES OF AMERICA

Book design by Jennifer Ann Daddio/Bookmark Design & Media Inc.

1 3 5 7 9 10 8 6 4 2

First American Edition

CONTENTS

ACKNOWLEDGMENTS

I am grateful to Michael Palgon, Kevin Tobin, and the entire Doubleday team involved with this book. I'd like to thank my editor at Doubleday, Darya Porat, not only for her faith and determination in bringing this book to an English language audience, but also for overseeing the book's translation and for her talents as a diligent, deft editor of the book's manuscript. Deep thanks to our wonderful agent, David Kuhn, and Billy Kingsland from Kuhn Projects, who skillfully guided us throughout this project. To Geoffrey Weill—thank you.

To Professor Elie Weisel, for the kind words.

Also to the late Chaim Stolowitzky, Dr. Mordecai Paldiel, Judge Arie Segalson, the late Elisheva (Helga) Rink-Bernson, and to the captain of the *Exodus*, Ike Aaronovitch.

And last but certainly not least, to my dear friend Michael Stolowitzky, without whom this book could not have been written.

Gertruda's Oath is a true story. All of the events described in the book are based on my interviews with family members and survivors of the Holocaust, contemporaneous documents, and my research of those events. However, because *Gertruda's Oath* is based in large part on the recollections of those involved (many of whom have since passed, including Gertruda), it was necessary for me to use my skills as an author to compose parts of the dialogue and to fill in details of certain events to facilitate the narrative. Michael and Gertruda's story, and the story of all those affected by the Holocaust, is poignant history, and is here told as close to fact as possible.

Gertruda's Oath

The smoke clouds of war slowly began to dissipate and the spring sun broke through, caressing the ruins that buried tens of thousands of human beings, flooding the devastated streets, and scattering sparks of light on the waters of the broad Vistula River that slowly bubbled up to wash away memories of dread and death.

On the hill, above scarred Warsaw, stood the ancient and magnificent mansion of the Stolowitzky family, which had miraculously survived the war intact. Four floors of hewn stone, carved edges, statues of ancient warriors on the roof ledge, impressive mosaic windows and painted wooden ceilings.

Only two of the original inhabitants of the mansion were still alive, a boy and his nanny, and they were on their way to another country, far away. In their new home, between peeling walls, rust spots spreading in the bathtub, and cheap furniture—that mansion with all its splendor and charm seemed like a daydream, the product of an overactive imagination.

The boy and his nanny, who adopted him as a son, lived in a small apartment in one of the alleys of Jaffa, in a tenement. From the window, they saw only dreary buildings, children playing in an abandoned yard, and women returning home from the market, carrying heavy shopping bags. Most of the day, the apartment was invaded by the noise of passing cars and the stench of garbage. In winter the smell of mildew permeated the rooms, and in summer the walls trapped a blazing stifling air.

In the mansion on the hill, everything, of course, was different. The big building with its spacious wings, its gardens, was properly heated in winter and properly cooled in summer. A pure breeze from the river blew in the windows and servants tiptoed about to avoid any undue noise. The closets were stuffed with expensive clothes. Luxurious meals were served in rare china dishes. The old heavy cutlery, polished clean, was gold, and the wine was poured into fine crystal glasses.

Michael Stolowitzky and his adoptive mother, Gertruda, had survived the war and now both of them were struggling to survive in the new land. He attended school. She was past her prime by now. Every morning she'd go to work as a cleaning woman in the northern part of the city and return in the evening, her joints aching and her eyes weary. Michael would greet her with a kiss, take off her shoes, cook her meager supper, and make her bed. He knew she was working too hard only to have enough money to send him to school and provide for all his needs. He swore that someday he would pay her back generously for everything she had done for him—for saving him from death, for devoting her life to him, for making sure he didn't lack anything.

Poverty and shortages weren't strangers to Michael Stolowitzky. He had experienced them throughout his journey of survival in the world war, but he also saw light at the end of the tunnel, the end of penury, the end of the daily struggle for existence. He believed that someday, in the not-too-distant future, everything would change and things would go back to the way they were, to the days when they knew wealth and comfort, days far from suffering and torments.

His rosy future was within reach, clear and concrete. Only a four-hour flight from Israel lay a blocked treasure, millions of dollars and gold bars deposited in Swiss banks by his late father, Jacob, the Jew who was called "the Rockefeller of Poland." Michael was his only heir.

The legacy, a small recompense for the suffering and loss of the war, filled Michael's thoughts and assumed a central place in his fantasies. When he was recruited into the Israeli army, he waited impatiently for his military service to end so he could work on getting the money. He was sent to a battle unit and was wounded in the leg by a bullet from a Syrian sniper during a firefight in the northern Kinneret.

Groaning in pain, he was taken to the operating room in the hospital in Poriya. When he opened his eyes after the anesthesia wore off, he saw his adoptive mother weeping. He held his weak hand to her and she clutched it to her bosom.

"Don't cry," he said. "I promise you that everything will be fine."

When he was discharged from the army, he returned to their small apartment and the very next day he went to look for work. No work was beneath him. He was a messenger on a scooter, running around all hours of the day among customers in Tel Aviv; he worked as a waiter in the evening; and he was a guard at a textile factory at night. It was important for him to save up money.

Two years later, in June 1958, he took all his savings and the surviving family documents and bought an airplane ticket to Zurich.

"How long will you be there?" asked Gertruda anxiously.

"Two or three days. I don't think I'll have to stay any longer than that."

"And if they won't give you the money?"

He smiled at her confidently. "Why won't they? You'll see, I'll come back with my inheritance and our whole life will change," he promised.

She went to the airport with him and kissed him good-bye.

"Take care of yourself," she said. "And take care of the money. Don't let them steal it from you."

"Don't worry," he replied.

He got on the plane, excited and anxious. In Zurich he rented a small room and couldn't fall asleep all night. He had only the name of one bank among those where his father had deposited his funds, and the next day he went there. He pictured the bank clerks bringing him heaps of money and his adoptive mother welcoming him when he got back to Israel, rich and carefree. He knew exactly what he would say to her:

"We're rich, Gertruda. Now we'll move to our own house, we'll buy whatever we want, and most important—you won't ever have to work again."

And she would wind her arms around him, and would say to him, as always:

"My dear, I don't need money. I only need you to be with me."

CHAPTER 1

Two Weddings

1.

Shrouded in a uniform decorated with the military medals inherited from his forefathers, the marquis Stefan Roswadovsky bit his lips in rage and drained another glass of brandy. He was a potbellied, ruddy-faced man, whose seventy-two years had passed in a nonstop journey of pleasures. Under his broad jaw, like a plump dumpling, hung a pink double chin, which grew and thickened as the rest of his body swelled with his gluttony.

From the yard came the rustle of carriage wheels entering the gate, and the taste of nausea, as the taste of impending disaster, rose in the marquis's throat. What wouldn't he give to prevent this?

Gloomy leaden clouds, like his mood, hung over Warsaw. A thin silent rain fell on the flower gardens of the mansion at Ujazdowska Avenue 9 when the carriage stopped and the driver jumped from his seat and opened the door. A man of about forty, lean and tall, in an elegant wool coat, got out of the carriage. His face was firm and his step supple and confident. The driver opened an umbrella over his head and walked him to the door. From the corner of his window, the marquis watched them in despair. In a few minutes, he knew, the door would be opened and the honor that had been the glory for generations, passing as a legacy from father to son, his family honor and his own honor, would be trampled and desecrated by a coarse foot.

A servant with a frozen face, wearing a black frock, led the guest in and took his coat.

"Will the gentleman please wait until I announce his arrival," he said submissively.

The servant silently entered Roswadovsky's office and bowed deeply.

"Marquis," he said, "Mr. Stolowitzky has arrived."

The marquis hesitated. "It won't hurt the Jew to wait a little," he grumbled. He needed more time to prepare for the meeting.

With a sigh, the marquis sank deeper into his armchair. His forefathers looked on from the velvet-covered walls, decorated army officers, bearing swords, astride noble steeds with gleaming hides. Next to them, in gold frames, were the portraits of their beautiful plump wives in splendid gowns, wearing gold jewelry and diamonds. Persian rugs, woven by experienced artists who toiled for days in the cellars of Isfahan and Shiraz, were spread from wall to wall, and beautiful furniture that could adorn royal palaces stood in various corners of the spacious office.

The elderly marquis stirred uneasily in his chair, nervously pulled his well-tended mustache, and labored to hide his revulsion at his meeting with the man waiting in the next room. Never had it occurred to him that he of all people, offspring of a noble Polish family, only ruler of the fate of hundreds of tenant farmers, owner of lands and precious art, would wind up in such an embarrassing and offensive situation that would roil his peace of mind and stir melancholy thoughts about the order of the world that had been turned on its head.

In the family of Marquis Roswadovsky, honor and position were supreme values, the core of life. Roswadovsky was sure of what his ancestors would have done if a Jew had dared to set foot in their house. None of them would have hesitated to throw him out and might even have thrashed the man who had the nerve to stand up to them and take advantage of their distress.

Never had members of the Roswadovsky family met Jews like the man now waiting in the vestibule. In Baranowicz in eastern Poland, where the family owned many estates, the Jews would be filled with dread and awe whenever the marquis's carriage passed by. They all knelt down and didn't dare raise their eyes to him. Where did those days vanish to, how did his authority fade? Could the floor of his splendid house in Warsaw, one of the many glorious family houses scattered throughout Poland, be defiled by the shoes of one of the Jews of his city, who came not to plead for his favors, but because the marquis himself summoned him urgently to help get him out of trouble?

Moshe Stolowitzky was the sort of Jew Marquis Roswadovsky didn't know. He was extraordinarily rich, very powerful and influential; not many men in Poland could boast of his great wealth. He had inherited a great deal of his wealth from his father, a resourceful businessman who had made the bulk of his money before World War I, producing and selling sleepers for railroad tracks, polishing millstones for flour mills, operating a tavern in Baranowicz where he lived, and trading successfully in real estate. When Baranowicz passed from the Poles to the Russians during World War I, many of its residents fled to Warsaw. Moshe Stolowitzky managed to save most of his fortune. Marquis Roswadovsky wasn't so lucky. In the dead of night, he escaped from the city, leaving behind quite a bit of his wealth, and found shelter in his magnificent house in Warsaw. But his money soon ran out, his debts mounted, and he had to settle them without delay. The only way to satisfy his creditors was hard and painful—he had to sell houses and plots of land. Buyers came and went. Some wanted to take advantage of the marquis's difficulty and offered unreasonably low prices. Others offered a little more but not enough. Until Moshe Stolowitzky came and finally made a decent offer.

The servant returned to the marquis a few minutes later.

"Mr. Stolowitzky's in a hurry," he said. "He claims he can't wait."

The marquis grumbled aloud. "He's got some nerve, that Jew," he growled.

The servant was silent, waiting for instructions.

"Fine, show him in." The marquis swallowed his revulsion.

A few minutes later, Moshe Stolowitzky stood in the doorway, looking directly at the marquis. He came to do business from a position of strength. He had no time for small talk or pleasant manners.

Reluctantly, the marquis entered into a business discussion with his guest, who conducted hard and uncompromising negotiations. In the next hour, Roswadovsky sold him buildings and lots in Baranowicz and also transferred to him ownership of the house in Warsaw. As always, when he was in desperate need of money, it outweighed honor, position, and every other consideration. With a heavy heart, the Polish marquis swallowed his offense and signed the bill of sale.

It was very hard for him to part from his property, particularly the beautiful house in Warsaw. It was a big mansion, furnished with ostentatious splendor, full of rare art, his pride and joy. In that house, Roswadovsky employed an army of servants, and there was a pantry stuffed with delicacies and a cellar of fine wines. At stately dinners, he entertained the Polish elite and wealthy businessmen, and it was painful to give all that up to prevent a scandalous bankruptcy.

His young mistress, a black-haired beauty, daughter of one of his tenant farmers, who lived in the mansion in Warsaw and made his visits there even more pleasurable, wept bitter tears when she had to pack her things and return home. The marquis stood helplessly at her side.

"What will happen to me now? What will happen to us?" she sobbed.

The marquis stroked her head and a tear gleamed in the corner of his eye. He had no answer.

Moshe Stolowitzky left the marquis's house with the feeling that he had made an excellent deal. He was known as an experienced merchant. His crafty mind and audacity paved his way to the offices of senior government officials, and he soon became *the* contractor for railroad tracks. The hundreds of workers he hired laid railroad tracks throughout Poland and then stretched rails for trains over Russia as well. Anti-Semitic manifestations didn't bother him because Jew haters didn't dare touch him. He was a welcome guest in the homes of heads of state and they were glad to be entertained in his own house.

The marquis requested a week to move out of his house in Warsaw. After the last moving van left the place for good, Moshe Stolowitzky moved in there with his wife, Hava, and their little son, Jacob.

2.

Moshe Stolowitzky wasn't only a rich man, he was also a proud Jew. He regularly read the Yiddish newspaper, *Dos Yidishe Tageblat,* he and his wife attended the Jewish theater, Wikt, established by the actor Zigmund Turkow, invested in the Yiddish film *Yiddl mitn fiddl,* which became a hit among Jews throughout the world, contributed to yeshivas and Jewish schools, and supported Jewish writers and poets. Every Friday baskets of Sabbath food were sent on his behalf to the poor of the city, and in his mansion, as was customary among major Jewish philanthropists, a box of cash was set up for grants to the needy who knocked on his door every single day.

His only son, Jacob, was destined to follow in his footsteps. Moshe hired teachers who taught him Hebrew and general sciences, bought him a subscription to the Hebrew children's newspaper *Olam Katan (Small World),* and was happy when the boy read stories about Hasids—pious Jews—and the holy places in the Land of Israel.

One stormy winter night, Moshe Stolowitzky sat in the first row in the Novoschi auditorium where about three thousand Jews gathered to listen to a talk by Ze'ev Jabotinsky. The short, bespectacled Zionist leader with a serious face called on them to ascend to the Land of Israel before Europe tossed them out. Moshe Stolowitzky admired Jabotinsky and read his writings devotedly, but he thought Jabotinsky exaggerated when he talked about the danger lurking for the Jews of Europe. Stolowitzky and his family, like most of their friends, saw Poland as their homeland and were grateful for the

Stolowitzky family mansion. Warsaw.

wealth they had amassed there. They felt good and comfortable and naturally it didn't occur to them that bad times were in store for them as Jabotinsky's gloomy predictions had foretold.

Before long reality proved to Moshe Stolowitzky that he was living in a fool's paradise. One Friday evening, the Jewish millionaire was relaxing in his velvet easy chair, facing the Ark of the Covenant in the Tlomackie Synagogue, the biggest and oldest synagogue of Warsaw. For a long time he listened with pleasure to the chanting of the well-known cantor Moshe Koussevitzky, and when it was over, he left the synagogue with a group of worshippers. His carriage was standing nearby and at home his family and a traditional Sabbath meal awaited him. Stolowitzky didn't get far. A group of anti-Semitic youths surrounded the group of worshippers, threw rocks, and shouted curses at them. The Jews stopped in their tracks, stunned. Most of them had witnessed anti-Semitic persecutions in the past, but never ones so brutal. Only when the attackers tried to snatch their prayer shawl bags did the victims recover and assault the youths. A brawl developed, lasting until the police came and restored order.

In his private carriage, Moshe Stolowitzky, bruised, his clothes torn, returned home. The event itself didn't worry him too much. He preferred to believe that isolated anti-Semitic incidents didn't indicate a dangerous trend. He was concerned mainly that his wife would take things more seriously than he, and so he told her only that he had fallen and bruised himself on his way out of the synagogue. She called a doctor, who bandaged him and ordered him to stay in bed for two days.

When he returned to the synagogue a week later, the rabbi mounted the pulpit when prayers had ended. His arm had been broken in the attack and was in a sling.

"I have decided to leave Poland and move with my family to Jerusalem," he called out in a clear and emotional voice. "Poland is a trap for every Jew. Take your things and leave here before it's too late."

Moshe Stolowitzky wished the rabbi good luck and returned home. He told his wife about the panic that had gripped the rabbi and about his decision to leave Poland.

"Maybe he's right," she responded pensively.

"Nonsense!" He raised his voice. "There's no reason to panic."

3.

June 28, 1924, was a hot, sunny day, and hundreds of Warsaw residents were strolling on the paths through the green lawns along the river. That afternoon, Jacob Stolowitzky introduced his parents to his fiancée, Lydia. He was twenty-two years old, and his bride-to-be was twenty, a handsome girl, thin, the daughter of a Jewish army officer from Krakow, studying political science in Warsaw. They had met at a party at the home of mutual friends and it was love at first sight.

Hava and Moshe Stolowitzky greeted their son's fiancée in the ballroom of their mansion and spoke with Lydia about her family and her studies. They liked her very much and didn't care that her parents weren't as rich as they were. She was Jewish and their son loved her and that was what mattered. At the festive dinner they made for Lydia and her parents, the guests toasted the young couple and they set the date for their wedding.

Three months later, the wedding ceremony gave the elite of Warsaw an unforgettable experience. Members of the government, senior officials, tycoons, artists, and intellectuals poured into the mansion and blessed the happy family. Dozens of servants passed among the guests offering abundant delicacies and champagne and an orchestra played until the last guest withdrew.

The young couple left for a honeymoon in Switzerland and when they returned to Warsaw, a surprise awaited them. Moshe Stolowitzky suggested they live in his splendid mansion and set a big wing aside for them.

Jacob and Lydia settled down comfortably in the spacious

house. Lydia ordered furniture from Italy and supervised the crew of servants of their wing—a housekeeper, a cook, two cleaning women, and a chauffeur. Jacob was integrated into the management of his father's business, which flourished more than ever. He traveled a great deal throughout Europe, signing contracts with various states and amassing a great deal of wealth.

The two of them badly wanted a child. Lydia dreamed he would grow up to be a doctor. His father wanted his son to be a businessman like him, who would someday inherit the family empire. Although they couldn't agree, both of them had every reason to believe that their child's future, like their own, would be a bed of roses.

They were wrong.

4.

Karl Rink expected much more from life than he got. He was a twenty-four-year-old bachelor with blue eyes and short hair who worked as a junior accountant for the chemical firm A. G. Farben in Berlin. His salary was barely enough to pay his rent and buy food. His office was small and dark and his work was boring. He dreamed of a different career, more lucrative and more interesting, which would guarantee him real success. Now and then he even went looking for such a job, but the only work he was offered was in accounting and that wasn't enough. He learned very quickly that for every good job that opened up, many people, more talented than he, jumped on the opportunity. Unfortunately for him, the chances of finding another position were growing dim.

The only refuge from his tedious routine was sport. Bicycle racing was the only area where Rink showed real talent. He belonged to the company sport club, trained on the weekend in all weather, riding on mountain paths, and he won trophies that were displayed on a shelf in his small apartment. Above them, in a glass frame, was a local newspaper article reporting on his victory in the district competition of bicycle riders.

On September 12, 1924, he hurried to finish work earlier than usual and returned to his one-room apartment in a dreary working-class neighborhood in west Berlin. He put on a dark suit and a tie, picked up his parents at their house in a distant suburb, and they all took a trolley to city hall, where Mira, her parents, and a handful of friends were waiting for him.

Mira, a plump, fair-skinned girl of twenty-one, was starting out as a clerk in the Department of Wills in the Ministry of Justice. She

Mira Rink with baby Helga. Berlin, 1926.

wore a white dress and stood arm in arm with Karl before the municipal clerk who performed their marriage.

Karl was a Christian and Mira a Jew, but their differences didn't diminish their love. Karl's father was a truck driver and his mother was a housewife. They seldom went to church and loved Mira like a daughter. Mira's parents owned a grocery store and were observant Jews. Even though mixed marriages were common in Berlin, Mira's parents strongly objected to her marriage with a Christian. Karl tried at length to convince them, and Mira also made considerable efforts to persuade her parents to let her marry her fiancé. In the end, they were forced to agree.

The young couple received a few wedding gifts, mainly glass and china dishes. Karl's colleagues collected a small sum and his manager gave him a week's salary as a present. The couple's parents threw a modest reception and bought them a new double bed.

Happy and in love, Mira and Karl went on a two-day honeymoon to a small town in the Black Forest. They rode bikes on winding paths among the trees, ate blutwurst, and danced to the music of a rustic orchestra in the local beer cellar until the weé hours of the morning. When they returned to Berlin, they settled in Karl's apartment, and at the end of the year they had a daughter, Helga. They brought her home from the hospital, put her in a cradle, and looked at her with loving eyes.

After everything they had been through, their life was calm. They loved each other and their baby daughter and pushed her stroller in the green parks on warm weekends. Mira was promoted in the Ministry of Justice, and Karl believed he would finally find the work he dreamed of. They both faced the future with confidence. They believed they would have prosperity and professional satisfaction, pure bliss.

They were wrong.

CHAPTER 2

A Prince Is Born

1.

In the spring of 1931, after the snow and rain of the passing winter ended and sunbeams started breaking through the clouds, Karl Rink was called to a meeting in the Nazi Party office. He knew that the sport club of his firm, like many sport clubs, worked under the aegis of the SS, the brutal senior arm of the party. But he had little interest in politics. He wanted to ride a bike, win races, set new records, finally find work he liked. The Nazi Party interested him in only one context: it poured money into the sport club, encouraged its members, and distributed prizes. He had never been in the party office and he was curious about this meeting.

A stocky man in an SS uniform greeted him, shook his hand warmly, and introduced himself as the person in charge of sports teams. He gave him a friendly smile and a silver-plated trophy for his achievements in the annual bicycle competition.

"Continue to excel," he told him. "The party loves men like you."

Karl Rink was pleased with the attention he had won in the SS office. On the first Sunday after that, he took Mira and their little daughter, Helga, to a café on the shore of the lake. It was a nice warm day and people in their Sunday best filled the cafés, licking ice cream, sipping coffee, and eating cakes, while others were sailing leisurely. Times were hard and the economic situation was getting worse, but those enjoying the lake shore in this charming corner of Berlin pretended things couldn't be better, as if all around them businesses weren't collapsing one after another, as if the rate of unemployment wasn't rising every day. Karl thanked his lucky stars that he had a source of income, that there was someone who appreciated his achievements in sport, and that the wife and daughter he loved most were sitting beside him.

But the delusion was short-lived. One morning, Karl was called to the office of his supervisor. He hurried there with the hope that he might be offered a transfer to a new and more important position. His happiness, it turned out, was premature. "You must know, Karl," said his manager, "that the economic depression has hit our firm hard. The number of orders has fallen a great deal, our losses get bigger from day to day, and in these circumstances we have no choice but to fire some of the workers. I'm sorry to say that you're on the list."

Being fired, after ten years of working, left Karl speechless. He rolled up the envelope with a small sum of money as recompense by the management, picked up his coat, left the building, and headed home.

When he opened the door of his apartment, Helga, then six years old, fell into his arms with a shout of joy. She wasn't used to seeing him come home so early. Mira was also surprised to see him.

"What happened, Karl?" she asked anxiously. "Are you sick?"

"No," said Karl in a gloomy voice. "I was laid off."

Mira turned pale. Even though unemployment rose from one day to the next, and the economic distress grew worse, she didn't want to believe that they, like many others, would lose their livelihood. Day after day, they met men in their neighborhood who had been laid off. They trudged along, avoided meeting the eyes of passersby. They seemed to envy anybody who was luckier and could still support his family. Now her small family had joined the ranks of the desperate. They would have to live on her modest salary, and both of them knew that wouldn't be enough.

"What will you do now?" she asked with dread.

"I'll look for work," said Karl, but in his heart he knew that wouldn't be easy.

They stayed up late, whispering about what was in store for them, thinking of acquaintances who might help. Karl said he would go to them the very next day.

In the morning, he went out to look for work, any work as long as it had a regular salary. Karl wanted to believe he would soon find somebody who would offer him a job. He knocked on the doors of people he knew, was answered politely, but didn't make any progress. For hours he wandered from one business to another, offered himself for anything, but returned home that evening empty-handed.

For whole days, he stayed out of the house to avoid his wife's muted painful looks. Over and over, impatient employers turned him down. The number of possibilities he hoped for quickly diminished. Since he didn't dare return home before nightfall, he often went to the neighborhood movie theater and watched the same film over and over, sunk in the seat, alone and crushed, gazing at the screen but not seeing a thing.

One day, after he left a failed job interview, he passed by an auditorium where a Nazi Party meeting was taking place. He went inside, met a few members of his sport club, and heard fiery speeches promising to improve the nation when the party rose to power. They called on the unemployed to join them to prepare a new order and restore Germany to its glory. Karl listened intently. A new hope was kindled in his heart, and when the audience was asked to join the party, he gladly signed up. In the following days, he didn't miss a meeting, was recruited to help the party, and learned to admire Adolf Hitler, the leader who could inflame his listeners and give them the confidence they needed for better days. With all his heart he wanted to help the rise of the new regime that would guarantee the nation and himself a better economic future.

2.

The Jews of Germany watched the rise of the Nazi Party with growing concern; like a giant octopus, it sent out choking arms in all directions. Hitler ruled the party with an iron fist. His declared purpose was to come to power by any means: destroying political enemies, kindling fear, and inciting the masses against the Jews of Germany, claiming that they were the main cause of the economic debacle, corruption, and unemployment.

Joining the party cost Karl Rink dearly. It created a widening rift in his relations with his Jewish friends, mainly with Mira's parents and family. Many of Mira and Karl's friends broke ties with them. Her parents refused to accept him in their house.

More than once, Mira tried to persuade her husband to resign from the Nazi Party. They talked about it for hours.

"Your friends are people without a conscience. They murder in cold blood whoever opposes them," she said. "They'll do everything to get rid of the Jews."

"You exaggerate," he said, dismissing her. "Attacking the Jews is just a means of winning the support of the people before the elections."

He believed naively in the purity of Hitler's intentions and said that as a member of the party, he had to work to promote the Nazi ideology. "You'll see how good it will be here when Hitler comes to power," he promised excitedly.

Mira looked at him sadly. "You're wrong," she said. "With Hitler, it will never be better for the Jews. The opposite."

"What do you understand about politics?" Karl cut her off.

They stopped arguing. Mira saw no point in trying to persuade him that she was right. She fell silent, but her heart was heavy.

Blind to the gloomy reality, Karl expanded his activity in the party and was soon asked to join the SS, which had become the elite organization of German security services. He was accepted with open arms and given a thorough medical examination by a doctor who wrote a positive report on his health. A psychologist questioned him about his parents, his childhood, his education, his friends, his family, his profession, and his hobbies. In almost every way, Karl was a perfect match for the SS. He was a pure Aryan, strongly motivated, and physically fit. There was only one problem: his wife was Jewish, but the SS commanders wanted him and believed that the problem would be solved sooner or later. He received a good salary and was sent for a three-week training course to a small, remote camp not far from Berlin. The course included memorizing *Mein Kampf,* Hitler's credo, strenuous physical exercises, weapons training, and harsh endurance tests. Students learned methods of interrogating and torturing detainees. They had to wring the necks of dogs and cats with their bare hands, lie in foxholes while vehicles passed over them, wrestle comrades to victory, do without food for three whole days in a row, be whipped and live in solitary confinement in a tiny cell underground. Karl sailed through the training.

At the end of the course, Karl swore loyalty to the Führer and pledged "fidelity and obedience" to his dying day. The SS symbol, two parallel lightning flashes, was tattooed under his arm. He received a black uniform, new boots, an armband with a swastika, and a personal dagger he attached to his belt.

When he returned home in his new uniform, Helga burst into frightened tears at the sight of him and Mira looked at him in horror.

Karl Rink. Berlin, February 1938.

"That's scary," she said.

"It's just a uniform." He tried to calm her. "A lot of Germans are wearing it these days."

She sighed. "I've got a feeling this won't turn out well, Karl."

"You have no reason to worry, Mira."

"Do they know you've got a Jewish wife?"

"I never hid that."

"And how did they react?"

"That really didn't seem to bother them."

She looked at him and turned pale. "It doesn't bother them now, but one day it will, believe me," she said.

"Nonsense," he protested. "They'll have to come to terms with it."

"In the course they must have taught you everything about their theory of race."

"They did."

"Which means that, sooner or later, they'll demand that you leave me or leave the SS. What will you tell them then?"

"I'll persuade them that there's nothing wrong with you," he said confidently. "I'll tell them that you stand by my side."

She sighed. "You're naive, Karl," she said. "You're so naive."

3.

As soon as Hitler came to power in January 1933, the writing was on the wall, flagrant and prophesying evil. It was supposed to demonstrate to the Jews of Germany that, from now on, nothing would stand in the way of the Nazi leader's intention to undermine their social, cultural, and economic position. And that is indeed what happened. Jewish officials in government offices were soon fired, along with Jewish lecturers in the universities and Jewish managers of public institutions. They were replaced with pure Aryan Germans.

Mira Rink was fired from the Ministry of Justice with a brief announcement. "The law doesn't allow us to employ you any longer," said the manager of her division. "We expect you to leave today." She received no payment when she was dismissed.

Ashamed, she went home and made lunch for Helga, who was about to return from school. When the eight-year-old girl came in, she was surprised to see her mother home at that hour. "I don't feel so well," Mira blurted out as an excuse. She noticed that her daughter was unusually nervous and tense. "My teacher told us he couldn't continue teaching," said Helga. "Tomorrow we'll have a new teacher." The Jewish teacher lived nearby. He had a sick wife and three children.

Mira calmed her daughter and kept her company while she ate lunch. She then helped her do her arithmetic homework. In the evening, when Karl came home from work, Mira told him that she had been fired, and so had her daughter's teacher.

"I told you," she said painfully. "Your Nazis won't rest until they finish with all the Jews of Germany."

He stroked her head affectionately and ignored the danger signals this time, too.

"I understand your concern," he said. "But this is only a show of strength. Hitler doesn't intend to make a big deal of the Jews. It's clear to him that he has to prove himself mainly with economics. Besides, you see how good it is that I have a steady job. How would we manage now without my salary?"

• • •

In the following days, Karl came home early, usually with a bouquet of flowers. He took Mira to the theater and the movies, bought her new books to read. It was important for him that she calm down and get used to the situation as fast as possible, that she be optimistic like him.

But Mira looked at reality with eyes wide open. Attacking Jews, narrowing their options, and destroying the sources of their livelihood continued at an increasing tempo. Jews were also fired from private jobs, the newspapers were filled with slander against them, Jewish products were boycotted, and her parents' grocery store lost all its customers. On November 14, 1935, the Nuremberg Laws were passed, stripping Jews of German citizenship and canceling all marriages with Jews.

"In terms of the law," Mira said bitterly to Karl, "you're no longer my husband and I'm not your wife."

As usual, he waved his hand in dismissal.

"You'll always be my wife," he said in a solemn voice. "Nobody can separate us."

4.

Lydia and Jacob Stolowitzky learned, to their grief, that money can't fix everything and even the wealthy sometimes need much more than what's in their pocket to make them happy. After a few years of comfort and love, their joie de vivre disappeared. They began moving around the mansion sadly, withdrawn. They stopped organizing parties and concerts, seldom invited friends. Many nights, Lydia wept into her pillow because, despite her efforts, she couldn't get pregnant. Her doctors were devoted and did all they could to help her, but eventually they had to admit that there was nothing else they could do for her. They doubted if she could ever have a child.

She tried all that was available to her. When the best doctors in Warsaw couldn't solve her problem, Lydia went to famous experts in Zurich and Vienna and tried the latest treatments. Sometimes they were painful, sometimes she had to stay in a private hospital in a foreign city far from home, but nothing stopped her. Her husband supported her all the way. "Money's no object," he said. "We'll pay what we have to just so we have a child."

Despite the big sums of money paid to them, the doctors couldn't help. But Lydia refused to despair. She began frequenting the courts of rabbis and miracle workers, spending a lot of money on charity, consulting fortune-tellers, and filling the house with amulets against the evil eye. When none of these worked, she finally felt she was about to collapse. The family doctor pleaded with her to take sedatives. Her husband took her on a cruise on the Danube and sent her on shopping trips to famous couturiers of Paris. But nothing could restore her emotional forces. She moved from place to place like a rag doll, depressed, barely talking. She often entertained thoughts of suicide. Deep in her heart she had already accepted that she would never have a baby. Close friends suggested she adopt. Her husband, Jacob, also supported the idea. But Lydia couldn't bear the thought. She wanted only a child of her own.

To the amazement of the doctors and herself, one day, after twelve years of fertility treatments, Lydia Stolowitzky discovered that she was pregnant. From that moment on, she stood straight, the light returned to her face, and she brightened up. She hired a nurse to stay with her throughout her pregnancy, and demanded that her doctors examine her every single day.

The daughter of Lydia and Jacob Stolowitzky was born in the mansion on the river on a cold, snowy day—and died only a few days later. Determined to bring another child into the world, the couple once again consulted their doctors, and in mid-February 1936 their son was born. The delivery was easier than Lydia expected and she was happier than she had ever been.

The parents named the baby Michael, after the angel of God, symbolizing grace, youth, and especially protection from the evil eye.

Jacob hurried to the synagogue to thank the Creator for the miracle and contributed a considerable sum to the poor. Lydia sat at her son's cradle for hours, weeping and laughing in turn, looking at him as if she couldn't believe her eyes. She furnished a nursery for Michael with toys and hired a nanny day and night. "He's my prince," she said to the nanny. "Don't take your eyes off him."

CHAPTER 3

Blackmail

1.

Like an excited child playing with his favorite toy, twenty-nine-year-old Emil stroked the wheel of the white Cadillac with his strong hands. He wore a black chauffeur's uniform and a white visored cap. He was a Polish Catholic, tall and dark, the private chauffeur of the Stolowitzky family. His loyalty was rewarded with what was most important to him: a good salary, a heated room, and three meals a day.

The Cadillac rolled over the pocked road from Warsaw to the village, the soft springs blocked the jolts from the potholes in the worn pavement, and Emil glanced now and then into the rearview mirror at his employers in the backseat. Jacob Stolowitzky, a short, high-strung thirty-six-year-old, in a hunting suit and leather boots, was smoking a thick cigar; his wife, Lydia, thirty-four years old, beautiful as a princess, in a dress as white as snow, was pleading with him to stop smoking; and their two-year-old son, Michael, rosy-cheeked and silent, in an immaculate tailored suit, was chewing on a piece of chocolate. In the front seat, next to the driver, sat the nanny, Martha.

Martha was thirty years old, short and thin, with a stern face. She took good care of Michael, imparted knowledge, and taught him obedience, manners, and courtesy. His parents were satisfied with his education. They raised him with love and didn't want him to lack anything. Not an hour went by that Lydia didn't come to see how he was, to hug and kiss him. She knew she would probably not have any more children. The doctors agreed that she would almost certainly not get pregnant again. She and her husband were sure that Michael would be their only heir.

Lydia and Michael Stolowitzky. Warsaw, May 1938.

. . .

Happy and carefree as they delighted in thoughts of the vacation in store for them on their summer estate, the Stolowitzky family sank into the soft leather seats of the American car and waited patiently for the trip to end.

The road went through sleepy towns and poor villages. Farmers looked in amazement at the magnificent car, the only one of its kind in all of Poland. Jacob Stolowitzky glanced at them with a cursory indifference, his wife rubbed French cream on her hands, and Michael glued his eyes to the window to look at the people in shabby clothes who gazed at the vehicle as if it had come from another world. Michael never saw people like that on Ujazdowska Avenue in Warsaw, around the four-story mansion. They weren't part of his world; he wasn't part of theirs.

Like his father, Jacob Stolowitzky was an experienced businessman, calculating and clever. He expanded the family business empire, acquired coal and iron mines, land, and houses, signed partnership agreements with companies all over the world, employed hundreds of workers, and deposited most of his money and gold in secret Swiss bank accounts, deducting part of it for charity. Emissaries from the Land of Israel who came to Poland were entertained generously in the home of the Jewish tycoon and always left with contributions, even though they could never extract a promise that he would ever settle in the Land with his family. "What will I do there?" he responded to their attempts to convince him. "I'm just fine here."

Poland was indeed good to him. Abundantly wealthy, the Stolowitzky family led an enviable life. They employed as many servants as they liked, bought clothes and jewelry in the capitals of Europe, and sailed on the Adriatic every spring on a luxurious yacht,

Jacob Stolowitzky. July 1929.

once even with the Duke of Windsor and his lover, Mrs. Simpson. They hosted dinners in their mansion for the elite of Poland and entertained famous guests from abroad, hired well-known artists to perform in the grand ballroom on the second floor of their house, and spent their vacations on their summer estate two hours away from Warsaw.

It was a large estate in a picturesque region. A thick forest and fruit and vegetable gardens covered a considerable part of the land, and at its edge was a clear, beautiful lake. Some of the wooden cottages in a clearing of the forest were for the family and their guests, and others for the workers who maintained the estate off season.

At last they arrived. Two armed guards hurried to open the big iron gate and bowed to the Cadillac that stopped at the central wooden home. As always, Emil carried Michael on his shoulders and galloped with him to the house. After he put Michael down in the big vestibule, Emil went to the garden and picked a bunch of flowers, came to Lydia, and gave them to her. "You never forget," she said. She smiled at him indulgently and her husband tapped him on the shoulder affectionately.

"How could I forget," replied Emil in a flattering voice. "You're like a mother to me."

The aged housekeeper of the estate greeted the family with obsequious bows and hurried to move their things from the car to their rooms. The rooms were furnished with expensive simplicity. On the beds were white sheets and soft down comforters; from the open windows overlooking the forest came pungent smells of pine trees and a symphony of chirping birds and animals. The weather was nicer than usual. Cloudless blue skies stretched overhead and flowers bloomed in the well-tended garden.

Throughout the day, many preparations were made around the estate. Close relatives, friends, and business partners invited to share their vacation were brought in carriages from the railroad station or arrived in cars driven by their private chauffeurs. Roars of laughter and pleasant conversations accompanied the abundant lunches served in gold dishes on a dining table that had belonged to the royal family four hundred years earlier. Children ran around and played on the lawns; babies and their nannies sunbathed.

Dinner was just as extravagant as lunch. When it was over, Lydia gathered her guests in the ballroom and presented a famous chamber orchestra brought especially from Warsaw. After the concert, the men smoked cigars and the women sipped warmed cognac. Servants put candy on pillowcases and prepared to shine the shoes the guests left outside their rooms at night.

At dawn the next day, accompanied by the forest guard of the estate, the family and their guests went out on horseback to hunt and fish. They hunted pheasant and fished for turbot and then sent them to the kitchen to be cooked for dinner. During the afternoon break, the servants spread white cloths on the banks of the lake and set them with various delicacies and bottles of wine. Lydia read her son a story and Martha, the nanny, went for a horseback ride.

When evening fell and everyone prepared to return to the house, they discovered that Martha had disappeared. Lydia and Jacob were frightened. Martha was extremely punctual and was never late or absent without a reason. Jacob waited a little while and when she didn't return, he gathered a group of riders and went out to search for her. They found her some way off, among the trees of the forest, lying on the ground, groaning in pain. The horse she had been riding was lying next to her with a broken leg. "He stumbled on a rock," she muttered. The servants improvised a stretcher of blankets and hunting rifles and carried her to the summerhouse.

The Stolowitzky family was devastated. Martha wasn't only a nanny; she had quickly become a beloved and appreciated member of the family. Michael sobbed and Lydia called Emil to take the injured woman to the hospital in Warsaw. She herself went with them. An initial examination revealed a bad break in her left knee and hemorrhages in her arms. The doctors were concerned. "Unfortunately," said one of them, "it will take a lot of time for her to recover."

Lydia didn't return to the summerhouse. Martha's condition depressed her so much that Lydia stayed for several hours at Martha's bedside, trying to relieve her pains and cheer her up. Never had she been so close to human distress, to grief and disaster. She felt Martha's pains and prayed for her recovery.

2.

It was supposed to be a happy day, a milestone in the life of Gertruda Babilinska. She and her family had been waiting for this day, and Gertruda was thrilled when it came at last.

In their small house in Starogard, near Danzig, three hours from Warsaw by train, the excited family dressed in their wedding clothes and set off for the church, where Gertruda was to be married. She was the oldest child, the only daughter.

Gertruda was charming, nineteen years old, tall and fair, a teacher in the local school. Her students and colleagues loved and admired her, and at the end of every school year, her students' parents showed their appreciation with an expensive gift. She planned to go on teaching even after she was married, at least until she had her first child.

Many good men had courted Gertruda, but she was in no hurry to accept them. She examined each of them carefully and ended the relationship when the suitor failed to touch her heart. She wasn't interested in marriage for money or status. She believed in love. She met Zygmunt Komorowski in the home of mutual friends. He worked in an import-export office in Warsaw, was a handsome and well-groomed man ten years older than her, and he liked Gertruda the moment he met her. He was impressed with her broad education, her expertise in German, and her pleasant ways, and he lavished compliments on her that made her blush.

Zygmunt was a man of the world, an experienced urbanite, who won her heart with his courtesy and his stories about the big city and the global business he was engaged in. After a few months of courtship, one evening, in the best restaurant in Starogard, Zygmunt proposed marriage. Gertruda, who believed that she had at long last found the love of her life, gladly accepted. He promised to take her to Warsaw, buy them a big apartment, support her in style, and give her lots of love.

The couple decided to get married in the local church of Starogard and to hold a reception afterward in the home of the bride's parents. Her mother and her relatives worked day and night preparing food for the party and walked, in a big group of family and friends, to the church in the town square. Gertruda, excited and tense, wore a white wedding gown she had bought in Danzig.

Family and close friends gathered in the church, and the bride's students stood outside and applauded her as she approached. Flushed, Gertruda clutched a small bouquet of violets and, in a trembling voice, thanked everyone for their good wishes.

In the church, everything was ready for the ceremony. An old man sat waiting at the organ. The priest smoothed his robe and Gertruda's parents shook hands warmly with the last guests. Everyone was waiting for the groom, who was about to arrive with his parents and sisters, but Zygmunt was late. A long time had passed when a messenger appeared in the church door with a short letter for Gertruda. In it, the man of her dreams told her that for unspecified reasons, he couldn't go through with the wedding. He concluded with an apology for the grief he had caused her and wished her good health and happiness. Gertruda burst into tears, ran home, and locked herself in her room.

For three days she lay on her bed in her wedding gown, didn't eat, didn't see anyone, and didn't stop sobbing. When she finally came out of the room with her eyes red and her face pale as a ghost, she told her parents quietly that she had decided, because of the disgrace, that she could no longer stay in the town. Her parents, still stunned by what had happened, didn't even try to change her mind and only asked what she intended to do.

"I'll go to Warsaw. I'll find work. I'll try to get over it. Nobody knows me there," she said.

"Just promise me that you'll come back," said her mother.

It was hard for Gertruda to promise. "How can I know what will happen to me?" she replied. "Maybe I'll find a new bridegroom there."

She went to the school to announce her resignation. The principal expressed his profound disappointment. He tried to convince her to stay. He said that her students were waiting eagerly for her, that the wounds would heal in time, and that the big city where she was heading generally didn't welcome strangers from remote towns. She paid no attention to his words and asked for a letter of recommendation. The principal gave her a warm letter and said an emotional farewell. She returned home, packed her few things in a small suitcase, hugged her parents, collected her little bit of savings, and boarded the train to Warsaw.

With the help of an acquaintance, Gertruda found a job as a nanny for two young daughters of a well-to-do family. She worked there for a number of years until the family left the city. Gertruda returned to her hometown but never managed to adjust to her old surroundings. After a few years of struggling, she again packed up her belongings and set out for Warsaw to find a new job.

The capital city greeted her with a downpour. She wandered through the streets, frozen, vainly seeking shelter beneath her umbrella. The wind swirled the raindrops and blew the umbrella out of her hands; she got soaked to the skin. She ran back to the railroad station, where she sat in the heated waiting room until her clothes dried. When the rain stopped, she left the station and began combing through the nearby alleys until she saw a sign in the door of one of the houses with peeling plaster announcing an apartment for rent. The staircase reeked of cooking smells, the landlady was coarse, but the rent was low enough to persuade her to take the apartment. Gertruda put her clothes away in the shabby wardrobe and looked out the window at Warsaw in the dark. The first lights came on in the windows of the city and suddenly the idea that she would stay there for an indefinite period of time made her afraid that she would encounter only more disappointment. Nevertheless, she had no choice. She felt she couldn't go back home again. She had to make every effort to fit in.

Her meager savings would last only a few weeks if she was frugal, and she knew she had to find work soon. She was also sure she couldn't bear to be idle for long, couldn't endure the days without people around her, and she knew she had to make a living.

The rain began again. Gertruda stretched out on her bed and fell into a nightmare sleep. When she woke up early in the morning, she hurried to a small café, drank a cup of coffee, and scanned the want ads in the morning paper. There were ads for shopgirls, cooks, and clerks. She ignored those and went on looking until one of the ads caught her attention. She read it over and over:

HONORABLE FAMILY IN WARSAW URGENTLY SEEKS A DEVOTED NANNY, NO HOUSEWORK, FOR A TWO-YEAR-OLD CHILD. LODGING AND A GOOD SALARY ARE GUARANTEED. PLEASE CONTACT THE STOLOWITZKY FAMILY, UJAZDOWSKA AVENUE 9.

The job was just what she was looking for. She loved children, could help them when they needed it, could listen to them. If the working conditions were good, she decided, she would take the job.

Gertruda left the café and set off for the address in the newspaper. The city stirred around her for another day of bustling activity. The sky was gray, stores opened one after another, and people hurrying to work filled the trolleys.

Her heart beat with excitement when she came to Ujazdowska Avenue. She loved the splendid houses where rich people and government leaders of the city lived and the shining cars that glided out through the cast-iron gates. There were no such houses in Starogard.

She rang the gold-plated doorbell of number 9. There was a long minute of silence until an elderly maid stood in the entrance.

"I came about the ad," said Gertruda.

Impassively, the woman scanned her from head to foot.

"Come in," she said. Gertruda stepped hesitantly into the vestibule. Around her, everything—every statute, every picture on the wall, the grand staircase to the second floor, the bouquets of flowers filling gigantic vases—radiated wealth she had never known. She had never heard the name Stolowitzky.

The maid took her coat and led her into a small room whose windows looked out onto a garden.

"I'll tell Mrs. Stolowitzky you've come," she said and left.

Gertruda sat down on the edge of the velvet sofa, careful not to dirty the expensive upholstery. She was afraid the mistress of the house would be a harsh and arrogant woman, like those wicked rich people she had read about in novels. She hoped the lady wouldn't be contemptuous of her simple clothes and wouldn't set demands she couldn't meet. Furtively she straightened her dress and tried in vain to hide her hands, which seemed too clumsy. Well, she said to herself, I really don't belong here; they must be expecting a nanny with experience taking care of rich and spoiled children, while I have only taught schoolchildren in a poor town. The longer she sat there, the surer she became that she had no chance.

The door opened and she saw a beautiful woman, elegantly dressed, who looked at her warmly. Gertruda got up, embarrassed.

"Sit down," said the woman softly. "Will you have some tea?"

"No, thank you."

The woman held out a delicate hand. "My name is Lydia. What's yours?"

"Gertruda."

"Thank you for coming," said the lady of the house. "You're very quick. We put the ad in only this morning and no one has come but you. Where are you from?"

Gertruda answered briefly.

"Do you have experience?"

"Yes, I do," Gertruda said. She gave the woman a letter of recommendation from the father of the household where she worked before.

Lydia Stolowitzky scanned it.

"He writes very good things about you," she commented.

Gertruda blushed.

"Are you married?" asked the woman.

"No."

"Tell me about your family."

Gertruda did.

The woman looked at her for a long time. "I assume you're not Jewish," she said.

"I'm Catholic."

Lydia Stolowitzky surprised her. "We're Jews," she said.

Gertruda looked at her in amazement mixed with fear. Jews? She didn't expect to work for people like that. In her town there were no Jews. Once a family of Jewish merchants did try to settle in the town, but various residents made their life so miserable that they were forced to leave. She had heard horror stories about Christian children murdered by Jews on Passover so that their blood could be used for the holiday ritual. There were other wicked rumors, half-truths and harsh libels about the Jews, and she was sure she couldn't stay in that house.

"I . . . I don't know if that would suit me," she said sadly.

"Why?" Lydia Stolowitzky wondered.

"Because you're Jews and I'm Catholic," she replied frankly.

The woman smiled. "Our previous nanny was also Catholic. That didn't bother her or us."

Gertruda stood up. "I'm sorry," she said.

"So am I," replied Lydia.

"I hope you find a suitable nanny," said Gertruda. "I'm sorry for taking your time."

She turned to the door.

"Before you go," said Lydia, "I want you to know that I like you. If you should decide nevertheless to take the job, come back to me. I'll be glad to talk with you again."

Gertruda went outside and a cold wind from the river, mixed with tiny raindrops, struck her face. She couldn't decide whether she had acted properly in turning down the offer, but she doubted she'd find a better one.

3.

For a whole day, she wandered around, helpless. More than anything she now needed somebody who would understand her and tell her what to do, but in the big, strange city, there wasn't anyone who could do so. Only one person, far from here, could come to her aid and she decided to go to him. With a heavy heart, Gertruda boarded the train at the Warsaw railroad station and went home. Cityscapes changed to green fields and farmers working their land. The smell of plowed earth, mixed with the bitter smoke from the locomotive, whirled in her nostrils when she stood at the open window in the passenger car. The smells and sights brought her back home, to where she was born, grew up, went to school, and made a living. She became depressed as the train slowed down and stopped at the small station of Starogard. Even though she had been gone only a couple of days, it was only now that she understood how much she missed her parents.

From the railroad station, she went straight to the small church in the middle of town and entered the open door to the empty hall. Candles were lit on the small platform and the statue of the crucified Jesus with a gilded crown of thorns looked at her. She knelt, dropped her head, and said a silent prayer.

Quiet footsteps passed by her and somebody called her name. She raised her eyes to the priest standing next to her, smiling.

"Gertruda, my child," he said quietly. "Welcome. I thought you left here and wouldn't return for a long time."

"I came back to ask your advice."

The elderly priest had known her since she was a child. He also knew her devout Catholic parents, regular churchgoers.

"How can I help you?" he asked.

She told him about her attempt to find work in the Stolowitzky house in Warsaw. "The problem is that they're Jews," she said softly.

The priest waited for her to go on, but she had nothing to add. She hoped he'd understand.

"You came for me to tell you if it's all right to work for Jews?" he asked.

She nodded.

"Did they make a good impression on you?"

"Yes."

"And what exactly bothers you about them?"

"Nothing specific, but I don't know their customs. I don't know if they'd let me go to church or even hang the pictures of the saints in my room. I'm not sure I'll feel comfortable there."

The priest put his hand on her shoulder.

"There are good Christians and bad Christians and good Jews and bad Jews," he said. "The most important thing is that they're good people, who will love you and whom you will love. I've got a feeling that you'll be happy there."

"I hope they really are good people," she said.

"So do I, my child. Go in peace and may God protect you."

She left the church, went to her parents' house, and told them about her conversation with the priest. They begged her to stay but she refused. Her father tried to persuade her to find work where there were no Jews.

The next day, all the way back to Warsaw, through the monotonous rattle of the train wheels, Lydia Stolowitzky's last words echoed in her ears: "Come back to me, I'll be glad to talk with you again." She hoped no one else had taken the job in the meantime.

Lydia Stolowitzky greeted her with a broad grin.

"I was expecting you," she said. "I had a feeling you'd come back to me. Come, I want you to meet Michael."

They went up to the second floor, to a fine nursery. A rosy-cheeked boy, sitting on the carpet and playing with an electric train, raised his blue eyes to her.

"Say hello to Gertruda," said his mother. "She's your new nanny."

The boy looked at her inquisitively.

"Want to play with me with my train?" he asked in a clear, ringing voice.

Her heart skipped a beat. He was so beautiful, so well-groomed, and so polite that she wanted to press him to her heart and kiss his soft cheeks.

"I'd love to play with you," she replied, and sat down next to him. When she looked around a few minutes later, Lydia had gone.

Gertruda's fears vanished in the following days. Life in the Stolowitzky house was easier and nicer than she had imagined. Lydia Stolowitzky never made her nanny deny her faith; she let her hang the pictures of Jesus and Mary on the wall of her room and put a crucifix on her nightstand. Lydia herself wasn't observant, and while her husband, Jacob, did contribute a lot of money to the synagogue, he didn't attend services frequently. He was a busy man and didn't spend too much time at home. Lydia was devoted to volunteer work in social organizations, read for pleasure, entertained a lot, and played the piano. Gertruda chose Sunday as her day off, when she attended church.

Michael came to love her as a member of the family. Her comfortable room was next to his and she was always willing to come to him. When he grew a little older, she taught him to read and write, and took him to museums, holding his hand. She loved taking care of him. She sent photos of the two of them to her parents and wrote them that she had never been so happy in her life.

In the evening, before he went to sleep, she sang him the lullabies her mother had sung to her when she was a little girl, and when he was sick, she sat at his bed day and night until he recovered. She watched him as the apple of her eye, bought him gifts with her own money. In time, he became much more to her than a child she was paid to care for: he was the child she had wanted so much to have but couldn't. "You're my dear son," she whispered in his ear every night after he fell asleep. "My only beloved son."

. . .

Gertruda walked around the big house quietly, trying not to bother anyone. She made friends with the servants and helped the cook when there were guests. Her salary was decent and she managed to save a large part of it.

Michael was a talented child. At the age of two, he began playing the piano, with a private teacher who came to the house twice a week, and he loved reading children's picture books. Gertruda adored how he looked, his pleasant manners, his clear voice when he sang popular songs with her. He spent more time with her than with his mother, loved to hear the bedtime stories she read to him, and missed her when she went to visit her parents.

On Sunday, when she went to church, he would go with her to the gate and wait for her in the yard. Often he wanted to go inside and see what was going on, but she refused to let him. "You're Jewish," she said. "You don't belong in church."

Once a week she went with him to visit Martha, the former nanny, who had now recovered. The two women became friends and Gertruda offered to give up her place if Martha wanted to return to work. Martha was glad, but Michael wasn't. "I love Martha," he told Gertruda, "but I love you more." Lydia insisted that Gertruda continue as Michael's nanny. That week, Jacob Stolowitzky paid Martha a large sum of money for her retirement.

Michael didn't budge from the new nanny: He wanted Gertruda to eat with him at the family table and not in the kitchen like the other workers, and when she told him that her birthday was coming, he begged his mother to give her an expensive gift. Lydia went to a fine shop, bought her a nice dress, made a small party, and gave her the gift. Gertruda wept with joy.

Her whole world was enclosed within the four walls of the Stolowitzky house, as if it had always been her home. Lydia treated her as a sister, the servants respected her as someone superior to them. They honored her and obeyed her and she was careful not to take advantage of her position. She had little to do with the outside world and when the principal of her old school pleaded with her to come back to teaching because the children missed her, she replied politely that she was happy where she was, with people who appreciated and loved her. She exchanged letters with some of her old friends, learned English by correspondence, knitted sweaters for Michael, and turned up her nose at the clumsy courtship attempts of Emil, the chauffeur. After her great disappointment in love, she wasn't interested in men.

4.

Hava Stolowitzky, Jacob's mother, died in her bed on September 22, 1938, after a long and difficult illness. Less than three months later, her husband, Moshe, suffered a stroke at a business meeting in his office and was taken to the hospital, where he lay unconscious for a week. When he finally came to, half his body was paralyzed and he spoke only gibberish. His son, Jacob, hired the best doctors for him, sat at his bed day and night, and no one was happier when at long last his father opened his eyes and looked at his son.

"I don't know if I'll stay alive," said Moshe Stolowitzky with a great effort. "Something is worrying me, my son. The situation in Germany is getting worse by the day. Hitler is building a big army, too big, and he's crazy enough to go to war to conquer all of Europe. I'm afraid that chaos will rule the world, and many businesses will fail. I intend to sell all my property and transfer the money to a bank in Switzerland. That money can be withdrawn in a crisis, invested wisely, and earn several times over. If I die, I suggest you do that instead of me."

Moshe Stolowitzky died a few days later. Thousands attended his funeral in the big Jewish cemetery in northern Warsaw. He was buried next to his wife, near the grave of the writer Y. L. Peretz. On the Stolowitzky couple's marble tombstone, inside a stylized iron fence, was a tablet of a hand contributing to a charity box, a reference to their generosity.

With the death of Hava and Moshe Stolowitzky, the mansion and the rest of the property was transferred to their son, Jacob. His wife, Lydia, spent a few months redecorating the mansion to suit her taste. Jacob worked hard to master the many deals his father left him and to guarantee his clients that every contract signed by his father would be honored in full.

Michael grew up like a prince in the fairy tales. His clothes were made by a well-known tailor, the cook made sure the child ate only high-quality food, and Gertruda didn't let him out of her sight from the minute he woke up to the time he went to sleep.

Lydia was very proud of the new look of the mansion and wanted to impress others with it, too. The housewarming for the new interior was celebrated with a ball for the dignitaries of Poland and the wealthy of Europe. The famous bass singer Feodor Chaliapin, accompanied by the best musicians of Warsaw, entertained the guests with opera pieces in the big ballroom. Wine flowed like water, and the mood was lively.

Jacob Stolowitzky followed his father's orders and sold most of his properties for good prices. With the help of his friend, the Swiss attorney Joachim Turner, he deposited the millions he received in a few banks in Switzerland. He was sure he was doing the right thing. His father's advice and his instincts about coming events always turned out to be right.

5.

Ever since her grim struggle to have a child, Lydia Stolowitzky had become superstitious and feared that someday their good luck would run out. Even though there was no obvious reason to fear an impending disaster, she was afraid that something bad would happen to her only son, that happiness would vanish, that the business would collapse. Her husband patiently put up with her long monologues and her accounts of bad omens, and tried in vain to dissipate her anxieties.

If Lydia wanted triumphant proof that her fears had some basis, she got it one Saturday afternoon. It was a warm sunny day and the Stolowitzky family was at the usual Sabbath meal. One maid cleared the plates of the first course and another brought the second. There was a good mood at the table. Jacob told of a new contract he was about to sign with the Soviet government to lay iron tracks from Moscow to Tashkent in Uzbekistan. Lydia suggested that, to honor the event, she would hold a reception and invite a famous violinist. Michael fluently and proudly recited a comic poem from a new children's book and everyone applauded him.

As they were finishing the soup and the maid was putting a pair of stuffed pheasants on the table, a knock was heard at the door. Everyone looked surprised, since family meals were a strict ceremony and the servants knew that they were not to be disturbed.

The door opened and Emil stood there. He bowed and apologized for the disturbance.

"Come back later," grumbled Jacob.

"This is urgent!" the chauffeur insisted.

"What's so urgent, Emil?"

"A woman gave me a letter for you and said it's a matter of life and death."

Jacob Stolowitzky put down his fork and opened the envelope. Urgent letters about business were an everyday affair. Messengers came and went from his house even on the Sabbath, but never had they dared disturb him at lunch.

His eyes ran over the note and his face turned pale. He gave the letter to his wife and Lydia gasped.

"What is this supposed to be?" She was amazed.

"I have no idea," said her husband. "I've never gotten a letter like this."

"I knew it," groaned Lydia. "I knew our good life couldn't last."

The unsigned letter said:

Mr. Stolowitzky,

If you don't want something bad to happen to you and your family, prepare a million zlotys in cash by tomorrow. Send your chauffeur to the entrance of Kraszinski Park. That will be the signal that you're willing to deliver the money to us. Afterward, we shall tell you what to do. We warn you not to go to the police.

He read the letter again and again, finding it hard to digest the words.

His wealthy businessmen friends were often targets of blackmailers. One of them was shot as he came out of his house after he refused to agree to their demands. For a long time, Jacob Stolowitzky had repressed the fear that such a thing could happen to him, too, someday. Now it was his turn.

He turned to Emil.

"Who gave you the letter?" he asked.

"A woman I don't know gave it to me at the house and disappeared."

"Describe her."

"Not young, thin, in a black coat. Her head was wrapped in a brown kerchief. She wore sunglasses."

"Were there other people with her?"

"I didn't see any."

"How did she know you work for us?"

"She waited at our gate. When she saw me she approached and waited until the gate opened for me, came to me, and asked if I worked for Mr. Stolowitzky. I said I did and then she gave me the letter for you and ran off."

Jacob dismissed Emil. Michael looked at his father inquisitively and Gertruda refrained from asking what had happened. Jacob quickly finished eating and withdrew to his room. From there he phoned the police.

An officer and two policemen soon came to the mansion on Ujazdowska Avenue. They collected testimony from the chauffeur and the servants, took the letter, and warned the family members not to go out alone. Jacob took his gun out of his desk drawer and put it in his pocket. Lydia canceled visits to her friends and closed herself in the house. Gertruda was ordered not to take the daily walk with Michael until the police caught the blackmailers.

For a few days nothing happened, and then Emil came with another letter. He said he was driving slowly at a busy intersection in Warsaw when the letter was suddenly thrown through the window of the Cadillac. "It was the same woman who gave me the first letter," he said.

This letter was also addressed to Jacob Stolowitzky.

Like its predecessor, it, too, wasn't signed:

> *We have learned that, against our demands, you did go to the police. We warn you for the last time: if your health and the health of your family are important to you, cut off all contact with the police immediately and pay the money. Send your chauffeur to park the car at the gate of Chopin Park tomorrow at five in the afternoon. We will see that as an agreement to the payment. Further instructions to come.*

"They're following us," Jacob said to Lydia with a worried expression. "They apparently saw the police come into our house."

"Or somebody told them about it."

"Who?" he asked in amazement.

"Any of the workers in the house. The servants, the gardeners, the cook . . . Every one of them could be a partner in that plot."

"We've always treated them like family. It's troublesome to think that one of them is plotting to harm us."

"What do you plan to do now?" she asked.

"Of course, I'll give this letter to the police. There is no way I'll give in to these criminals."

6.

The windows of the mansion on Ujazdowska Avenue overlooked lively Chopin Park. Parents strolled with their children, nannies pushed baby buggies, happy families spread blankets on the lawn and feasted on delicacies.

Michael begged Gertruda to take him for a walk in the park. Ever since the blackmail letters had come, they had been warned not to leave the house. But weeks passed and nothing happened. It was hard for Michael to be cooped up inside, and Gertruda consulted with his mother.

"Take him for just a short walk," Lydia agreed. "But on condition that Emil watches you."

Emil was relieved of all his work. The sky was clear when they left the house and entered the park. In the chauffeur's pocket a gun was hidden, given to him by his employer. Jacob Stolowitzky demanded that Emil stay very close to the nanny and the child.

The three of them ate ice cream in a café on the shore of the lake. Gertruda saw nothing suspicious. She shut her eyes and dozed off in the sun. Michael licked all his ice cream and Emil lit a cigarette.

Soon they headed home. Gertruda and Michael strolled arm in arm and Emil walked behind them. As they were walking, a mass of bushes suddenly loomed up at the side of the path and a man and a woman darted out of it. They attacked Michael and tried to get him out of Gertruda's arms. The nanny hugged the child with all her might and shouted for help. The man punched her in the nose, and he and the woman continued to pry the child from his nanny's arms. A few men walking nearby ran up to Gertruda and Michael. The two kidnappers let go and started fleeing. Emil pulled out his gun, shot at them, and started chasing them. Gertruda clutched Michael to her heart and he burst into tears. She asked the men who surrounded her to walk them back to the mansion. When they got home, Lydia gave her son and the nanny one look and was in a panic. She quickly bolted the door behind them.

"What happened?" she wanted to know.

Gertruda told her.

"You're hurt."

"It's nothing," said the nanny. Her nose was bleeding and her body ached from the blows, but she didn't complain. The important thing was that Michael was safe. She wouldn't have forgiven herself if the kidnappers had won.

Lydia brought bandages and antiseptic.

Emil came back some time later. "I chased the bastards, but they were too fast for me," he said sadly. "I couldn't catch them."

7.

The police inspectors heard Gertruda and Emil's story. The two of them were questioned at length and asked to describe the two kidnappers. "Was it the same woman who gave you the letter for Mr. Stolowitzky?" one of the inspectors asked Emil.

"Yes," he replied. "It was the same woman."

"Did you see where they escaped?"

"They left the park and ran to a car that was waiting for them. They got into it and drove off. I shot at the car but it disappeared."

"What kind of car?"

"A black Mercedes."

"Did you see the license number?"

"I didn't have time."

The inspectors came to Jacob Stolowitzky in the middle of a business meeting downtown. They closed themselves up in his office and told him about the chain of events.

"Somebody apparently revealed to the kidnappers that your child was about to go to the park," they said. "They laid in wait to kidnap him. Who could have told them about the planned walk?"

"Only the nanny, Gertruda, and the chauffeur, Emil, knew in advance about the walk," he said.

"How long has the nanny worked for you?"

"More than a year."

"You're satisfied with her?"

"Very."

"And the chauffeur? How long has he worked here?"

"Six years."

"Who hired him?"

"I did. We put an ad in the paper and he came with good references."

"Have you had problems with him during the time that he's worked for you?"

"Never."

"He may well have cooperated with the kidnappers," said the inspector. "Remember that he was the person who brought you the two extortion letters. He also knew in advance about the visit to the park. He did shoot at the kidnappers but didn't hit them. He may have missed on purpose. I think we should arrest him."

"Do you have any proof?"

"We don't have any proof, but we do have our suspicions."

"That's not enough," Stolowitzky insisted. "Emil is a devoted and loyal employee. He wouldn't dare do something bad to us."

"People are willing to do a lot for money," said the inspector. "Nevertheless, we do have to consider the possibility that he's involved in it. Trust our instincts. After he sits in prison awhile, he'll tell us everything. To be on the safe side, you should look for another chauffeur."

"Absolutely not," protested Stolowitzky. "I guarantee that Emil wasn't involved in this. We're very satisfied with him and have no doubt that he's loyal and honest."

Nevertheless, the police decided to hold Emil for questioning. Bowed and sad, he went with them and came back only two days later.

"They picked on me for no reason," he complained to his employers. "They threw me into a cell with common criminals and questioned me day and night. But, in the end, they didn't find anything against me."

CHAPTER 4

Kristallnacht

1.

The meeting hall of Karl Rink's SS unit was packed with men young and old, all wearing black uniforms. Outside was early November cold, and inside the hall, dense with clouds of cigarette smoke, a tense expectation prevailed.

Rink, however, was relaxed and at ease. Ever since he had joined the SS, he had mainly provided security for the senior members of the party. No one mentioned his Jewish wife and he was sure that fact was forgotten. To his great joy, Mira's fears had also subsided a little over time.

At seven on the dot the commander of the unit, Reinhard Schreider, stormed into the hall. He climbed onto the stage and raised his hand. "Heil Hitler!" A forest of hands went up and the hall echoed with shouts of "Heil!"

A silence fell when Schreider, his face enraged and his voice thundering, began his speech about an incident that had made headlines: a few days earlier, a Jewish student named Hershel

Greenspan had entered the German embassy in Paris and shot to death the diplomat Ernst von Rath in revenge for the Nazis' expulsion of his family from Germany.

"We've all heard about the awful crime in Paris," shouted the commander hoarsely. "And you know who's guilty?"

"The Jews!" the hall thundered unanimously.

"If the Jews think we'll ignore what happened," added Schreider, "they're very wrong. We will give them what they gave us. Tonight, all over Germany, demonstrations are being held against the Jews, and I call on every one of you to recruit as many friends as possible and go out into the streets."

He gave clear orders: to destroy the shops and apartments of Jews, to burn down synagogues, to locate Jewish businessmen and outstanding figures in the community and arrest them on the spot. Thousands of other activists of the Nazi Party all over Germany received similar orders at the same time from their district commanders.

Karl Rink went out into the cold street, into the night that would be remembered as the abomination of "Kristallnacht." He knew he was expected to act as a loyal SS man, that his comrades were relying on him to carry out the order to strike the Jews. His commanders appreciated his devotion, his obedience, his loyalty to the principles of the organization. He had been promoted faster than others, got a job in SS headquarters, a good salary, and a motorcycle. As a loyal member of the party, he always carried out every order from his superiors. Now, on the evening of a pogrom against the Jews, he hesitated for the first time.

He thought of Mira, her parents, and her family. Ever since they had gotten married, he treated her family like his own flesh and blood. When he was with them, he didn't talk about his work, never said a word against the Jews, never harmed them or their property, as his companions did, and he was offended when the family broke ties with him when they learned of his activity in the SS. This evening, he was ordered explicitly to commit acts he had never thought of doing, but he was part of a unit whose members had sworn to obey orders and he had no idea how to avoid carrying out the mission.

He was forced to go with them that night when they assaulted Jewish shops in Berlin and smashed display windows, had to watch them burst into the apartments of terrified Jews, beat them up, and destroy their furniture. He tried to stay as far away as he could without arousing suspicion, and he breathed a sigh of relief when things returned to normal in the morning. He made his way home slowly, past heaps of smashed furniture thrown out the windows of Jewish houses. He tiptoed inside, careful not to wake his wife and daughter. He got into bed silently but couldn't sleep, picturing the pale faces of the Jews who were victimized by the Nazi thugs. He knew he wouldn't dare tell Mira and Helga about it.

He woke up late in the morning. Helga had already gone to school and his wife looked dejected.

"I heard about what happened last night," she said. "Tell me the truth, Karl. Were you there, too?"

"I was, but I stood aside."

She looked at him directly.

"How long will you be able to stand aside, Karl? How long before you'll have to hurt Jews yourself? I could still somehow understand your motives when you joined the party. Many unemployed people had to do that. It was a time of great dreams, of belief in

Hitler's power, even though I knew and told you explicitly that someday the Jews would fall victim to the Führer's lunacy. You don't fit
that group of thugs. You don't fit because you're my husband and
the father of our daughter. Don't forget for one moment, Karl, that
I'm a Jew, and Helga is a Jew like me according to Nazi law. For her
sake and mine, promise me you'll leave the SS."

Karl was perplexed. He was torn between his wife and the party,
but his faith in Hitler was still strong, in spite of everything.

"The party has done a lot for us," he said. "I was unemployed,
we didn't have a penny, and suddenly Hitler came and everything
changed. There are also decent people in the SS, Mira. What they
did to the Jews was the result of anger about the murder in Paris.
Everything will calm down, I promise you."

"Don't you understand that the situation will only get worse?"

"You see things in the wrong light, Mira."

He was pouring himself a cup of coffee when, suddenly, the
doorbell rang. Karl went to open it and stood face-to-face with an
SS man he didn't know.

"Schreider wants you to come to him," said the messenger.

"When?"

"Right now."

Ever since he had joined the SS, Rink had never had a chance
to meet the commander of his unit in person. He wondered why
Reinhard Schreider had summoned him to an urgent meeting.

"What could he want with you?" Mira wondered. "Maybe he
wants to punish you for not taking part in the destruction?"

Karl didn't reply. He left the house, started his motorcycle, and
went to SS headquarters.

2.

Life in the Stolowitzky mansion went on as usual even as war clouds were lowering over Europe. The rapid development of the German army, the annexation of Austria to the Third Reich, and Hitler's rule over the entire Sudetenland in Czechoslovakia did stir concern in Poland, but the Stolowitzky family continued going to the summer estate, entertaining guests, and skiing in the mountains. Business was flourishing and money flowed in. There were no more blackmail and kidnapping attempts. "There's no reason to worry," Jacob would say to soothe those around him and himself. "In the end, Hitler won't dare go to war." He was optimistic about the future. He knew that even in the worst case, he wouldn't be especially hurt. Most of his money was in a safe place—in the armorplated vaults of the banks in Switzerland.

Meanwhile, every afternoon, when it wasn't too cold or rainy, Gertruda went for a walk with Michael. Before they left they would report to Lydia for a final check. Michael would ask his mother seriously: "Are we dressed properly for the Stolowitzky family?" And Lydia would smile and reply: "Of course, you're dressed just fine." She would give Gertruda a few zlotys and wish them a nice time.

Gertruda and Michael would go out the gate, usually accompanied by Emil, cross the street, go into nearby Chopin Park, pat the peacocks walking around freely, eat ice cream or cake in Café Belvedere, and sail in the colorful boats on the lake. They also loved to ride downtown on the trolley, watch the trains coming and going at the busy station, and look into the display windows packed with goodies.

Emil occasionally drove them out of town. They went to little villages whose residents looked admiringly at the rich people from

Warsaw, bought apples and cherries from farmers at the side of the road, and strolled on paths among the vegetable plots. Emil didn't hide his attraction to Gertruda. He courted her ardently and showered gifts on her, which she politely refused. She continued to ask him to leave her alone.

On a spring day in 1939, when Gertruda and Michael went out as usual, the sky was blue and a bright sun stood overhead. They strolled on Yeruzalimska Street, and at a small kiosk Gertruda bought chocolates for Michael and herself. When they sat down on a bench and munched on the treat, a brown puppy came to them, wagging his tail. Michael patted him and the puppy licked his hand.

"You think Mother will let me bring him home?" he asked.

"No, Michael," replied Gertruda. "You know she doesn't like animals."

"Too bad," said Michael. "He's so sweet."

They got up and walked off but the dog followed them. Gertruda waved him away firmly. He tried to ignore it, but she was more stubborn. At last, the dog withdrew sadly, his tail between his legs, and slowly crossed the street. A trolley approached and the driver rang the bell to warn the dog away from the tracks, but the dog didn't pay attention to the danger. Michael gripped Gertruda's hand in fear and shouted to him, "Watch out!" The dog didn't move any faster and slowly crossed the tracks, the trolley coming closer. Michael quickly dropped Gertruda's hand and ran to the dog. The trolley honked again. Michael jumped between the tracks and picked up the puppy.

Gertruda shrieked in terror. She swooped down on Michael and started pulling him from the path of the advancing trolley. The dog wailed and escaped from the boy's arms, while the trolley hit

Michael's knee and threw him onto the street. A burst of blood stained his trousers.

Gertruda anxiously bent over the child, who was groaning in pain. "Please, God, help us," she sobbed. She pictured Michael's mother getting the news of her son's injury and holding her responsible. How could she bear the thought that she had been negligent in taking care of the child she loved so much?

The trolley stopped and terrified passengers surrounded the nanny and the injured boy on the pavement. Somebody made his way over. "I'm a doctor. Let me through," he called. He was a young man, simply dressed. Gertruda whispered a prayer as he examined Michael. The doctor quickly took off his own shirt, tore it into strips, and used them as bandages to apply pressure. Then he picked Michael up and ran a few streets to the nearby hospital, with Gertruda hurrying along behind him. He took the child into the emergency room, called for doctors, and rushed to the operating room with them. The operation took a long time, and Gertruda kissed the doctor's hand when he told her that Michael's condition had improved and he would certainly recover soon and return home.

"Are you his mother?" he asked.

"No, I'm the nanny."

"Go home and tell his parents," he said. "I'll stay with the boy until they come."

In fear and trembling, Gertruda walked to the Stolowitzky house and told them what had happened. Lydia was shocked, but Gertruda's fears were groundless: Lydia didn't say a word about Gertruda's responsibility and didn't throw her out. She only asked her to come with her immediately to the hospital. When they got there, they found Michael sedated and the young doctor standing next to him. Gertruda told Lydia of his devoted care.

"I don't know how to thank you," said Michael's mother.

"There's no need to thank me. I only did what I had to," he said, and left before she could say another word.

Lydia and Gertruda sat by Michael's bed all night. The next morning, when the child opened his eyes and smiled wanly, the young doctor returned. He patted Michael and promised he would soon get out of the hospital.

"What's your name?" asked Lydia.

"Joseph Berman."

"You must be Jewish," she said. "So are we."

"Nice to meet you."

"God sent you to us. You saved my son. Thank you."

When Michael was released from the hospital two days later, Gertruda put him to bed. Emil found out Dr. Berman's address and Lydia drove with him to the doctor's house. They came to a lovely apartment house downtown and climbed up to the third floor. A brass plate fixed to the door said: DR. JOSEPH BERMAN, SPECIALIST IN LUNG DISEASES.

The doctor's wife opened the door to them. Sounds of children playing came from the apartment and she looked inquisitively at the refined woman and her uniformed chauffeur.

"Is the doctor at home?" asked Lydia.

"Yes. He's with a patient now. Come in, please."

They sat down in the corridor across from the doctor's treatment room. An old man came out soon after, followed by the young doctor, who was amazed to see the visitors. Lydia stood up and handed him an envelope.

"That's for you," she said.

He opened it and found a large sum of money.

The doctor shook his head.

"I didn't treat your son for money," he said quietly.

She felt embarrassed.

"But that's your work . . . you're entitled to payment."

He gave the envelope back to her.

"That wasn't part of my work," he said. "I was glad I could help."

It was hard for Lydia to understand why he refused her payment. Never had anyone refused money from her.

"Nevertheless I want to reward you for what you did," she insisted.

He smiled. "Your thanks are enough, madame."

She quickly put the envelope on the nearby cabinet and hurried out the door.

3.

Karl Rink entered SS headquarters with mixed feelings. He knew that Unit Commander Schreider wouldn't bother to summon him if he didn't have a good reason. Karl straightened his black uniform, tightened his swastika armband, and tried to guess what his commander might say to him.

The building was humming with uniformed men running around in the corridors and congregating in groups. He knew most of them and exchanged greetings.

In the anteroom of the unit commander's office, Schreider's third in command, Kurt Baumer, gave Rink a friendly smile. Baumer was Rink's close friend, his only friend in the SS. The two of them had lived in the same neighborhood as children and had come a long way to reach their present positions.

"The commander is expecting you," said Baumer.

"What does he want?"

"I have no idea."

Baumer led Rink to Schreider's big office. On the wall was a large photo of Hitler and the swastika flag hung behind the desk.

Karl straightened up, raised his right hand, and shouted "Heil Hitler!"

Schreider sat up in his leather chair and returned his greeting with raised arm. He was stocky and bald, with a tic in the corner of his mouth.

"Leave us alone," he said to Baumer.

"Karl Rink." He addressed his underling in an official tone. "You've been with us now for seven years, correct?"

"Seven years and two months."

"You've won a lot of praise, Rink. I've read the reports on your activity, your devotion to the Führer. There are good chances that you'll be promoted and given more responsibility."

"Thank you, Commander."

"But I wanted to clarify a few things. First of all, I got a report on the activities of our men in the retaliation we carried out against the Jews. Among other things, I was told that you didn't really take part in the operation."

"I was there."

"You were. But what did you do?"

"I participated like everybody else."

"It was reported to me that you stood aside, didn't beat up Jews, didn't smash shop windows. Why?"

"I did my best," said Karl quietly.

Schreider didn't take his penetrating eyes off him,

"Your wife is Jewish, Rink, correct?"

"Yes."

"And I assume you'll tell me that has nothing to do with your standing aside in demonstrations against the Jews."

"It has nothing to do with it," Karl lied weakly.

"You live together or apart?" Schreider wanted to know.

"What do you mean, Commander?"

"You know, of course, that the Nuremberg Laws annulled all marriages between Aryans and Jews. In fact, you're forbidden to be married to a Jew."

"I know."

"They tell me that you continue to live with your wife, against the law."

"Correct."

"Rink," the SS officer continued, "our Führer is leading Germany and the whole world to a new age. Revolutionary changes are in process. We need good men who will give a hand and carry out the exalted mission assigned to us. We need you, Karl."

"I'll carry out every order, sir."

Not a muscle moved in Schreider's face.

"Of course, it's clear to you," he said harshly, "that you'll have to decide between us and your wife. You can't be faithful to the party and to the Jews at the same time. You have to separate from her."

"She won't get in the way." Karl Rink tried to persuade the commander. "The fact that my wife is a Jew has never stifled my devotion to our ideal."

"Look, Rink," hissed Schreider, "so far we haven't pressed you because we thought you'd come to the right conclusion by yourself. Now you have to decide: either her or us. There's no other possibility."

"May I ask something?"

"No." Schreider's patience ran out.

"I need a little more time."

The commander glared at him.

"A loyal SS man," he said, "has to be able to sacrifice everything for the Reich. We expect only one thing will be important to our

people: victory. Family may not be the top priority for an SS man.
Are you clear?"

"Yes," muttered Rink.

"When will you divorce her?"

"Soon."

"That's not good enough, Karl. Get divorced this week."

Rink stood helpless, desperately seeking an answer.

"This week," Schreider repeated the order. "Understood, Karl?"

Karl Rink rode his motorcycle aimlessly in the wet streets of the city.
He didn't hurry home. He needed time to think, to decide, and it
was hard, harder than any fateful issue he had ever confronted in his
thirty-eight years. He loved Mira, and yet he felt loyal to the SS.
There were many things in the organization that he loved, other
things he didn't like, mainly the treatment of the Jews. In the SS,
they preached the purity of the Aryan race morning, noon, and
night, blamed the Jews for all the troubles afflicting Germany.
Newspapers described the Jews as abominable leeches sucking the
blood of the Germans. He loathed those attacks, but still believed
they were merely pitfalls on the way to the goal. His problem was
that his loyalty to the party was as strong as his love for his wife. He
was unhappy that Schreider had wrung a promise from him to end
his marriage within the week. How could he part from Mira after
such a happy life together?

When Karl came home, Mira was sitting in the living room,
listening to an opera on the radio. Ever since she had been fired,
she hadn't been able to find another job. No one dared hire Jews
anymore.

Mira lowered the volume and looked up at her husband. She
waited for him to tell her about the meeting with Schreider.

He dropped onto the easy chair across from her.

"Schreider gave me an ultimatum." The words broke in his mouth.

"Let me guess: he told you to choose—me or the party."

"Yes, that's what he said."

"I warned you it would be that. What did you tell him?"

"I said that you won't get in the way of my activity."

"That convinced him?"

"I don't think so."

"He wants us to get divorced?"

"Yes."

"And what did you decide?"

"I said I'd do it, but I didn't mean it."

"What does that mean?"

"That means that I have no intention of getting divorced."

"What will happen if Schreider discovers the truth?"

"I hope he won't."

Karl got up and paced around the room.

"The party is important to me, Mira," he said after a long silence. "The party is my future, the future of all of us, Germany's future."

"Your party will bring down a disaster on all of us."

"You're wrong, Mira."

She sighed.

"*You're* wrong, Karl, not me."

4.

The rainstorm in mid-June 1939 collapsed trees and made roofs fly in the poor neighborhoods of Warsaw. As always, it also disrupted phone lines. Nevertheless, through the deafening beeps and static of the phone in his office, Jacob Stolowitzky could hear a woman's distant voice sobbing in despair.

He clutched the receiver in his clenched fist and put it tight to his ear. After a long moment, he managed to identify the voice. It was the wife of the manager of his plant in Berlin.

"Try to calm down," he said. "I don't understand a word."

Her weeping slowly subsided.

"The SS arrested my husband yesterday," she groaned. "They're holding him in jail and won't release him."

"Why?"

"Because he's a Jew, Mr. Stolowitzky. That's what he's guilty of."

Stolowitzky turned pale. The arrest of the manager of his big steel plant in the industrial area of Berlin had come at the worst time, in the middle of negotiations with the railroad company of France about supplying hundreds of miles of railroad track. Only the German factory could quickly provide such big quantities of track. Any disruption in the operation of the plant was liable to undermine negotiations with the French. Suddenly, the enormous profit of the deal seemed uncertain.

"Where is your husband?" he asked.

"I have no idea."

Stolowitzky gave her a few words of comfort and called the German Ministry of Defense. He had good friends there, senior officials he did business with. He often traveled to Germany to meet them and entertained them in the best restaurants. He was sure they could help him now.

He managed to reach two of them, but this time they treated him coldly.

"The Nazis are running things now," they said. "You'll have to talk with them."

"I'll leave for Germany today," he said eagerly. "I'll meet with anybody I have to to release my manager."

"Not a good idea for you to come now," one of them advised him before he hung up. "Germany today is no place for you. Remember that you're a Jew. They're liable to arrest you, too."

Jacob Stolowitzky walked around his office helplessly for a long time. It was hard to plan his next steps.

The phone rang. The wife of his plant manager was back on the line.

"Mr. Stolowitzky," she said in a choked voice. "The SS came back to the factory today and threw out everybody with Polish citizenship. Ordered them all back to Poland."

Stolowitzky was proud of his Polish engineers. He had chosen them carefully and sent them and their families to Berlin. Without them, he knew, his plant faced a total shutdown.

"It's awful, Mr. Stolowitzky," the woman added. "Berlin has turned into hell. Anti-Semitism is rampant, the Jews are thrown out of their jobs or are arrested, every one of us is doing all we can to escape from here."

The conversation was cut off.

Jacob Stolowitzky clutched his head in his hands. He had been following events in Germany in the newspaper, had read about increasing abuses against Jews, but his plant was under foreign ownership. After all, he himself was a foreign citizen who did business with the German government. It didn't occur to him that Germany would dare do anything bad to foreign citizens.

He went home despondent, recalling the bleak deathbed prophecies of his father who had seen what was happening and understood the inevitable process of incitement against Jews. Angrily, he told his wife about the arrest of the manager and the expulsion of the engineers.

"I have to consult with my lawyer in Berlin," he said. "I'll go there today."

She tried to stop him.

"The Germans will arrest you, too," she said. "There's talk of war in Europe. Wait until things calm down."

He took her hand.

"I have to," he said. "Don't worry. I'll be back in a few days."

One of the maids packed his traveling case, and he said goodbye to his wife and son. On his way out, he met Gertruda.

"I'm going," he said. "Take good care of Lydia and Michael."

She looked at him with dread. Her senses told her that he was going on a dangerous trip.

"Yes, sir, I'll take care of them as best I can," she replied.

Emil carried his suitcase to the car.

"To the railroad station," Stolowitzky ordered his chauffeur.

He got into the first-class carriage and sank into the soft seat. As the train moved, Jacob Stolowitzky looked out the window at Warsaw receding in the distance.

He was sure he'd be back in a few days.

5.

School ended as usual, late in the afternoon. Twilight was falling as Helga left school and walked home, wrapped in her coat, wool gloves warming her hands, along a street where signs of the Kristallnacht pogrom were still evident. The display windows of shops had been smashed and JEW was written on their doors. Her heart stopped at the sight of SS men dragging an old Jew into a gray car. For a moment, she imagined she saw her father among them, wearing a uniform and pitiless like them, but he wasn't there. She thought of his relationship with her mother, destroyed recently because he insisted on staying in the SS. She pictured family memories from the recent past, walks in charming landscapes, sailing on the lake of Berlin, a picnic in the forest, joyous birthday celebrations. In all those scenes, Karl Rink appeared as a devoted father, smiling, and happy. She remembered days when she was proud of him. What had happened to her father, she asked herself, what had made him change his skin, turn his back on his way of life, stick with the beasts who ruled the country she loved with a regime of thugs?

As she was still sunk in her thoughts, a group of boys blocked her way. She tried to get away from them, but they surrounded her and called her names. Their leader, a strong, fair-haired boy, approached the girl, pulled her hair, and cursed at her. Helga tried to resist but he punched her and pushed her down on the sidewalk. Her nose started bleeding. The boys laughed. "Stinking Jew," shouted their leader, and he kicked Helga. "That's only the beginning. We'll be back here tomorrow."

In pain, she stumbled home. She wiped the blood off her nose, hoping her mother wouldn't notice. But Mira saw it at once.

"What happened?" she cried in amazement.

Helga told her.

Mira washed her daughter's face and bandaged her nose. Helga locked herself in her room. The house felt dreary. Mira walked around like a shadow of herself. She thought of what had happened to her daughter and knew that such things would happen again, maybe worse. Yes, she'd tell her husband everything, but she didn't believe he could do anything. She knew it wasn't easy for him, that he was torn between the party and his family. Her heart ached at his refusal to resign from his job with the SS. She smoked nervously and drank a glass of wine, unable to think properly.

Karl Rink didn't come home much and today, just when his wife and daughter needed him the most, he wasn't there. When he did come, late at night, Mira was lying on the sofa in the living room, smoking.

She gave him a brief account of the incident. Karl Rink sighed in pain, went to his daughter's room, and hugged her.

"Don't worry," he said in a soothing voice. "It will pass. Everything will be fine."

Helga lowered her eyes. She knew that nothing would be fine, nothing would go back to the way it was.

"Do you know who did that?" He pointed to the bandage on her nose.

Yes, she knew. His name was Paul, the neighbors' son. In the past he had always smiled at her. She couldn't imagine that someday that nice boy would turn into a monster.

6.

On June 20, 1939, the train from Warsaw to Berlin was unusually empty. Jacob Stolowitzky sat tensely in his compartment, upset by the gloomy thoughts about the danger lurking for his business in Germany. His only consolation was his upcoming meeting with his attorney. He wanted to believe that, in spite of everything, things could still be done legally in Berlin.

Facing him, in the first-class compartment, sat a German couple. The husband rode silently the whole way, and his wife clutched a whining baby. A waiter passed among the compartments, offering hot drinks and food. Jacob Stolowitzky wasn't hungry. Nausea climbed up his throat and grew worse every moment.

At the border station, the train stopped and German guards entered the car, carefully examining Stolowitzky's Polish passport.

They asked the reason for his trip to Berlin. He said he was traveling on business.

"Jew?" they asked.

"Yes."

They grimaced. "What business do you have in Berlin?"

"I've got a factory."

"It won't belong to you for long," hissed one of the guards mockingly, and his companion asked, "When do you intend to return to Poland?"

"This week."

They stamped his passport reluctantly and left.

When the train continued, Jacob Stolowitzky looked out the window and saw military traffic on the roads. Trucks packed with soldiers and cases of ammunition moved along slowly in long columns, towing machine guns and field kitchens. In the railroad station in Berlin, there were more soldiers carrying equipment and weapons.

Jacob took a cab to his lawyer's office. He saw JEWS OUT written on smashed display windows of shops on the main streets and Nazi thugs marching on the sidewalk with wooden cudgels in their hands.

The lawyers' office was locked, and a sign on the door read: CLOSED UNTIL FURTHER NOTICE. After feverish searching, Stolowitzky came to his lawyer's house. He saw a man who seemed to have grown old overnight. He invited him in. The lawyer corroborated all his client's fears: the Nazis were quickly taking over factories owned by Jews, limiting the movements of the Jews, and imposing heavy punishments on anyone who dared violate their increasingly strict orders.

"None of us knows what will happen tomorrow," said the lawyer. "They took away my license, I lost almost all my clients who no longer want any contact with Jews. My colleague, a Jewish lawyer, who dared complain to the police against a Christian businessman, was beaten up, stripped naked, and forced to walk in the street with a sign hung around his neck by the police reading: I WILL NEVER AGAIN COMPLAIN TO THE POLICE. Many of us are escaping from here. Others are staying at home and shaking with fear." He revealed that in a few days, he and his family were moving to Palestine. "I tried to sell my property," added the lawyer. "But there are no buyers. Everyone is waiting for the Jews to leave and our property will go to the rabble for free."

"What can I do to save my business?" asked Jacob Stolowitzky anxiously. "Is there any point in going to court?"

"No," said the lawyer sadly. "They'll just throw you out."

Stolowitzky glanced from the window to the bustling street. Life appeared to be going on as usual, but in fact it was hell.

"I've got only one piece of advice for you," said the lawyer. "Go immediately to the railroad station and return home before it's too late."

"The situation is that bad?"

"Worse. There are signs that war is approaching. If I were you, I would also weigh the possibility of taking the whole family and getting out of Poland. In my opinion, that's liable to be one of the first targets the Nazis are planning to hit."

The train to Warsaw was to leave at dawn the next day. Jacob Stolowitzky took a room in a hotel near the station and ordered a phone line home. Two hours later, he heard Lydia's voice.

"How are things in Berlin?" she asked.

"Very bad. I'm coming home."

Emil met him at the railroad station and drove him home. Jacob was tired. He sat down in the backseat and was silent all the way. Lydia greeted him in the vestibule.

"What happened?" she wanted to know.

He told her.

She gave him a telegram from his agent in Paris.

He read it quickly:

The contract with the French company is ready to be signed, except for a few clauses that demand your approval. You should come at once.

Stolowitzky's eyes sparkled with joy.

"At long last, good news," he said to his wife.

"You're going to Paris?" she asked.

"Of course."

He went to Michael's room, hugged and kissed him.

"I'm going again," he said. "When I come back, I'll bring you a terrific present."

"When will you come back?" asked Michael.

"In a few days."

He phoned his agent in Paris and told him he would be there the next day.

A few hours later, in the train that left for Paris at dawn, he thought, One door was closed, but another door has opened.

7.

Karl Rink was restless. His head was spinning and he was on edge. With clenched fists, he walked around the house of the boy who had hit his daughter, trying to decide what to do with him. He remembered the days when everything was fine in Germany, days when he could have complained to the police about the boy who had attacked his daughter and expected something would be done about it. But everything was different now. The police certainly wouldn't accept a complaint against someone who hit a Jewish girl, and he couldn't do much himself either. He couldn't go into the boy's house in an SS uniform and threaten him and his parents. One complaint from them to his superiors, and he would land in jail immediately. But Karl couldn't just drop it. He just couldn't let it go.

He knew the boy's face and went on watching for him near his house, hiding behind an announcement board filled with Nazi manifestos. At nightfall, he saw him coming home, followed him, pulled out his gun, and hit him on the back of the head with the barrel. The boy collapsed with a groan of pain. "That's for the girl you beat up," he hissed. "If you touch her again, your punishment will be much worse."

"Who are you?" groaned Paul. He couldn't recognize Karl in the dark.

"Never mind," growled Karl and hit him again with his gun.

Paul wept bitterly. "But she's a Jew," he tried to explain.

"Promise you won't go near her again," demanded Karl.

"Promise . . . promise . . ."

Karl Rink turned around and disappeared, and the boy stumbled home. His mother was scared when she saw him.

"What happened to you?"

"Somebody beat me up."

"Who?"

"I don't know. I didn't see in the dark. He said it was because I took care of some Jewish girl in our class."

"My poor boy." His mother clasped him to her breast. "The Jews are a curse. Don't go near them. Hitler will take care of them."

. . .

When Karl returned home, he found Helga and her mother sitting next to each other. The windows and doors were locked.

"Paul won't hurt you anymore," he said.

"You're sure?"

"Trust me. I know."

"I'm not sure I'll go to school at all," said Helga. "If not Paul, some other anti-Semite will come. I'm scared I'll get worse than a punch in the nose."

He wanted to comfort her but he didn't know what to say. She looked out the window. It was raining again.

"Father," she said, "Mother and I don't feel safe here. It gets worse from day to day and you can't take care of everybody who decides to attack us because we're Jews."

He went to her and wrapped his arm around her shoulder.

"I love the two of you," he said. "I love you more than anything else in the world. Please, have a little patience. The persecution of the Jews won't last forever."

His hand gave her a wave of warmth, as in the past.

"Thanks for trying to persuade us." She made a great effort to get the words out of her mouth. "But that won't help, Father. You won't dare to look directly at the truth, you delude yourself that you can go on for a long time being in the SS and being part of a Jewish family. It's only a question of time until something bad will happen to you and to us."

Karl gave her a long look and then he said to his wife: "Helga may be right. The only solution is for you to leave here with her. If you stay in Berlin, there's no guarantee you'll be able to go on living calmly."

"I'm not going anywhere," said Mira. "This is my home. I can't leave my parents. They're elderly and not in good health and they need me. Nobody will throw us out of here."

He sat down across from her with an expression of pain on his face.

"Don't be stubborn," he demanded.

"Leave us alone, Karl. Go away from here. Go back to your friends."

"You have no right to risk your life. You have no right to risk Helga's life."

"She's a big girl. Let her decide for herself what to do."

Helga stood at the window and looked outside gloomily. She hadn't seen her father smile for a long time.

"Did you hear what your mother said?" he asked.

"I heard."

"I'm not going," Mira repeated.

"Mother, Father's right," said the girl. "We can't live here. I want you to come with me."

"I'm staying, Helga."

"Then," Karl pleaded with his daughter, "you'll have to go alone."

"I want Mother to come with me," said the girl tearfully.

"Mother can't, Helga," said Karl.

"I don't know . . . let me think about it."

"Think fast," Karl Rink urged her. "Very soon all the borders will be closed and it will be too late."

CHAPTER 5

Kidnapping in Broad Daylight

1.

At the Paris railroad station, Jacob Stolowitzky was met by his French sales agent, who drove him to the Ritz Hotel where a suite on the top floor was reserved for him. "The contract is almost done," said the agent. "There are just a few issues that haven't yet been agreed upon. I hope we can sign very soon."

Jacob told him about his gloomy hours in Berlin.

"From the way things are turning out in Germany, I have no doubt that my factory will be closed," he said. "A lot of money will be lost there."

"The French are worried about the situation in Germany," said the agent. "Your factory may not be able to supply the iron tracks. What will happen?"

"I'm in touch with big factories in Britain," said Stolowitzky. "I can fill every order with them."

. . .

Despite the optimism about finalizing the French contract, the matter took longer than Jacob expected. The thick file included all the work plans, deadlines, details of personnel that would be recruited. Work on that file had taken more than two years. Now, at the last minute, they were worried that Stolowitzky wouldn't be able to deliver the goods. Within two days, he had gotten commitments from the British plants, met with representatives of the French railroad company, his agent and lawyers who had negotiated contacts with the French from the beginning, and together they went over all the questionable paragraphs. According to the contract, Jacob Stolowitzky was supposed to create railroad tracks to replace old tracks along many hundreds of miles all over France. In exchange for the work, the French promised to pay him an enormous sum.

Jacob Stolowitzky wasn't happy about the delay in Paris. He wanted to get back home to Warsaw, to his wife and son, to catch up with his business there. But discussions with his French clients were also important. The deal would be one of the biggest he had ever made, and now, after the blow he had suffered in Berlin, it was even more important.

He called Lydia several times and apologized for not being able to come home sooner. She understood. This wasn't the first time he had been away from home on business for a long time.

"Don't worry about us," she said. "Everything's quiet here and we're all fine."

2.

Wolfgang Erst was a dull-witted thug, a former construction worker who rose in the ranks of the SS with wild demonstrations against

Jews and secret murders of opponents of the Nazi regime. He obeyed his superiors blindly and they knew they could count on him not to utter a word about what went on in the inner sancta and torture cells of the organization.

When Reinhard Schreider summoned him to his office, Erst was excited and happy. He had the feeling that his commander would compliment him on his activities and even announce his promotion. But Schreider did neither of those.

He leaned toward the thug and only said: "I've got a special assignment for you, Erst."

"Yes, Commander."

Schreider pushed a note to him with a name and an address.

"You know who that woman is?" he asked.

"No," replied Erst.

"Have you heard the name of her husband, Karl Rink?"

"No idea."

"She's a Jew married to one of our men. Two weeks ago he promised me to divorce her. I want to find out if he has."

Erst peeped at the note and gathered it into his hand. For him, such an investigation was no big deal. He had carried out more complicated ones.

"I'll take care of it right away," he said. "You can count on me."

"I know."

Erst and two of his men set out to find what Reinhard Schreider wanted to know. When Erst returned to Schreider, he told him: "We didn't find any impression of divorce. Mira and Karl Rink live together as usual. He sleeps and eats at home, and he doesn't seem to have taken any step toward divorce."

"Bring the woman to me," ordered Schreider.

Ever since she was fired from her job, Mira stayed home most of the time. In the morning, after the attack on Helga, she would walk her to school to protect her, then went grocery shopping and visited her parents once a week. When the time came to pick up her daughter from school, she would leave the house again, come back with Helga, and stay there until the next day.

"Tomorrow, when she goes to the grocery store," said Erst, "we'll arrest her without a scandal and we'll bring her to you."

3.

Early in the morning, Peter and Maria Babilinska boarded the train from their town. Peter was a farmer who grew cabbage and potatoes and also worked in the post office. His wife made jam, which she sold at markets.

The two of them were tense and worried, eager to get to their daughter in Warsaw. They hadn't seen her in a few months.

Gertruda was surprised when the maid told her that her parents had arrived. She brought them in and made tea, which her parents didn't touch.

"How are you?" asked her father.

"Fine." She wondered why they had come. Ever since she had started working as a nanny, they rarely visited her. She herself had visited them only three times since she had started working in the Stolowitzky house.

"Your mother and I are going through hard times," sighed the father. "You've been here more than a year and . . ." He fell silent in embarrassment. Gertruda waited for him to go on.

"We have come to take you back home," said her father, and her mother nodded.

Gertruda looked at her father in amazement.

"You're not young anymore," added Peter. "And we're not getting any younger either. Our greatest wish is to see you married and to hug the grandchildren you'll bring us."

"I feel good here," she said. "I don't think I want to get married now."

"You're a Christian," he tried another tack. "You don't belong in this house."

"I take care of a child," she insisted. "He needs me, especially now. His father is away and his mother is alone. I can't leave."

"You can, Gertruda."

A tap was heard at the door and Lydia came in. Gertruda introduced her parents.

"We came to take our daughter home," said Maria. "The time has come for her to get married and take care of her own children and not those of others."

Lydia stared at the nanny.

"When are you going?" she asked.

"I'm staying here," she answered.

Lydia's lips trembled. "I understand your parents' concern," she said. "Maybe you really should go with them."

Gertruda addressed her parents. "I'm sorry," she said. "I want to stay here."

Maria and Peter knew their daughter's firmness, her stubbornness. They stood up heavily.

"Think about what we said," said Peter. "We'll wait for you at home. Come soon."

"Thanks for coming all the way here," she replied. "But I don't intend to change my mind."

Her mother burst out crying and let the tears roll down her cheeks.

"You see how hard it is for Mother without you," said her father. "Don't break her heart."

Gertruda hugged her mother.

"I love you," she said. "But I'm an adult. Let me do what my heart commands."

The mother kissed her, as if they were parting forever.

"Promise you'll take care of yourself," she said.

"I promise."

Dejected and pained, her parents left the room. Lydia said to Gertruda, "I just want you to know that Michael and I are glad you decided to stay with us."

4.

By the late 1930s, the Nazi Party controlled everything. It sent people to prison and concentration camps who opposed or were likely to oppose its regime; it scattered spies all over the state, passed laws and regulations designed to spew the Jews out of German society and force them to leave the country. The residents of the state quickly got used to the new situation. Most of them still believed firmly in Hitler and his promise of good things to come. For the time being, they turned a blind eye to phenomena they might not have been able to endure in other times. They got used to seeing many difficult scenes: a car stopping at a curb near an apartment house, a few men in black leather coats dashing out of it and pounding up the stairs. A few minutes later, they come down with a frightened prisoner, throw him into the car, take off quickly for an unknown destination, and life goes back to business as usual. This happened to quite a few politicians who opposed the criminal behavior of Hitler and his followers; it happened to writers, artists, intellectuals who criticized the Führer; it happened to many Jews.

Mira Rink constituted an explicit stumbling block that had to be removed. Karl Rink was supposed to divorce her, but he refused and thus sealed his wife's fate. His bosses decided for him.

In late August 1939, Mira went out to buy food in the grocery store near her house. She stayed there a little while and then made her way home, her mind filled with thoughts about the great problem that endangered her marriage. Her love for Karl was unshakable. He was the first and only man in her life, and it was hard for her to accept the fact that he still believed in the Nazi Party and took part in its activities.

She passed by some Jewish neighbors who cast furious glances at her, not for the first time. Some of them, who had been her close friends in the past, broke off with her as soon as her husband joined the SS. It was hard for her to bear it, but she had to repress her grief.

Before she arrived home, three men in black leather coats blocked her way.

"Frau Rink?" asked one of them.

She nodded. Erst and his two men seized her arms without a word and threw her into a brown car that started moving quickly.

"Who are you?" she shouted, even though she immediately could guess.

They clenched their lips.

"My husband is an SS officer," she tried to explain, but they looked at her with frozen eyes and were silent. For a moment, she thought of opening the car door and trying to escape, but she understood at once that that was impossible. They wouldn't let her run away.

At an old stone building in the southern part of the city, the car stopped. Mira Rink looked around and didn't recognize the place. She had never been there in her life.

The three men pushed her inside the building and led her through narrow corridors to a big room. SS officer Reinhard Schreider looked up at her from his desk.

"Leave her here," he said, and the three left the room.

He calmly offered her a glass of water, which she refused.

"You know," he said, slowly and seriously, "that the law forbids marriages of Jews and Aryans?"

"I know."

"You're a Jew and your husband is an Aryan, correct?"

"Correct."

"You understand that in your married life you're both violating the law?"

"I married him long before the law went into effect. We love each other, and we've got a fourteen-year-old daughter."

"Recently, I agreed with your husband that you'd get divorced."

She pretended to be surprised.

"I have no idea what you're talking about," she said.

"I am obliged to inform you that for the sake of order, every one of us must obey the law. You, Frau Rink, had to get divorced."

Suddenly, she was filled with fear. There was something cold and alien in the voice of the man facing her. She knew that he expected only one answer from her.

"Absolutely not," she insisted, nevertheless. "We have no intention of breaking up our marriage."

His face grew furious.

"That's very bad, Frau Rink."

She stood up. "Can I go now?" she asked.

"No," he raised his voice. "You cannot go now!"

He picked up the phone and issued an order. The three men who had grabbed Mira Rink entered the room.

"Take her to the yard," he ordered them.

By the time she understood where they were taking her, it was too late. The paved yard was surrounded by a high stone wall. They ordered her to face the wall and emptied the magazines of their guns into her body. The sounds of the shattering were blocked in the stones of the wall and Mira collapsed on the ground. The three of them dragged her body to a nearby pit dug to hold victims like her.

5.

Karl Rink was swept away in the flow of the uniformed men to the big SS assembly hall. Under the gigantic swastika flags fixed on poles along the walls, thousands waited for the Führer's arrival. He came in an open Mercedes that made its way through the crowd hysterically roaring "Heil Hitler." He entered the hall and climbed onto the stage. Hitler's talk was electrifying and Karl was hypnotized. Like all those gathered there, he also saw before him a determined savior, and when Hitler shrieked, "Deutschland über alles," a tremor of excitement went through him. He felt again like a partner in a glowing political plan, a wonderful vision of the future to march Germany into a period of unprecedented flourishing.

Afterward, he got on his motorcycle and rode home. In recent months, whenever he went home, he felt a heavy oppression. It was hard for him to bear his wife's suffering, his daughter's piercing questions, the sense that they didn't understand him. As he rode, he came up with the idea of mobilizing friends and relatives to try to persuade Mira to stop pressuring him until things settled down.

• • •

All the lights were on in the apartment when he arrived. He heard his daughter weeping in her room. When he stood in the door, she looked at him with red eyes.

"Mother's not here. I don't know where she is . . . I called you at the office but you weren't there."

He looked at his watch. It was after ten at night.

"Where could she be?" he asked, refusing to share his daughter's dread.

"She went out this morning to buy food and didn't come back."

"Maybe she went to visit somebody?"

"She's never been out so late . . . I'm afraid something happened to her."

He pleaded with her to go to sleep. "When you wake up in the morning, Mother will certainly be here," he said, trying to calm her.

"Look for her, Father," pleaded Helga. "Look for her before it's too late."

Karl climbed on his motorcycle and went looking for his wife. His first stop was her parents' house. They were asleep when he arrived. His mother-in-law opened the door and grimaced when she saw him. She and her husband hadn't exchanged a word with him ever since the attacks on the Jews had begun.

"Is Mira here?" he asked.

"No. What happened?" the mother asked, frightened.

"She left home and hasn't come back."

"What does that mean?" Her voice was accusing.

"I don't know."

"Find out from your friends, Karl," she said. "I'm sure those bastards took her."

Her husband came out of his room and stood aside. He heard the exchange.

"Bring her back home!" he called out angrily. "Bring her back before something awful happens to her!"

Karl visited a few friends. Mira wasn't there either. He went to the hospitals, checked the police stations, but nothing turned up. He returned home helplessly, and suddenly, his thoughts took him to the SS. No, he said to himself, his comrades in the organization couldn't have done that. Nevertheless, he phoned his commander. Schreider was still in his office.

"My wife has disappeared," he said. "Do you know anything about that?"

"How should I know?" Schreider played innocent.

Karl walked around the apartment on pins and needles. His wife's mysterious disappearance put him unbearably on edge, and the more he thought about it, the more he understood that something or someone had deliberately caused her disappearance. He returned to SS headquarters, asked the help of his friend Kurt Baumer, talked with the commanders of the interrogation division, with those in charge of prisoners, with every senior official he came upon. All of them denied any connection to his wife, but Karl didn't believe them.

When he arrived home, Helga was still awake, weeping bitterly.

"Did you find Mother?" she asked.

"Not yet," he replied.

He felt that the chances of finding Mira were getting slimmer with every passing hour. He had no idea what he could do to bring her back home.

6.

Karl Rink didn't get any sleep all night between the twenty-fourth and twenty-fifth of August 1939. He thought of his wife who had disappeared and tried to breathe some hope in his heart that she'd soon come back. But even if she did, who could guarantee her safety and the safety of Helga if Karl wasn't at their side day and night? How could he ensure that the anti-Semites wouldn't attack them? How could he know that those attacks wouldn't end in disaster?

In the morning, he put on his civilian clothes, left the house, and rode his motorcycle to the edge of the city. On the second floor of a faded apartment building was the office of a charity organization called "Help for Jewish Youth," whose task was to get young Jews out of Germany and take them safely to the Land of Israel. There, he had heard, they were sent to agricultural settlements called kibbutzim, where all their needs were met. The SS knew about the organization but ignored its activity, since its purpose coincided with the Nazi goal of getting rid of the Jews as fast as possible.

The director of the organization, a social worker named Raha Frayer, was talking on the phone with some contributors when Karl Rink entered her office. She glanced up and gestured to him to wait. In his civilian clothes, he looked like any worried parent who wanted to send his children out of Germany to a safe place. Raha Frayer finished her phone call and turned to Karl.

"I'm an SS man," he said, surprising her. She looked at him fearfully and sensed that something bad was about to happen. A sudden visit of SS men couldn't be a happy event.

But Karl smiled at her reassuringly.

"Don't be afraid," he said. "I'm here because of my daughter."

He told her everything. "I want to get Helga out of Germany before it's too late."

"You came at the very last minute," she told him. "The day after tomorrow, a group of children is taking a train to Switzerland. From there they go to Italy, and from Italy they'll sail to Palestine, where the children will be sent to kibbutzim. If your daughter can be ready by the time the train leaves, I promise you we'll make sure she gets to Palestine."

She went to the next room and brought back a young man in simple clothes.

"This is Karl Rink," she said, introducing Helga's father to him. "And this is Yossi Millman, of Kibbutz Dafna, the leader of the group going to Palestine."

Karl asked if they knew which kibbutz his daughter would be sent to.

"Not yet," answered the leader. "That will be decided only after we get there."

Karl hurried home. Helga was sitting at the window and looking out despondently, waiting for her mother to come back.

"Unfortunately, you can't stay in Berlin anymore," said her father. "You've got to leave here."

"And Mother?"

"When she comes back home, I'll try to persuade her to go, too."

"I want to wait here for her to come back."

"That could take time, Helga. Time isn't on our side."

"You can find Mother. You've got connections."

"I tried and it's not so simple."

She couldn't keep the tears out of her eyes anymore.

"I can't go without Mother. I've never been alone. Find her and we'll all go away from here together."

He hugged her. "I want us all to be together, too," he said. "But

that can't be right now. If you don't leave here, things I don't want
to happen are liable to happen to you."

She sobbed into his chest.

"I don't know what to decide," she murmured.

"Trust me, Helga."

"Where do you want to send me?" She forced the words out of
her mouth.

"To Palestine. The war won't reach there."

"I don't know anybody there."

He gave her a detailed account of his meeting with Raha Frayer
and described in rosy colors what was in store for her in Palestine.
"You'll be much better off there than in Germany," he said.

"And what will happen to you?"

"I'll stay here. I'll look for Mother and I'll try to take care of
myself. There are two more days until the trip. You should start
packing."

She hesitated.

"There is no choice, Helga. You have to go. I promise you that
the minute I find your mother, I'll send her to Palestine, too."

"I want you to come, too."

"I've got obligations, Helga. I've got to stay here, at least for a
while."

She wiped her tears.

"I'll miss you both very much," she said.

Early in the morning, Karl Rink rode his motorcycle through the
still deserted streets of Berlin. Helga rode on the backseat, holding
a small suitcase in one hand and grasping her father's body with the
other. This time, too, Karl wore civilian clothes so as not to attract
attention at the railroad station, which was packed with uniformed

men. The father and daughter hurried to the platform where the train to Zurich was waiting. The group of Jewish children was already onboard one of the cars. Their parents stood on the platform, looking sadly at their loved ones through the windows and wiping away tears.

Karl accompanied Helga to her seat in the car and hugged her, barely keeping himself from crying.

"See you soon," he mumbled, without believing it himself. He kissed his daughter, pulled some money out of his pocket, and gave it to her.

"Don't forget Mother," she demanded.

The engine tooted.

"Have a good trip," he said. "Take care of yourself."

"Write to me a lot, Father."

Karl Rink left the car, froze on the platform, and watched anxiously as the train pulled away with his only daughter. He felt as if one of his limbs had been cut off. His wife had disappeared and his daughter had gone to another country. Deep in his heart he feared that he would never see either of them again.

7.

On August 31, 1939, all the obstacles were cleared away at long last and the contract between Jacob Solowitzky and the French railroad company was signed at a joyous ceremony. In the offices of the train company, bottles of champagne were opened and joyful speeches were delivered. Jacob Solowitzky ignored news of Germany's intentions to go to war and prepared to return home.

He stayed in Paris one more day to buy gifts. At a famous couturier on the Champs-Élysées, he bought an elegant dress for his wife. For Michael he bought a fleet of toy cars and racetracks. And he remembered to buy small gifts for each of the servants.

He returned to the hotel and asked for a phone line home to tell his family when he would arrive.

"Sorry, sir," said the operator. "All lines to Warsaw are disconnected. Please try again later."

He tried to send a telegram, but couldn't do that either.

He didn't understand what was happening. Never in all his travels had he been unable to call home. He felt uneasy. Something wasn't right but he didn't know what.

He went down to the hotel restaurant and ate a light meal. When he went back to his room, he tried again to call home. The lines were still disconnected.

Stolowitzky asked the operator to keep trying. For hours he waited in vain for a line. At last he fell asleep and woke up in the morning to a tap on his door. A waiter put breakfast next to his bed. He sat up, muttered thanks, and put the tray on his lap. As he was drinking his coffee, he turned on the radio. The news delivered by the announcer froze his blood:

The German army has invaded Poland.

September 1, 1939, a gray and rainy day, would be recorded as one of the worst days in human history. In the morning, like swarms of hungry locusts, two thousand German fighter planes covered the skies of Poland, as 1.8 million German soldiers and twenty-six hundred tanks invaded the state from three sides. Rumors about big military operations Germany was preparing had been in the air for some time. Poland feared the expected events and called up the reserves, but other than that, made no real preparations to greet the invaders.

The Polish army, much smaller than the force of the attacker, fought bravely and inflicted losses on the Germans. Tens of thousands of invaders were killed, almost three hundred planes were brought down, and about 240 tanks were destroyed. It was a hard blow for the German army, but not hard enough to make it retreat. In fact, the Poles had no chance from the very first shot. The Germans conquered one village after another, one town after another, and killed civilians mercilessly.

The German army invasion of Poland stunned the whole world. Even though the Germans were still far from the capital city of Warsaw, the thunder of cannons was already echoing in the city day and night. Agitated people gathered in the streets. The central railroad station teemed with scared families who had snatched up all their valuables, left their homes, and tried in vain to board a train to take them out of the country. Trucks and private cars filled with refugees flooded the roads leading out of Warsaw.

Lydia Stolowitzky walked around her house confused and helpless. Her husband's absence only increased her despair. For the last two days she hadn't heard a word from him, and that wasn't like him. When he traveled, he always made sure to send her telegrams or call every day and report on where he was and tell her exactly when he would be coming home. This time he hadn't. She had no idea where he was in Paris or what his phone number was. She tried to call her parents in Krakow, but the lines were disconnected.

Dejected and desperate, Lydia understood that she couldn't stay in Warsaw for long, that she had to flee to safety. But she couldn't imagine how. Only now did she realize that she had never had to make a truly fateful decision. In her pampered life with Jacob Stolowitzky, the only decisions she had made were what to serve for dinner or which artist to invite for a private appearance in her home. Now she herself would have to decide her fate and the fate of her son, and that burden was already unbearable.

8.

The news of the invasion of Poland couldn't have come at a worse time for Jacob Stolowitzky. Just when he had to be home, to support his wife and son and find a way to get the family to safety, he was far away from them, helpless, unable to save them.

At first he thought of hurrying to Warsaw before the Germans got there and moving his family to a safe place. He had enough money to guarantee that that would be done in the best way. He called his travel agent, hoping to find a way to get home, but was met with rejection. All trains and buses to Warsaw were canceled until further notice. Again Stolowitzky wanted to call home, but couldn't. Surprisingly, the operator asked him: "Haven't you heard of the war, sir?"

Not knowing what to do, he took a cab to the Polish embassy, where pandemonium reigned. Officials ran around panicky in the corridors, pleading with the operators to get them an urgent line and paid no attention whatsoever to him. He made his way to the ambassador's office. They were old friends and whenever the millionaire from Warsaw was in Paris, they had dinner together at an expensive restaurant.

"Help me get back home," Stolowitzky asked the ambassador, even before he said hello.

The ambassador gave him a wan smile and said: "Forget it. There's no chance you'll get there. The Germans are advancing rapidly. They'll soon be in Warsaw."

"But . . . my wife and child . . . I can't leave them there alone."

"Unfortunately, I can't help you."

A new idea suddenly popped up in Stolowitzky's mind. "I could hire a driver and get to Warsaw with him," he said. "Maybe it's not too late."

"You're endangering your own life," the ambassador warned him. "The Germans would arrest you at the border and you probably wouldn't get out alive."

Jacob Stolowitzky believed the ambassador was right. His life would indeed be in danger if he went to Warsaw. Nevertheless, he wasn't willing to give up so fast. He took a cab to the office of his Paris agent to discuss the possibilities of sending a chauffeur to Warsaw to try to get Lydia and Michael out. The agent immediately called in his private chauffeur and suggested he do it. Stolowitzky gave the man a suitcase full of money to bribe whomever he needed to, and promised the chauffeur a big sum if he came back with his wife and son. The chauffeur agreed, wrote down the address of the mansion in Warsaw, and set off.

In the next days, Jacob spent most of his time in his agent's office, waiting for the chauffeur to come back. Meanwhile, he learned that, because of the German invasion of Poland, the French railroad company worried that a period of uncertainty was in store for Europe. As a result, the terms of the contract would be frozen until the situation was cleared up.

But the contract was the last thing on his mind. He was already imagining his wife and son arriving in Paris safe and sound. That was what he wanted most right now.

It took four days for the chauffeur to return, alone. He said that he had been stopped at the Polish border by German soldiers and not allowed to continue. Stolowitzky felt that his world was collapsing.

He had a bad premonition.

9.

The slim hope that the Polish army would block the Germans before they reached Warsaw dissipated like a light cloud in a storm wind. The news from the front was bad and the Polish government's attempts to calm fears failed to convince anyone. Alarm sirens wailed day and night, cannon thunder approached the city, German planes dropped bombs on apartment houses and residential areas, and the streets were filled with people and vehicles trying to get out of the city.

One by one, the servants in the Stolowitzky house on Ujazdowska Avenue disappeared. First the cook ran off, then the gardener, then all the others. Only Lydia and Michael, Gertruda and Emil the chauffer remained.

Lydia felt her self-confidence draining away. At any moment, she expected her husband to come back home and take charge. He had promised her to come back in a few days.

The roar of the bombs terrified Michael, and Gertruda couldn't dissipate his fears even when she sat at his bedside every night. For whole days he didn't let go of her hand or let her out of his sight. Her cool head, solid body, and firm step served as an indispensable support for the child.

Lydia, who had never made a dinner by herself in her life, was helpless when the cook left her, so Gertruda took over. She bought food in the black market, cooked, set the table, and washed the dishes. She gladly got up early in the morning and went to bed late at night. She took care of Michael and his mother, kept the house clean, and even trimmed the rosebushes in the garden.

Emil clearly lusted for her. His boss's absence from Warsaw left him a lot of free time and idleness frayed his nerves. Ever since Gertruda had come to work there, he had dreamed of the moment when she'd be his. She inflamed his imagination, her refusal of his advances didn't discourage him, and now he felt emboldened. Lydia was nervous and yearned for her husband, the servants had disappeared, and Gertruda had become an easy prey.

She was standing at the stove in the kitchen, making dinner. Night fell and cannon shells shook the walls of the house. Gertruda was tasting the soup when a strong hand grabbed her waist from behind. She shrieked in panic and tried to remove the hands gripping her. Emil laughed. "What happened, you don't like that?"

"Don't touch me!" she shouted. "Lydia will fire you when she hears about this."

He continued laughing and didn't let go of her. "Lydia can't do anything to me," he said. "I'm the only man in this house. You all need me. She wouldn't dare stay here alone with you and Michael."

Gertruda twisted but he was stronger than she was. When she tried to shout, he put one hand over her mouth and raised her dress with the other. Her legs kicked him in vain. Emil laid her on the floor and attacked her with his full weight. She groaned in despair and prayed.

The voice of a frightened child was heard on the kitchen stairs.

"Gertruda, are you here?" called Michael.

She couldn't answer. Emil froze. "Don't move," he whispered in her ear.

"Gertruda," Michael continued. "I can't fall asleep. I need you."

He came into the doorway and he looked for her. Emil cursed, got up, and slipped out of the kitchen. Gertruda lay on the floor, her body aching. Michael bent over her.

"Are you sick?" he asked.

"No, darling, I just fell down. Help me get up."

The little boy held out his soft hand to her and she got up slowly. Trying to cover the rips in her dress, she walked to Michael's

room, put him in bed, and then hurried to her room to change her
clothes. Tears fell from her eyes.

10.

The group of Berlin children sailed from Italy and reached the Land
of Israel on a cold rainy day in October 1939. The group numbered
a dozen boys and girls aged thirteen to sixteen who had attended
Jewish schools in Berlin and knew a little Hebrew. They were
stuffed into crowded cells in the ship's hold, hurled on the waves
day and night, didn't talk much, preferred to withdraw into themselves, and feared for the fate of their parents. Sad and uncomfortable, they waited in the port of Haifa in a crowded warehouse until
they were taken to the kibbutzim. They carried small suitcases and
looked often at the photos their families had left with them.

When the representatives of the kibbutzim arrived, Helga and a
few other children were taken to Kfar Giladi, where they met with
their guides who would tell them about life on the kibbutz. A few days
later, the children of the Berlin group received Hebrew names and
Helga became Elisheva. She lived in the same building as her traveling companions, studied with the children of the kibbutz, and worked
at various jobs. They spent their free time with adoptive families who
tried to give them warmth and love. Elisheva was grateful for the way
she was treated by the family that adopted her, one of the veteran
families of the twenty-three-year-old kibbutz. She liked life on the
kibbutz, although she was still bound to her past. She avoided talking
about her family, said only that her father and mother had stayed in
Berlin, and didn't reveal the truth about her father to anyone.

She learned to milk cows, pick oranges, and lead goats to pasture
in the mountains of the Galilee. She usually walked around bare-

Helga (Elisheva) Rink, seventeen years old.
Kfar Giladi, Israel, 1942.

foot, her delicate feet quickly adjusting to the dirt paths, the stones, and the thorns. The sun tanned her pale face and her bare arms. In the kibbutz, her long silences and her solitude in the lap of nature were accepted. She took many walks in the field sunk in thoughts of her father and mother, the friends she had left behind. At night, she couldn't sleep. The winds of war were blowing hard now and she knew that sooner or later, her father would find himself on the front. She was worried about his safety and waited for his letters.

A few weeks after her arrival at Kfar Giladi, Helga received a letter from her father:

My dear daughter,
    I'm sorry to tell you that, despite my many efforts, I haven't been able to find any traces of Mother so far. None of the many people I asked for information about her could help me. The

*people I work with deny they had anything to do with Mother's
disappearance.*

*Every evening I return home depressed. I look at her things,
at your things left behind, and my heart is torn with longing. My
great hope is that we'll all soon be reunited and happier than we
were.*

*Meanwhile, I've been told that I have to go to Poland. I hope
I won't be assigned work I don't like.*

*I long to know how you spend your days. Do you feel well?
Have you started school and made new friends? I am attaching a
small sum of money for you. In recent days, the post office
service has been disrupted because of the war. I won't be able to
get letters from you, but I hope I can still keep writing to you.*

Missing you.

Father

Karl Rink gave the letter to a friend who was going to Switzerland
and promised to forward it from there. Since he didn't know where his
daughter was, Karl addressed the letter to Yossi Millman of Kibbutz
Dafna who had escorted the group of children from Berlin to the Land
of Israel. Millman sent the letter to Helga. She hid it and wanted to
answer her father, but the letter she got had no return address.

For years after that, Karl Rink didn't write to his daughter and
she couldn't write to him.

11.

Jacob Stolowitzky was a strong and determined man who had overcome many difficult obstacles in his life, ones that could easily have
brought down other men. But never had he felt so helpless and use-

less as in those damp days in Paris in the autumn of 1939. He listened to the radio and read the newspapers, neither giving him any good news. They reported on the rapid advance of the German army in Poland, the great destruction and the corpses littering the road, the collapse of the Polish army.

Lydia Stolowitzky, too, had never felt so desperate as in those days. The news from the front was bad. Columns of tanks and personnel carriers loaded with German soldiers were making their way toward Warsaw, villages and towns were conquered with no resistance, planes bombed various areas of the country indiscriminately, and hundreds of bodies of Polish soldiers and civilians were reeking alongside the roads. Lydia couldn't get in touch with anyone in her family or with friends in the top levels of government who might be able to help. There was a sense of fear and disorder in the air; rumors of the brutality of the conquerors spread.

Most of Lydia's friends and neighbors had already fled Warsaw. The manager of her summer estate somehow got to the city to plead with her to hide in the isolated farm. She refused, "No place in Poland is safe today," she said. "The Germans will certainly get to the farm, too."

She gave him some money to pay the workers and said she was sorry not to go on paying them in the foreseeable future.

"Never mind," said the man. "We'll wait for you until the war is over."

That very day, Isaac Geller, a rich diamond merchant who lived nearby, knocked on the door of the Stolowitzky house. He was a frequent guest of Lydia's and a close friend of Jacob's. Michael often played with his son in the diamond merchant's house at Ujazdowska 15.

"We've decided to escape from here," he told her. "The Germans are liable to enter Warsaw any day. You should also get out."

"Where should we go?" asked Lydia in a choked voice.

"Vilna. It's safer there."

She didn't know what to say. She knew that she should leave Warsaw. But she was afraid that if she did, her husband wouldn't be able to find her.

"Have you gotten a phone call from Jacob?" asked Geller.

"No. The lines are cut."

"Before we go, can I help you with anything?"

"Thanks. I just want Jacob to be here."

But Jacob Stolowitzky didn't come and the roars of the cannons grew louder. The Lithuanian city of Vilna, now under Soviet rule, was 375 miles from Warsaw. According to the Molotov-Ribbentrop Pact, which had been signed a few weeks earlier, Germany and the Soviet Union agreed not to attack each other. Therefore, many Jews saw Vilna as a safe place. After serious hesitations, Lydia also decided to try to get there.

"Pack only what you and Michael need," she told Gertruda. "We can't take everything."

Emil was ordered to prepare the car for a long trip the next morning. He bought gasoline on the black market, got spare tires and tools for car repair, emptied the trunk of everything superfluous, and also packed his own things.

At dawn, when gray mists still shrouded Warsaw and the roars of the cannons sounded closer than ever, Emil loaded the trunk with the overflowing suitcases Lydia had prepared. She took ancient silver, valuable paintings, jewelry, all the cash in the house, and the family photograph album. Gertruda packed the pictures of Mary and the crucified Jesus that had hung above her bed and dressed Michael in a heavy winter coat.

From a hiding place in the house, Lydia took her husband's gun and hid it in her purse. "I hope we won't need to use it," she said in a worried voice. They got to the door, but Lydia didn't have the strength to leave. She returned, and for a long time she walked around the rooms whose windows were shuttered. Her eyes lingered on the furniture she was leaving behind, feeling as if she would never see it again. In the bedroom, she locked the door and stretched out on the big bed covered with a scarlet velvet spread. At long last, all alone, away from the servants, the nanny, and her son, she burst into tears.

Emil's impatient voice filtered through the door. "We shouldn't waste a minute, Mrs. Stolowitzky. We have to go."

Her body felt as heavy as lead when she got off the bed. She wiped her tears with a handkerchief and applied makeup to her face. More than ever she needed her husband now, his soothing voice, the security she felt when he was there.

She gathered up her passport, clutched to her chest her purse with money and valuable jewelry, and slowly left the house.

"The war will end soon and we'll all come back," Gertruda said, trying in vain to make her voice sound reassuring. Deep in her heart she was afraid that the situation would only get worse.

Lydia sighed deeply as she hid the house key in her purse. "Who knows what will happen to us?" she wondered aloud.

The car drove off.

"When will Father come?" asked Michael, his face sad.

"Soon, Michael, soon," murmured Lydia.

"I miss him."

"So do I."

CHAPTER 6

Gun Threats

1.

On the main streets of Warsaw, traffic moved mostly in only one direction—toward Vilna. Convoys of civilians, most of them Jews, in trucks and cars, on bikes and in horse-drawn carts, made their way to the safe city, protected for now from the war. The refugees looked worried. They were leaving friends and family, all their property, unsure of what was in store for them.

The Stolowitzky car crawled along. Emil honked the horn in vain to clear the street. Three hours after they had left Warsaw, the Cadillac had managed only to leave the suburbs, as traffic was also moving slowly on the narrow village roads.

Two farmers came to the window of the car selling apples.

"I want an apple," said Michael.

"Stop a moment," Lydia instructed Emil. Reluctantly, the chauffeur stopped. Lydia opened her purse and searched for money. At that moment, one of the farmers pulled out a knife and pointed it at her.

"Give me the purse," he growled.

Emil pressed the accelerator and tried to speed up, but the man clung to the window. One hand held the window door and the other went on waving the knife. Michael burst out crying.

Lydia clutched her purse to her chest. There was a loaded gun in it.

The knife came close to her face, scratching and threatening. Trembling with fear, Lydia pulled out the gun and pointed it at the man's face. He let go of the door and yelled for his companion. The two of them approached the slow-moving car as those inside the car looked at the two of them with dread.

"Give me the gun!" ordered Emil.

Lydia gave it to him.

The two farmers were now hanging on both sides of the car. A second knife suddenly popped up in the hand of the other farmer.

Emil stopped. He pointed the gun coolly at one of the farmers. "No, no," pleaded the man. But Emil pulled the trigger. He then shot the second farmer.

The two men collapsed in puddles of blood. None of the many refugees marching on the side of the road paid any attention to them.

Emil put the gun down next to him and went on driving as if nothing had happened. Lydia burst out crying.

"How could you be so cruel?" she shouted at Emil.

"This is war," he grumbled. "In war, there is no pity. If you don't kill, you get killed."

On the side of the road, people walked along silently, carrying suitcases and bags stuffed with personal belongings. An elderly man with white hair was walking among then slowly, a small suitcase in his hand. He looked up at the car, his eyes met Lydia's, and she recognized him immediately. He had worked as an accountant in her husband's office in Warsaw for more than twenty years. He was a childless widower who devoted most of his time to work. Jacob Stolowitzky appreciated his devotion and personal honesty.

"Stop the car and take him," Lydia called to Emil.

The chauffeur twisted his mouth reluctantly. "It will be crowded," he warned.

"Take him!" ordered the woman.

Emil stopped next to the man.

"We're going to Vilna," said Lydia. "If you like, you can come with us."

He smiled gladly. "Thank you," he said, and squeezed into the seat next to Emil.

On the outskirts of Vilna, a big traffic jam snaked along the border patrol checkpoint. The car advanced slowly. Lydia looked at the city in the distance. She didn't know Vilna, but she was sure she could get along there. She had enough money to support them for a while.

"I've got the address of an apartment to rent," said the accountant, as if he had been reading her mind. "I thought of living there, but you need an apartment more than I do. I'll get along somewhere else."

He gave her a note with an address.

It was late afternoon when they crossed the checkpoint, and it had started raining. Passersby hurried on their way without even a glance at the procession of refugees from Warsaw. They were used to seeing such long lines every day since the war began.

The Cadillac drove through the narrow streets. Lydia asked Emil to take them to the apartment for rent. Emil drove for a while in silence and suddenly he turned into a deserted sidestreet and stopped.

"What is it?" Lydia was terrified.

Instead of answering, the chauffeur pulled out the gun and waved it at her.

"Get out of the car and leave everything here!" he lashed out.

Lydia froze in fear.

"What are you doing, Emil?" she cried. "Have you lost your mind?"

"You heard what I said," he repeated coldly. "Now get out."

Michael shrieked in panic and Gertruda clutched him to her breast.

"Get out!" shouted Emil. Lydia had never heard him raise his voice or seen him scowl as now.

They stayed in the car, hoping he'd change his mind.

But Emil started shouting again. "Get out!" he cried. "You're wasting my time."

The accountant in the front seat attacked Emil and tried to get the gun away from him. A shot was heard and the man was pushed back and slumped on the seat. A big bloodstain spread over his suit. Emil opened the door and kicked the man out. The old man lay dead on the street.

Emil's eyes were crazy. He pointed the gun at his passengers. "The next bullet is for anyone who doesn't get out!" he roared.

Lydia clutched her purse with her money and jewelry. Her face was as white as a ghost.

"How dare you do this to us," she called out in a broken voice. "We always treated you so well, like a member of the family. We didn't listen to the police when they suggested we fire you after the kidnapping attempt on Michael."

Emil laughed. "You made a mistake," he said.

"What do you mean?"

"The police were right. The two kidnappers were friends of mine. All we tried to do was get a little money out of you. Too bad we didn't succeed."

"Bastard!" cried Lydia.

"Enough!" shouted Emil and grabbed the purse out of her hands.

"At least leave us a little money," she pleaded. "Don't let us starve to death."

He shoved her out of the car. Gertruda and Michael followed. Emil turned the wheel and drove off.

2.

They stood stunned in the darkening alley. Lydia leaned on the wall of a house. Her knees buckled as her world collapsed around her. Gertruda hugged Michael, whose body was shaking with weeping and dread.

"Why did he do that to us?" sobbed the child. "We loved him so much."

"He went crazy," said Gertruda softly. "Don't be afraid. He'll change his mind and come back to us."

Lydia wrapped herself in her fur coat, the only valuable object she had left. A cold wind whipped her face.

"What shall we do?" she asked desperately.

"First of all, we have to find someplace to live," Gertruda recovered.

"But we don't have any money."

"I've got a little bit," said the nanny. "I hid a few zlotys in my stockings. Emil probably didn't imagine I had any money."

Lydia hugged her. "You're our guardian angel," she said.

They went back to the main street. The note with the address was lost. Gertruda knocked on doors and asked people if they had a room for rent. Some people didn't even open the door. Others answered an impatient no. Two or three mentioned enormous sums for wretched holes.

It was night by the time an old woman was finally willing to rent them rooms in her house, at Mala Stefanska 6.

The landlady was a small, vigorous woman, with a hard face and disheveled silver hair. With her hands on her hips, her eyes and voice piercing, she yelled out to the women and child: "I hope you're not Jews."

"We're not," answered Gertruda.

"Where are you from?"

"Warsaw."

"Why did you come to Vilna?"

"Food got very expensive because of the war, I didn't have any work, we had no money left. We thought it would be better for us here."

She said that her husband was a soldier in the Polish army and had fallen in battle. The woman questioned her about her husband to make sure she was telling the truth, set a rent, and demanded payment for a month in advance.

"I don't have all the money now," said Gertruda. "But I've got enough to pay you a portion. I hope I can start working soon and then I'll pay you the whole sum."

"What's your profession?"

"I'm a teacher, but I'm healthy and am willing to do anything. I can be a nanny, a secretary. I know a few languages."

The woman grimaced. "I don't believe anybody's interested in a teacher, a nanny, or a secretary these days."

"I'll try, anyway."

"And who's that woman?" She pointed at Lydia, who had shriveled in a panic behind Gertruda's back.

"That's my cousin."

The woman grumbled under her breath.

"You have to remember one thing," she roared. "Anybody who lives in my house has to act modestly. You can't entertain men here or come back home late at night. I want you to promise me that the child won't make any noise. Clear?"

"Thank you," said Gertruda, and she gave the woman the rent money.

The landlady led the tenants to the second floor and opened one of the doors. The apartment had two big rooms, furnished with old pieces. Attached to the ancient stove was a sooty chimney pipe that went through the wall over a dusty window. With gnarled hands, the woman kindled pieces of wood in the stove and the cold in the room quickly dissipated.

"You're lucky," she said. "In Vilna there aren't any apartments left to rent."

Michael disappeared into the other room and returned with a shout of joy, holding a toy car.

"That's my grandson's," said the landlady.

"Can I play with the car?" asked Michael anxiously.

"Yes, but don't break it."

"Is there something to eat?" asked Michael. "I'm really hungry."

Gertruda asked the old woman if she could sell them dinner.

"I've only got soup," grumbled the landlady.

"Fine. We'll have soup."

The old woman brought a pot of potato soup and three plates and held out a hand for money.

They were hungry and devoured the meal. Afterward Gertruda made up the bed for Lydia and Michael. "I'll sleep on the chair," she said.

The night was cold and there were no more sticks for heating. Lydia and Michael slept in their clothes, wrapped in coats. Gertruda shivered with cold on her chair. In the morning, she bought tea and a few slices of bread from the old woman.

"Try to find the Geller family, our neighbors from Warsaw. They also fled to Vilna," said Lydia. "They can probably help us."

"I'll look for them," Gertruda promised.

She went to the city but quickly understood that the chances of locating the diamond dealer's family were very slim. Thousands of refugees had come to Vilna and filled every empty apartment. Convoys of refugees continued to flow into the city nonstop. The railroad station was teeming with families who couldn't find a place to rent. Many people were lying on the chilly floor with bundles of belongings, in despair.

For hours Gertruda wandered the streets, went into shops and restaurants, and asked for work without any luck. She sat down on a bench and considered her next step. There weren't many possibilities. She needed work desperately and didn't dare think what would happen if her money ran out before she found something.

Suddenly, she heard a car, looked up, and saw the Stolowitzky's white Cadillac passing by. Her heart skipped a beat. For a moment she wondered what to do, and then she leaped up and ran after it. Traffic was heavy and the Cadillac moved slowly. Gertruda soon caught up with the car. She didn't know what would happen when she met Emil, but she believed she could persuade him, tell him how miserable Lydia was, and convince him to give back at least part of the loot.

Her heart pounding, Gertruda approached the car. "Emil!" she called to the man behind the wheel. He turned his eyes to her. It wasn't Emil.

"Excuse me," she said, surprised. "This is our car."

The man was about forty years old, ruddy, with a fur hat on his head.

"I don't know what you're talking about," he growled. "I bought it this morning."

"From whom?"

"Don't bother me," he grumbled. "It's none of your business."

He closed the window in her face and turned his head away.

So, she thought, Emil sold the car and is probably living the good life now with the money he got for it and with what he stole. She decided to keep the meeting with the new owner of the Cadillac to herself. She didn't want Lydia to become even more depressed.

In the evening, after more vain efforts to find work, Gertruda returned to the house on Mala Stefanska. She was approaching the door when a young man came out of the adjacent house. Their eyes met and her mouth dropped open in amazement. She immediately recognized the doctor who had taken such good care of Michael after the accident on the trolley tracks.

"Dr. Berman!" she called. "What a coincidence."

"You're living here, too?" The doctor was amazed.

Gertruda told him what had happened to them and he shook his head with grief.

"The war turns men into monsters," he said. "How will you get along?"

"I have no idea."

"If there's anything I can do for you?"

"At the moment, no. Thank you, anyway."

He said that he and his family had come to Vilna a week before.

"The city is flooded with refugees," he said. "People take whatever work they can find for pennies."

"How long will this last?" asked Gertruda anxiously.

"God knows. How is Michael?"

"He's fine, just a little scared."

"We live on the second floor of number 8. My wife and I will be glad if you all come to dinner. It won't be a royal feast, but you won't go away hungry, I promise."

3.

For the first time since he had joined the Nazi Party, Karl Rink wasn't so sure, wasn't devoted so blindly to the party, or to the belief that only Hitler could lead Germany on the right path. Although he was proud to serve the party with all his might and didn't hesitate to carry out the orders of his superiors in the destruction of Communists and members of other opposition groups, he had private reservations about SS methods, which seemed too extreme for him. Every single day he tried to find Mira, asked everybody he knew for whatever information they might have. In his heart he suspected that the SS had had a major role in his wife's disappearance, but his companions and commanders kept lying as he struggled to find out what had happened to her. He asked to see lists of detainees and victims to be sure his wife's name didn't appear. Those who made the lists claimed they were forbidden to show them to anyone.

Helpless, Karl Rink returned to his empty house every evening and had a hard time deciding what to do. If he resigned from the

SS, he knew he would be sent to the front immediately and his life would be in great danger. If he didn't resign, he would have to carry out orders that went against his grain. From any angle, he seemed to be at a dead end.

In his long sleepless nights in the empty apartment, he missed his wife and daughter and was sorry he hadn't taken Helga's advice to leave Germany with their small family before it was too late. With a heavy heart, he returned to SS headquarters every morning and reluctantly carried out orders he was given, wanting to believe the war would end soon, along with the nightmare that haunted him.

One evening, Karl Rink was summoned to a special meeting in Reinhard Schreider's apartment in eastern Berlin. The commander lived alone in a luxury apartment on the ground floor in the quarter populated by many Nazi supporters. Karl Rink attended the meeting along with a group of officers about to join the German forces in Poland. All those present knew that the missions in Poland were only the beginning. If they carried them out well, they would be promoted to functions in the European countries conquered by the Nazis.

The meeting in Schreider's apartment seemed like a social event. Expensive wines and rare delicacies were served and the guests chatted animatedly until they were joined by a balding man of about forty with a swarthy face, in an SS officer's uniform.

"Gentlemen, I am honored to introduce you to Hans Frank," said Schreider.

The guest's name was familiar to everyone in the room. Frank had served in the German army in World War I, was one of the founders of the Nazi Party, served as minister without portfolio in Hitler's government, and was known as a die-hard anti-Semite.

"Today," added Schreider, "Hans Frank was appointed General-gouverneur in Poland. You will all soon serve under his command."

Frank spoke briefly. He said that he intended to impose law and order in Poland and mainly to take care of the Jews.

At those words, Karl Rink's mind wondered painfully why he hadn't resisted getting involved with the occupation force of Poland while there was still time. He looked at Hans Frank and knew he would support any and all kinds of torture of the Jews of Poland, and like all his colleagues, Karl would have to carry out the General-gouverneur's orders. He could have found some pretext to stay in Berlin and devote his free time to searching for Mira. He wondered what had moved him to be silent when he was told of his impending departure for Poland: Was he afraid of being an exception again, as on Kristallnacht? Was he trying to demonstrate his devotion to the SS?

Frank thanked the guests for their attention, made a toast, and wished them luck. Six years later, the war crimes court in Nuremberg would condemn Frank to death by hanging after he was found guilty of sending tens of thousands of Jews to the death camps.

A few days passed and before they set out, Schreider said good-bye to his officers who were assigned to Poland. He shook Karl's hand and wished him luck.

"Can I make a personal request?" asked Karl.

"As long as it's brief," said Schreider. "I'm very busy."

"I want to know the truth about my wife."

"Listen, Rink. You're wasting your valuable time. Your Jewess must have run away from you. I always claimed that you can't rely on the Jews. Say thank you that she's not there."

"I loved her, sir," said Karl.

"The SS is your only love, all of ours," Schreider replied, scolding him.

The conversation was over.

When he left Schreider's office, Karl Rink met his friend, Kurt Baumer, the commander's third in command. Baumer gave Karl passes for the train to Poland and to appear at German headquarters.

"I've got the impression," said Karl sadly, "that the truth about my wife's fate is being hidden from me."

Baumer gave him a long look.

"Let me give you some advice," he said. "Forget the whole thing. Nothing good will come of your attempts to find out where your wife is."

Karl sensed that Baumer knew a lot more than he was willing to reveal. Nevertheless, he understood that he couldn't get any real information from his friend about Mira's fate.

They parted from each other with a sad handshake.

4.

At dawn, Gertruda opened her eyes. The wooden logs she had bought with a portion of her last pennies had turned into gray ashes. The fire had gone out and she was shivering with cold. Lydia and Michael were sleeping on the bed, wrapped in their coats. Gertruda quietly went into the small kitchen, which contained a few pots, dishes, and an old aluminum kettle. The pantry was empty. She filled the kettle with tap water and put it on the electric hot plate in hopes that the steam would dissipate the chill in the apartment, if only a little bit.

She counted the few coins she had left and headed for the grocery store.

A heavyset man blocked her way in the staircase.

"You're the new tenant?" he asked.

"Who are you?"

"The landlady's brother."

He moved closer to Gertruda and she could smell alcohol on his breath.

"Is there anything you need?" he asked. With a shudder of horror, she saw that his eyes were scanning her body.

"Not at the moment."

"You need money? I can give you some."

"No need," she said. "I plan to start working. I'll have money."

He smiled. "I'm always around," he said. "I'll drop in to visit you from time to time to see if you're all right."

"Thank you, I don't think that's necessary."

"I'm sure it will be," he laughed. "Wait and see."

He moved aside and let her pass.

A convoy of refugees was going down the main street on horse-drawn wooden carts. Wrapped in blankets, the newcomers sat among their belongings. The face of a sad child emerged from a colorful blanket. Gertruda averted her eyes and went into the grocery store. The selection was small and the prices were dreadfully high. . She bought tea and sugar, a loaf of bread, and a little butter, and calculated that, at those prices, her money would run out sooner than she had thought.

By the time she got back to the apartment, Lydia and Michael were awake. She made them tea and a slice of bread and butter. Lydia thanked her, and Michael asked if he could have another slice.

"What will happen?" Lydia asked anxiously.

"Don't worry," Gertruda said, trying to calm her. "We've got a place to sleep and a little bit more money for food. Many refugees don't have even that."

Lydia sighed. "But the money will run out, and what will happen then?"

"I promise you we'll find a solution."

She didn't know how she could say such a thing. But she firmly intended to make every effort to ease Lydia and Michael's suffering.

Refugees she met suggested to Gertruda that she ask for help from the Jewish aid institutions in the city. She stood in line for hours and received a coat and a jacket for Michael and a pass for the soup kitchen. Lydia refused to go there, but hunger got the better of her. She had no choice and joined Gertruda and Michael for lunch at the soup kitchen. The room was packed with hungry refugees and there was barely room for the three of them. On the simple wooden table, they were served turbid soup and steamed vegetables. Michael ate eagerly, but Lydia couldn't put a thing in her mouth. The sharp transition from life in the mansion to the despondent atmosphere of the soup kitchen was hard for her. She looked at her neighbors at the table. Most of them wore tattered clothes, their hair was disheveled, and they were noisy. She dropped her eyes and murmured, "I can't stay here, I feel terrible."

They returned home and Lydia collapsed on her bed, weeping and desperate.

"Find me Jacob," she asked Gertruda. "Make every effort to locate him. Only he can get us out of here."

Getruda didn't know what to do. In Lydia's purse, stolen by Emil, were all her personal documents and the phone numbers to contact Jacob Stolowitzky. Gertruda didn't know where to turn, but she tried to comfort Lydia.

"I promise to try," she said.

In the evening, Lydia's condition grew worse. She felt like she was choking and she had chest pains. Gertruda called Dr. Berman, and he suggested taking her to the hospital immediately.

"Your heart is in bad shape," he said. "You need medical care day and night."

She refused firmly.

"I want to be with my child," she said. "Without him, my life isn't a life."

The next morning, after nursing Lydia all night, Gertruda went to look for work. She went in and out of stores, restaurants, workshops, but even if there was a job, no one wanted to hire an inexperienced worker. Only in the hot and crowded railroad station buffet did they finally agree to hire her as a dishwasher.

"We can't pay you any money," said the owner. "But we will give you food you can take home."

It wasn't what she'd hoped for, but it would help. She rolled up her sleeves and washed dishes until nightfall. In a pot she borrowed from the buffet owner, she carried a hot meal to the rented apartment. She filled the plates and ate with Lydia and Michael. Her thoughts returned to the house on Ujazdowska Avenue, where recently feasts had been served, but it seemed so long ago . . .

5.

Only uniformed men were in the special train from Berlin to Warsaw. Karl Rink sat in the car reserved for SS officers. His companions were excited about their expected sojourn in Warsaw, with Polish girls and the opportunities to steal money from the Jews. He refrained from joining the conversations.

At the Warsaw railroad station, they were picked up by an SS car and driven through the streets of the city, which had been heavily damaged by the German attack. Many houses had collapsed and smoke was still rising from the ruins. In the streets, mostly German soldiers were to be seen.

They drove to SS headquarters, where they were given their assignments. Karl Rink was appointed staff officer responsible for distributing orders limiting the Jews' freedom. A young officer, who introduced himself as his deputy, led Karl to his office. On his desk, he found a first draft of edicts that Hans Frank was about to impose on the Jews of Poland, ordering every Jew to wear a band with a yellow star of David on his right arm, every Jewish shop or business to show a Star of David. Kosher slaughtering was forbidden, and every Jew had to submit a detailed report of his property.

After settling into the new office, Karl Rink was taken to the apartment he was assigned. It was next to a large house abandoned in panic by its inhabitants when the Germans entered Warsaw. Most of the furniture was left in the three-room apartment. Family pictures hung on the walls: men in tailored clothes, some of them with well-tended beards, women in elegant dresses, and children in suits. There were also wedding pictures of a couple, a group picture in front of a synagogue, and framed academic degrees. Some of them were documents of the Jewish teachers' college. Rink also surveyed the library, which included a few books in Polish, but mostly holy books and books in Hebrew.

"I'll send somebody to get rid of those Jewish things," said Karl's escort.

"No need. Leave everything for the time being. It doesn't bother me."

He wanted the apartment to have a Jewish character, to remind him of his wife and daughter.

6.

The telephone froze in the hands of attorney Joachim Turner. "That's awful," he exclaimed.

At the other end of the line, Jacob Stolowitzky's voice from Paris was shaking. Turner was his loyal friend and confidante. He took care of transferring money to banks in Switzerland, and was authorized to withdraw any sum his friend instructed. In the unexpected phone call he received in his office in Zurich, Turner heard for the first time about Stolowitzky's wife and son stranded in occupied Poland.

"Help me," pleaded Jacob Stolowitzky. "Promise the Germans any sum they want to let Lydia and Michael leave there and join me."

"Any sum?"

"Any sum you find proper."

Turner was the attorney for several well-known businessmen in Zurich. Even before the war, he had negotiated on their behalf with German firms that supplied large quantities of coal to the Swiss. He was sure the Germans now needed every penny to move their war machinery and would be likely to accept Stolowitzky's millions in exchange for getting his wife and son out of Warsaw.

"I'll take care of it immediately," Turner promised.

That very day he went to the German embassy in Bern and saw the ambassador himself. The German was interested in the proposition.

"How much money are we talking about?" he asked.

"Ten million dollars," Turner threw out.

The ambassador blurted out an exclamation of surprise. He wanted details and the attorney gave him the names and address.

"I'll check it out immediately," said the German.

The attractive proposal was sent through diplomatic channels at once. Orders went out from Berlin to the occupying authorities in Poland to locate Lydia and her son, guarantee their safety, and await further orders. Stolowitzky phoned Turner every day to see if he had new information, and when there was none, Stolowitzky was deeply disappointed.

After a week, Turner was summoned to the German embassy in Bern.

"We did the best we could," said the ambassador. "Our people tried to find the woman and child, but it turns out they are no longer at the address you gave me. The building itself was empty when our forces entered Warsaw. It is now German headquarters. We also investigated the tenants in the area and nobody knows what happened to them."

"Do you have lists of Jews who were arrested or killed?"

"We don't yet have orderly lists. If we do have more information, I'll let you know, of course, without delay."

Stolowitzky was stunned. Until that moment, he had clung to the hope that his money would induce the Germans to find a way to locate Lydia and Michael and send them out of Poland.

"What do you suggest I do?" he asked the Swiss attorney.

"Pray," replied Turner.

7.

Overnight, Vilna, teeming with Jewish life, prayer houses, synagogues, and well-known rabbis, became a shelter for refugees streaming there from all over Poland. Law and order collapsed. Robberies, rapes, and murders took place every single day and the police simply could not handle every case.

The refugees packed the city. They were everywhere, seeking housing and work, humiliated by anti-Semites and exploitative employers. They stood in long lines at foreign consulates and pleaded for entry visas to countries far away from the front. Only those with contacts and sharp elbows managed to get the precious permission. Lydia sank into a deep depression, lying in bed for whole days and praying that the nightmare would end and that her husband would come back.

Michael couldn't understand the sudden change in his life, the passage from the mansion to the miserable room, his mother's helplessness. He didn't know what war was, but he did understand that something awful had happened, that bad people made them leave the house. He was silent a lot, played with cards that Gertruda had cut out for him from cardboard boxes and drawn on, and was upset when Gertruda wasn't with him. She herself was out of the house from early morning to nightfall. He waited for her eagerly, for the food she brought and the stories she told him every night at bedtime.

· · ·

Lydia's health quickly deteriorated. A woman who had been full of life, gaiety, and vigor turned into a desperate broken vessel. She suffered pains and had a hard time standing up. For a few days Lydia lay sick in bed, until one night Gertruda awoke in panic at the sound of the sick woman's groans. When she went to her, she discovered that Lydia was unconscious, and Gertruda called Dr. Berman. "She should have been taken to the hospital long ago," he said.

In the old Jewish hospital building, on Zavalna Street, a few nurses were dozing at the reception desk. A dim light cast gloomy shadows on the walls and the patients' groans seeped out of the rooms. Gertruda asked the nurses to call for help and they sent for a doctor from one of the nearby rooms. The elderly man put on a shabby lab coat and his fatigue could be seen on his face. He told two orderlies to get a stretcher, and they rushed to the apartment where the sick woman was lying. Dr. Berman was there. The elderly doctor examined her carefully and consulted in secret with Berman. "I hope we're not too late," he said.

Carried on a stretcher in the dark empty streets of Vilna, covered with a thin blanket that kept dropping off and exposing her body to the chill of the night, Lydia Stolowitzky was taken to the Jewish hospital. Dr. Berman accompanied her and tried to ease her pain as much as he could, but there was little he could do. He did manage to get her into a room that was less crowded.

"I'm afraid her heart won't hold out," he whispered to Gertruda.

The next day, on her way to the railroad station buffet, Gertruda stopped in church and said a prayer for the sick woman. It didn't help. In the middle of the night, Lydia suffered a serious heart attack. She lay helpless in bed, often unconscious for hours.

Gertruda sat at her bed. Dr. Berman and Michael insisted on

staying with her in the hospital. Michael slept on the cold floor, wrapped in a thin blanket given to him by one of the nurses. Close to dawn, Lydia suddenly woke up.

"Michael," she muttered.

Gertruda woke up the child.

"Your mother wants you," she told him.

Michael went to his mother. She raised a weak hand and stroked his face.

"My child," she whispered. "My beloved child . . . don't ever forget me."

"All right, Mother," he said in a sleepy voice.

Lydia beckoned to Gertruda.

"I have to tell you something," she said into her ear.

"Yes, madam."

"I'm about to die, my dear."

"Don't talk like that," Gertruda begged her. "Rest. It will pass."

The sick woman shook her head.

"It won't pass, Gertruda. I want you to promise me something."

"Whatever you want."

"I don't know what happened to my husband . . . I don't know if he's alive or if he'll ever come back. Michael is all I have left. He's the most precious thing in the world to me. I want to die knowing that at least he will remain alive. Swear to me that you'll take care of him."

"I'll take care of him as if he were my own son."

"No one must know he's a Jew . . . teach Michael to be careful . . . one word too many or one hasty act would lead to a great catastrophe."

"I know, madam."

"I've got distant relatives in Palestine. When the war is over take him to them."

"I swear to you I will."

"I don't have any money to leave you," sighed the sick woman. "Take my fur coat. It will help you get through the winter."

With a great effort, she raised her weak hand.

"Take off my wedding ring," she said.

Gertruda obeyed.

"Wear it now. From now on, you'll be Michael's mother."

Gertruda's heart pounded as she put the ring on her finger. More than any other moment on that sad night, that act indicated the end of the real mother's role and the beginning of the nanny's motherhood. Lydia stroked Gertruda's hand.

"You're Michael's angel," added Lydia in a dying voice. "He loves you and you love him. I want you to know that my heart is thankful for everything you have done and will do for him."

"It's I who thank you for the great privilege you've granted me."

"And one more thing," Lydia spoke with what remained of her strength. "In the banks in Switzerland there is a lot of money my husband deposited. A lot of money . . . and gold . . . take the money. It will help Michael and you to build a new life."

"Yes, madam."

"Write down . . . there are millions in the Banque Credit in Zurich . . . there are also millions in . . ."

She didn't go on. Her head slumped and her eyes closed. A deep silence fell in the room. Dr. Berman bowed his head and Gertruda said a silent prayer. Michael looked at them in fear.

"Please," Gertruda asked God, "help me keep my oath."

She had no doubt she would do everything to keep her promise to the dying woman. She knew it wouldn't be easy, that the weeks and months ahead would place countless obstacles in her way, that it would be hard, if not impossible, to snatch the child delivered to her care out of the claws of the cruel fate in store for him.

. . .

Lydia Stolowitzky died that night and her death certificate was given to Gertruda.

For a tiny sum, a Vilna carter took the dead woman to be buried in the cemetery. A gloomy bearded man dug the grave and lowered her body into it wrapped in a tattered shroud. Ever since the war had begun, he had dug many graves like this for refugees who couldn't stand the hardships in the new city. The number of deaths increased from one day to the next, and only seldom did the family members of the dead have any money to pay for the burial. Anyone who did have money was buried in the local Jewish community cemetery. Paupers were buried far away from there, in simple graves with wooden signs with handwritten names. Lydia Stolowitzky, one of the richest women in Warsaw, was buried in a pauper's grave.

The gravedigger said the kaddish, the memorial prayer for the dead, and instructed Michael to repeat after him. The child blurted out the foreign words in his thin, tearful voice. Gertruda hugged him and wept.

They walked home to save carfare. The two of them knew that from now on, the bonds between them would be so thick that only death could undo them.

CHAPTER 7

Midnight Expulsion

1.

For some time, Jacob Stolowitzky still believed that everything would turn out fine. It was hard for him to get used to the possibility that he would never see his wife and son again, that his business had come to an end, that his own fate was shrouded in fog. He stayed in Paris on the advice of his French agent, and he chose to believe in the vague promises of the railroad company that as soon as the situation was clarified in Europe, the contract would be carried out.

Reality smashed all his delusions one by one. The German mobilization went forward, almost without any obstacle. France felt the heavy burden of oppression and growing uncertainty. People congregated at the newspaper stalls, swallowed the headlines about the German army advances, and asked themselves and those around them if the French army could stand against the invaders. In the streets of Paris, refugees who had managed to flee from Poland at the last minute were walking around, their faces pale and their eyes darting around in fear that, even there, German army units would

burst forth before them. Nevertheless, as a way to make the impending disaster disappear in their minds, some of the French refused to change their daily agendas. They filled the restaurants, ate
oysters, and were eager to drink fine wine, nightclubs were open for
business as usual, musicians and opera stars were received with
cheers and flowers.

With all this going on around him, Jacob Stolowitzky felt in his
heart that his loved ones were no longer alive. Despite all his efforts, his connections, and his money, he couldn't locate his wife
and son. All telephone lines and postal service to and from Warsaw
were down and reports from Poland told of the deaths of many Jews
at the hands of the Germans.

With every passing day, Jacob's tension and dread increased.
Stolowitzky ran around the city like a caged lion, anxiously following the news about the fall of one country after another into the
hands of the Nazis, and hoping they would encounter a crushing
defeat if they tried to invade France. With a heavy heart, he went
to meet refugees from Poland and tried to find out if they knew
what had happened to his wife and son. One of them suggested
something that had never occurred to him, that many Warsaw Jews
had fled to Vilna.

Jacob Stolowitzky didn't hesitate. He rushed to the Russian embassy and requested an entrance visa to Vilna, but he was rejected
on the spot. "No chance," said the clerk. "We have explicit instructions from Moscow not to give visas to Vilna."

Stolowitzky didn't give up. His money had always opened every
locked gate, and he was sure it would now, too. He pulled some
money out of his wallet and put it on the clerk's desk without a
word. To his surprise, the clerk returned it.

"Sorry," said the Russian impatiently. "I can't do a thing."

Stolowitzky hurried to the office of his Paris attorneys and asked them to get him a permit to enter Vilna. "I'll pay whatever I have to," he said. The lawyers promised to try but they also drew a blank. He contacted Joachim Turner in Zurich and asked him to go to Vilna to look for Lydia and Michael. Turner agreed, but he couldn't get an entry visa either.

More desperate than over, Stolowitzky locked himself in his hotel room and did what he hadn't done since he was a child: he wept. The omnipotent businessman was now alone and abandoned, helpless. All at once, his money had become worthless. There wasn't anyone he could turn to for help, no hope that would improve his mood. He knew that his chances of getting to his wife and son were dwindling by the minute.

Gray, monotonous days went by. He grew thin and there were black circles of sleeplessness around his eyes. He stopped going to the restaurant at the Ritz. The grand atmosphere, the dishes, and the elegant service reminded him of home, the dining room where his family had sat before their life was shattered to bits. Twice a day, he grabbed a quick bite at a small restaurant on nearby Rue Rivoli. He didn't talk to the other diners. He'd eat quickly, pay, and return to his room, his face pale and his eyes dim. The only one who asked him how he was every single day was the waitress in the restaurant. Her name was Anna and she was twenty-eight years old, ruddy-cheeked, and always wearing a smile. She knew most of her customers, talked with whoever wanted to chat, and was quiet with those who preferred to be silent. She knew only that Jacob Stolowitzky came from Poland and lived at the Ritz. He always ate alone and his face was sad.

One day, Jacob didn't appear for dinner and Anna was worried. When she finished working, she went to the hotel and knocked on his door. He opened it wrapped in a blanket and feverish. Without asking him, she immediately sent for a doctor and bought him the medicines the doctor prescribed. Then she brought him a meal from the restaurant. He was so weak, he couldn't hold on to the dishes, so Anna fed him herself.

When he recovered, he thanked her warmly for all she had done for him. Until now, in Paris, he felt solitary and alone, depressed. Anna was the only beam of light in his life.

"Why are you so good to me?" he asked.

"Because I can't bear to see people suffering."

He told her about his family, how he couldn't get in touch with his wife and son, his fear that they had been killed, the collapse of his business. She tried to cheer him up: "Maybe your wife and son are somehow still alive."

"I don't think so," he sighed. "They're not used to harsh conditions. They won't hold out in the war."

"I wish I could help you more," she said.

He looked at her affectionately. "You've done so much for me," he said. "I'm glad I met you."

She gave him a long look. He was a Jew and she was a Catholic, and he was many years older than she, but that didn't matter to her. For her, he was much more attractive and interesting than most of the men she knew. She felt that her affection for him would turn into a strong love.

"I'm glad I met you, too," she said and blushed.

She told him that she was born in the Italian town of Pontrepoli, a few miles from the French border. Her father had died when she was a child and her mother worked in an institution for disabled people. A relative, the owner of the French restaurant, suggested she come to Paris to work for him as a waitress.

She spent her free time with Jacob, and he found himself thinking of her a great deal in the long nights. More than anything else, he needed a close and understanding soul, human warmth, and

Anna was at hand, full of goodwill and endless devotion. The bond with her became important, encouraging, vital.

2.

"Don't tell anyone you're a Jew," Gertruda warned Michael.

The two of them were sitting in front of the fireplace, where a few pieces of wood the landlady sold her were burning. In another hour, the fire would die out and it would be cold again. Very cold.

"I won't tell anybody," the child promised.

"Everybody has to know I'm your mother."

"So what shall I call you? Mother?"

She hesitated. Michael had only one mother. Gertruda was the replacement, not the real mother.

"No, don't call me Mother."

"So, I'll call you Mamusha."

A wave of warmth washed over Gertruda's body. Mamusha was the perfect name. An affectionate name children gave their beloved mothers.

"Yes, call me Mamusha."

His mother had died, his father was gone, he was separated from his home, and Michael fell into the biggest breakdown of his young life. He withdrew into a long silence and often burst into tears. He had to have the only living soul left to him in the world, her caressing hand, her soft words, her vitality. Gertruda worked fewer hours so she could devote herself to his care. Every day, she took him with her when she went to pray in church and walked with him in the streets of Vilna so he could get some fresh air. The weather was usually rainy and cold and the city didn't welcome refugees. Under one umbrella, the two of them walked in the

Michael and Gertruda. Vilna, 1942.

crowded streets and inhaled the cooking smells from the restaurants. Gertruda was extremely careful with her few remaining pennies. In the farmers' market she bought only what was cheap: potatoes, cabbage, beets, and stale bread. She cooked a lot of soup. She couldn't afford to buy meat.

Bad news came from Poland. The Germans had just taken over the whole country. Gertruda felt some relief when she assumed they wouldn't dare violate their alliance with the Russians and invade Vilna, too.

Rent and food expenses ate up almost all her savings. For whole nights she lay awake, considering how to earn some money. Michael was losing weight and had no appetite. She was afraid he would get sick.

Dr. Berman showed up as an unexpected savior. Life in Vilna

was good for him. He was well known as a specialist in lung dis-
eases and the number of his patients was constantly increasing.
One evening, he knocked on their door and made downtrodden
Gertruda an offer she couldn't refuse.

"I need a secretary to schedule my appointments," he said. "I'll
pay you generously. What do you say?"

She jumped at the chance and the next day she started working
in his clinic in his apartment next door. That day, Dr. Berman gave
her an advance on her salary and she bought food for herself and
the boy.

Dr. Berman opened the doors of his home to them. Yanek, the
doctor's oldest son, was the same age as Michael, and they played
together most days. Esther, the doctor's wife, often invited them to
share their dinner.

The winter, meanwhile, was harsh and desperate. Heavy snow
covered Vilna and the cold invaded their small apartment. They sat
in the double bed, hugging each other to keep warm. They drank
dozens of cups of boiling tea to fight the chill and waited eagerly for
a miracle to get them out of the situation they had fallen into.

3.

Every night, before she fell asleep, Gertruda Babilinska would leaf
through her Polish passport and her worries grew worse. Only her
name appeared on the passport. Michael appeared in his mother's,
which had been stolen by Emil. Gertruda was sure there were hard
times ahead for the two of them. She didn't know if she'd stay in
Vilna, she didn't know where the winds of war would blow, but she
did know that if she didn't find a way to put Michael on her passport, as her son, as her flesh and blood, she couldn't really protect

him. She had to find a way, at any cost, to hide his Jewishness and attach him to her officially. Adding his name to her passport would be the only proof that Michael was her son. But without documents to prove the child was hers, it wouldn't be easy.

One morning, she left the house determined to find a professional counterfeiter who could help her. Black market speculators stood on every street corner. She asked a few of them if they could find someone who could make changes to her passport. One elderly speculator told her: "What you want, lady, costs a lot." When she heard the sum, she left, feeling helpless.

On her way home to Michael, she stopped at the Ostra Brama Church across from the house, went inside, knelt at the altar, and prayed for someone to help her. When she stood up, she saw the priest Andras Gedovsky standing in front of her.

"Is everything all right, Mrs. Babilinska?"

"Not really," she said. She didn't dare tell him about the Jewish child.

"Can I be of some help?" he asked.

She chose her words carefully. "My husband was a Polish army officer who was killed in the war. I fled here with my son and didn't have time to take my passport. I'm afraid to walk around without it."

"The child who comes to church with you is your son?"

She nodded. Ever since she had started introducing Michael as her son, she had made sure he came to church with her every Sunday.

"Yes, Father. He's my child."

"A lovely child. What's his name?"

"Michael."

The priest sighed. "This war is causing so much suffering for so many people," he said. "Come with me. I'll try to help you."

With high hopes, she accompanied him to his office. He sat

down at his desk, asked for her personal details, and wrote on church stationery:

> *To whom it may concern: the widow Gertruda Babilinska, born*
> *in 1902, Polish citizen and devout Catholic, one of my flock,*
> *has lost her documents. I certify that she is the mother of*
> *Michael, born in 1936.*

Gertruda thanked the priest excitedly, put the document in her purse and returned home.

4.

The idea of getting married wasn't his. It was Anna's.

She said, "France isn't a safe place for us. The French are afraid the Germans will invade them, and a lot of Jews are fleeing from here. We should go to my mother in Italy."

She suggested they get married. As the husband of an Italian citizen, said Anna, Jacob Stolowitzky wouldn't have any trouble crossing the Italian border with her. In May 1940, Italy was not yet involved in the war. Until the war was over, she added, Jacob could live with her in the family house in the small town of Pontrepoli.

"And what will happen if my wife is still alive?" he asked.

"If that happens," she promised, "I'll annul our marriage immediately."

On the morning of May 9, 1940, Anna and Jacob appeared at the city hall of Paris and were married in a civil ceremony. There were no family members, friends, or acquaintances present and twenty minutes after they entered city hall, they rushed out to catch the train to Genoa. Neither of them knew that the very next day the German army would cross the border and make its way to Paris, facing only slight and ineffective resistance from the French army.

Because of the fear that many refugees from France would flood into Italy, the Italian border control was stricter than ever. Border guards checked Jacob and Anna's marriage certificate and let the two of them cross the border without incident. From the railroad station in Genoa, they took a taxi to the small town where her family house was.

Anna's mother, a plump woman with a stern face, looked harshly at Jacob when she met him there for the first time. She wasn't happy that he was a Jew or that there was such a big age difference between him and Anna, but she held her tongue. After all, Anna was her only daughter. She had raised her alone for many years and didn't want to create a rift between them now.

The family house was at the edge of the town, amid apple and pear orchards, separated from the other houses. A narrow dirt path led from the street to the one-story structure where the couple lived in a quiet side room, overlooking a broad square. The windows could be left open all day without fear that any stranger could peep inside.

Anna's marriage stirred only passing interest in the town. Anna told her friends that she had met her husband in Paris, where he had various business dealings. She said that her husband had a chronic disease that kept him indoors most of the time. The townspeople soon got used to seeing her alone, buying fruit and vegetables in the farmers' market and meat at the butcher. Every Sunday she went to church with her mother and together they attended family events of friends and neighbors. Jacob generally stayed home and only at night did he go out for a short stroll in the deserted lanes.

Anna wanted children. Girls her age in the town who were blessed with several offspring often asked her why she didn't get pregnant and she had no answer. She pleaded with her husband to bring children into the world, but he wanted to wait until the war was over. Only then, he said, could he plan the new chapter of his life without worry.

5.

One evening, on her way home from the clinic, a stocky and familiar man blocked Gertruda's way in the staircase.

"Where are you hurrying?" asked Denka, the landlady's brother.

"My child is waiting for me," she answered quickly and tried to get around the man, but he didn't let her.

"Wait a minute," he said.

She had to obey.

His clumsy hand moved forward and tried to stroke her head, but she quickly dodged him.

"Let me go," she pleaded.

"Wait a minute. I wanted to offer you a good deal," he said.

She pretended she believed him. "What deal?"

"There are people who will pay you a lot of money for information you can give them."

She knew he was spying for the Russians. Everybody knew.

"You know that Jewish doctor, Berman, if I'm not mistaken." She shuddered. How did he find out about her relations with the doctor? Was he watching her when she worked in Dr. Berman's clinic? "All you've got to do is tell me if he says anything against the Russian government, if he's got friends who get together secretly, if you see them with weapons."

"I didn't see or hear anything," she answered quickly.

"You can hear and see, if you want to. With the right information you can go far, maybe even get a regular salary. What do you say?"

"I'll think it over," she concluded to get away from him.

His lips twisted into a grin.

"Your cooperation can also bring us closer together," he said. "I know you and I can have a very good time together."

"Let me go, please."

He clutched her body. His lips sought hers, but she averted her face.

Somebody entered the staircase and Denka let go of her at once.

"Good evening, Mrs. Babilinska," he said obsequiously. "It was nice talking to you."

She hurried up to her apartment with a feeling that she hadn't seen the last of that loathsome man.

6.

The Molotov-Ribbentrop nonaggression pact soon proved to be worthless. The break between Stalin and Hitler was inevitable, and on June 22, 1941, when the colorful flowers were blooming in the fields of Lithuania, the German army attacked the Russian lines and made their way to Vilna.

At eleven o'clock that morning, on Radio Moscow, the Soviet foreign minister announced in a furious voice that the Germans had violated the nonaggression agreement and were advancing toward

Vilna. The sirens of Vilna immediately began wailing and the thunder of air raids was heard in the suburbs.

It was a warm, sunny Sunday. Families were strolling in the
public parks, the churches were full, and at the side of the road,
Jewish refugees were selling their last valuables. All at once, the
siren and echoes of bombings broke the silence and sowed terror.
The sky was covered with German bombers dropping bombs on the
houses of the city, spraying the streets with machine-gun fire,
spreading death and destruction. The shouts of the wounded went
on echoing in the streets even after dark. The hospitals didn't have
enough room for so many wounded, and many of them lay abandoned in the streets. The planes returned to bomb again at night,
when columns of German armored carriers were two days away
from Vilna.

• The heavy bombing terrified Gertruda and Michael. She
dragged him to the cellar to hide among the thick stone walls. All
the tenants of the upper floors of the house also hurried down
there. The air in the cellar was stifling and compressed, there was
no food or water, children wept bitterly, the elderly quietly choked.

When they learned of the impending German invasion, the Lithuanians burst into cheers of joy. Many of them had been working underground to undermine the Soviet authorities and enable a fast
and effective German occupation. They sincerely believed that, in
gratitude for their sympathy for the Germans, Berlin would grant
Lithuania independent status. Right under the nose of the Soviet
authorities, the Lithuanians planned to establish their own government institutions and were ready to welcome the German army and
carry out every assignment, including the destruction of the Jews.
Like the Germans, they, too, believed that the Jews were a misfor-

tune and an obstacle that had to be removed. In manifestos that saw the vision of an independent Lithuanian state as a miracle, the Lithuanians were called upon to kill Jews and confiscate their property. In fact, the Lithuanians murdered hundreds of Jews and robbed them even before the Germans arrived.

The Jews in Vilna followed the events with dread. In truth, there were even some Jews who wanted the Germans to come, convinced that the occupiers would impose order and restrain the Lithuanian lust for the destruction of the Jews. But most Jews of Vilna, both local residents and refugees, were sure that the burden of the German occupation would be harsh. In despair, they hesitated whether to stay or flee toward the Russian border to find shelter far from the reach of the Germans and Lithuanians. The former choice was easier but much more dangerous. The latter required packing up some clothes and vital items and fleeing, mostly without a penny, to the unknown. No possibility promised anything good; neither was better than the other.

Gertruda chose to flee to Russia. She told Dr. Berman of her decision. The doctor wished her luck and said that he and his wife had decided to stay. "We've got two children at home," said the doctor sadly. "They wouldn't survive the hard trip to Russia."

Gertruda crammed everything she could into a small suitcase— clothes, two loaves of bread, a few apples, and a bottle of water— and left the apartment with Michael. She didn't tell the landlady of her intentions, to make sure the apartment would still be hers if she had to return.

Gertruda and Michael hurried to the railroad station. Cars belonging to the Soviet authorities sped past them on their way to the Russian border. Now and then German bombers sallied forth from the blue sky and swooped over Vilna and the columns of refugees. Cars burst into flames on the side of the road, and bodies lay wherever the bombs fell.

The railroad station in Vilna was full of people who crowded into long lines at the ticket counters. Elderly people fainted, children wept, and here and there fights broke out. Gertruda and Michael were crushed in one of the lines. After she bought tickets, Gertruda had only a few pennies left, but that didn't worry her. The desire to get Michael out of the impending danger was her only consideration.

The train to the border town of Radoshkowitz left two hours late. In the compartments and the corridors, hundreds of people rode sitting and standing, more than the train could hold. Dozens were lying on the roofs of the cars, holding on to ledges to keep from falling. The locomotive could hardly pull the train and it often broke down. The train was attacked four times by German bombers. They hit some of the cars and killed dozens of people. The bodies of those killed were thrown to the sides of the track. The wounded were taken off at the intermediate stations, in the vain hope that they might receive medical treatment.

Vilna was 125 miles from the Russian border, a trip that took no more than four hours in normal times. But the trainload of refugees took close to forty hours to cover the distance. Michael suffered in silence all along the way. He munched on dry bread, drank a little water, and hid under the bench. When the German planes dropped their bombs, he clutched Gertruda's hand.

The train finally stopped at the Radoshkowitz station, where many Jews were standing on the platform, waiting to return to Vilna. Gertruda didn't understand why, but there was no time for questions. Exhausted and hungry, but with a spark of hope in their eyes, the travelers ran to the border station. They hoped their share of torments would cease, at least for the time being.

Gertruda and Michael ran with all the rest and arrived panting at the Russian position. Armed soldiers stopped them and asked them for entrance permits to Russia. Because the bombing of Vilna had started on a Sunday, most of the passengers couldn't get hold of the necessary documents since the visa offices were closed. They pleaded with the border guards to let them cross into Russian territory, but the soldiers firmly refused and suggested they return to where they had come from.

No one was in a hurry to return. Stunned families gathered at the border station. People wept and begged the border guards. Others offered the last of their money and jewelry, but the soldiers were adamant. Only now did Gertruda understand why the platforms of the railroad station were full of Jews wanting to go back to Vilna. None of them had a permit to enter Russia.

Gertruda turned around without a word and started walking to the railroad station, holding Michael's hand. She had no money left for a ticket, but most of the others weren't any better off. They packed the train to Vilna and hoped they wouldn't be thrown off before they got to their destination. Their faces were sad and their eyes were tearful. They knew that every minute of the trip brought them closer to the hell they had wanted to flee.

In Gertruda's compartment was a young woman carrying a baby. She pleaded with the passengers to give her a little food, but no one paid any attention to her. Gertruda took out a few slices of bread and gave them to the mother. The woman grabbed the bread and devoured it. A few minutes later, she came to Gertruda and whispered in her ear. "You did a great mitzvah," she said. "I don't have anything to pay you for the bread, but I do have something else for you." She said she had made a living in Vilna by reading palms. "Give me your palm," she said. "I'll tell you your future, for free." Gertruda gave her her hand and looked curiously at the woman as she examined it.

"The dangers haven't passed," she said. "You'll have to be very careful."

"And the child?"

"I see him with you all the time. He's very tied to you. If you leave him, he won't stay alive."

"When will we finally have peace?"

"After a long time. The war will end and you'll be free to do what you want. I see a gigantic ship you'll board with the child, but the voyage will be hard. I also see a lot of blood, violence, dead people."

"A ship? Where will it take us?"

"To a place where you can build a new life. But a curse lies on that ship. Something bad will happen to it."

"I don't know what ship you're talking about."

"Neither do I, but someday you'll know."

"You suggest that I don't board the ship?"

"Your fate will make the two of you board that cursed ship and there's nothing in the world you can do to prevent it."

The train moved.

"Where are we going?" asked Michael when clouds of black smoke from the locomotive came through the open window.

"Back home, to Vilna," Gertruda answered.

"I don't want to," he decreed. His sharp senses warned him what was waiting for them for them in Vilna.

She stroked his head lovingly.

"Don't worry," she said. "I'll take care of you."

7.

A taste of bitter insipidity had filled Karl Rink's mouth ever since he had come to Warsaw. He was tormented by pangs of conscience for not continuing to search for his wife, and his regrets for Mira and Helga gave him no rest. He was sorry he hadn't followed his daughter's advice to flee from Germany with his family when that had been an option. Every week, he wrote a letter to his wife and sent it to their apartment in Berlin, hoping she would be there and could answer. He never got a reply.

Work in SS headquarters in Warsaw was as dreary as all routine office work. Karl collected orders to limit the movements of the Jews, sent people to post them on the walls of houses and on announcement boards, transmitted them to all the Jewish institutions and organizations that were still operating. Under his direction, gangs of soldiers were sent to make sure the posted orders were carried out. Jews who didn't wear identifying armbands or didn't mark their businesses with a Star of David were immediately arrested and sent to forced labor camps. Jews who were caught on trains after they were forbidden to travel on them were also arrested. Step by step, the property of the Jews also began to be confiscated.

Karl Rink finished work in the evening and then returned to his apartment. He avoided going to the nightclubs and concerts that were reserved for German officers. He didn't spend much time with his colleagues. In his nightmares, he saw them snatching and murdering his wife, while his hands were tied and he shouted with pain and despair.

. . .

On the night of Yom Kippur, German radio announced that all Jews had to move to the ghetto in Warsaw within five weeks. There was no room to hide or flee to avoid the evil decree. The Jews knew that not carrying out the order of the occupying authorities would be punished by death. The ghetto was the only possibility to stay alive. Tens of thousands of Jews started gathering up their belongings and loading on handcarts and on their backs every item they could carry. The area of the ghetto was small and the crowding was unbearable. Six or seven people, sometimes even more, lived in every room. Anyone who couldn't find a place to live had to stay in the street.

When the Jews moved to the ghetto, Karl Rink's job, for all intents and purposes, was done. He walked around idly, loathed the SS officers, the haughty men who filled the offices of the headquarters, and hoped he would soon be returned to Berlin. But his superiors had another plan. A few months after the Jews of Warsaw were concentrated in the ghetto, Karl was transferred to Vilna, which had been occupied by the German army. "There are a lot of Jews there," he was told. "We have to make order among them, as in Warsaw."

8.

Gertruda and Michael's trip back to Vilna was filled with torments and empty of hope. The train was crowded; the passengers were hungry and tired, and most of them didn't have enough money to buy dry bread at the stations where they stopped. The trip was mainly at night, for fear of German bombers. No one could sleep; sick people groaned in pain; some even died. Gertruda and Michael, under the bench, on the iron floor of the train, had to lie for hours without moving, pressed against other people. Their bodies hurt, their bellies rumbled with hunger, and their mouths were dry with thirst.

The train reached the Vilna railroad station in the afternoon. Hundreds of passengers burst out, dragging their meager belongings. The swastika banner was already flying over the station. German army tanks and motorcycles filled the street. Groups of armed soldiers strode proudly under the hot summer sun.

Two trucks parked across from the station and a group of armed Lithuanians with white armbands blocked the way of the travelers who had just arrived on the train. They demanded documents.

Gertruda took out the letter written by Father Gedovsky and gave it to the heavyset man wearing a Lithuanian army uniform, with a rifle slung over his shoulder. The man scanned the document stating explicitly that Gertruda Babilinska and her son were Catholics. The Lithuanian looked at her suspiciously.

"That's your son?" he asked.

"Yes."

"Where's your father?" The Lithuanian bent down to Michael.

"Died in the war," answered the child. That was exactly what Gertruda had taught him to say to anyone who asked.

"Where are you coming from?"

"Radoshkowitz," replied Gertruda.

"From the Russian border?"

"Yes."

"Why did you go there?"

"My parents are in Russia," she lied. "I wanted to join them."

"Why did you come back here?"

"Because I didn't have permission to enter Russia."

He examined her with a long look.

"You're a Russian spy," he said bluntly. "All Poles are Russian spies."

The Lithuanian hostility for the Poles was infamous. The Lithuanians did all they could to slander them to the Germans. After the destruction of the Jews, the Lithuanians planned to expel the Poles as well. In independent Lithuania, within the German Reich, there wouldn't be room for either.

"That's not so!" Gertruda defended herself. "I'm not a spy!"

"I'll have to arrest you," growled the Lithuanian.

She turned pale. Arrest meant torture, which could be the end of her and of Michael. She had only a split second to find a way to dodge the danger.

Her lips twisted into a seductive smile. "Do you mind if we talk about it at my house?" she asked.

His eyes flashed. "Where do you live?"

She gave him a wrong address.

"Come to me after your shift," she winked. "We can talk quietly. We'll have some cognac."

"I'll come this evening," he said. "Don't leave the house. Wait for me." ,

He returned the priest's letter to her and let her go back to the city. When she left, she saw a few dozen Jews—men, women, and children—being ordered to get into trucks. Anyone who had difficulty was pushed in there by force.

The trucks left the city and made their way to a thick forest about six miles south of Vilna. They drove along a dirt path into the forest and stopped where the Russians had dug gigantic pits to store oil tanks. The German attack had interrupted the work in the middle and the Russians had fled before they had time to bury the tanks.

The Lithuanians rushed the passengers out of the trucks, concentrated them in the small clearing, organized them into groups of ten to twenty people, confiscated any valuables they had, and ordered them to strip. Then they shoved every group to the edge of the pits and blindfolded the Jews. Some were stunned, others prayed, women shrieked hysterically; none of them had any doubt what was about to happen.

The Lithuanians' weapons spat fire and the naked victims knelt and fell straight into the pits. They were covered with stones and tree branches and more groups were brought to the valley of killing. Groans of the dying died out as evening fell.

9.

It took only a few days for the German army to turn Vilna into a fearful and evil city. Plants were closed, businesses went bankrupt, and the number of unemployed increased from one day to the next. Many local citizens were recruited into units that worked for the Germans, and anti-Semitic feelings that had long lodged in broad strata of the civilian public were allowed free rein. Many informants helped the Germans arrest those suspected of sympathizing with the Russians, and the jails were filled with prisoners taken from home or snatched on the street. Dr. Berman lost most of his patients and Gertruda lost her job.

New decrees against the Jews were issued from German army headquarters at a rapid rate. It was a system of cruel tortures planned to make the victims twitch, suffer, and despair, until the final blow of death landed on them. The Jews were forbidden to travel on public transportation, to own a telephone or a radio, to sit in cafés, to attend the movies or the theater, to go to the barber, to walk on the main streets, and to have any contact with non-Jews. They had to wear yellow armbands.

· · ·

The German occupation office on Zevalna Street, in the middle of the city, turned into a threatening fortress, the symbol of an omnipotent ruler. Long lines of citizens soon twisted at its door, wanting to find out the fate of their family members arrested for interrogation, to get a peddler's permit, or to offer themselves for work for the Germans. Most of them didn't speak German. Gertruda, who was fluent in that language because she had grown up in an area with a German majority, thought she could use that knowledge to make money. She went to those standing in line and offered herself as an interpreter. One of the peasants asked her on the spot to write a request for him in German.

"I can't pay you in money," he said. "But I can give you fruit and vegetables in exchange for your work."

She agreed immediately. The man wanted her to write a request for him to get a license for a stand in the farmers' market. Gertruda knelt on the sidewalk and wrote a letter. He went to his wooden cart and brought her pears and potatoes. That day she wrote two more letters and was paid with a loaf of bread, cabbage, and pieces of smoked fish.

The following days were even more lucrative. She was asked not only to write letters, but also to interpret for people who had a meeting in the offices of the German government. The first meetings scared her. She was afraid that the Germans would want to know who she was, would interrogate her, would get to her Jewish child, and would arrest both of them. But the need to make a living outweighed her fear. She looked directly at the Germans in uniform, spoke with them politely and confidently. To her joy, none of them showed any special interest in her.

She was successful and soon became well known as an interpreter who could communicate with the Germans. She brought home food, giving some of it to the landlady as rent and selling another part to her neighbors.

Sometime later, she no longer needed to hunt for customers in the street. People who heard of her started coming to her apartment or summoned her to their homes to write requests for them. The pantry filled up and hunger no longer stalked her and Michael.

Gertruda strickly forbade Michael to go into the street without her permission. The Germans often checked the identity of passersby, constantly looked for Jews who were passing as "Aryans," stopped suspicious people, interrogated them with torture, and executed many who couldn't allay their suspicions. Michael was liable to endanger his life whenever he walked in the street.

10.

The running of hobnailed boots echoed in the street, and orders in German disturbed the night silence. Rifle butts banged on doors. Frightened people crept out of their beds, hearing the order to move immediately to the ghetto. Karl Rink took part in the operation to move the Jews to the ghetto and felt bad at the brutality of his comrades who turned the evacuation into a vicious amusement. He had to accompany the expulsion crews quite often.

In the staircase of the house where the Berman family lived, frightened Jews gathered. They had a hard time understanding the exile order placed on their door. Gertruda met Dr. Berman in the courtyard.

"We have no choice," said the doctor. "If we want to live, we'd better pack up and move."

The Berman family loaded their things on a rickety truck. The landlady stood in the doorway and spat at them. "You lied to me!" she shouted. "You didn't tell me you were Jews." In the empty apartments, the warmth of people forced to leave in a hurry dissipated.

The truck groaned on the way to the ghetto and moved along slowly in a convoy of vehicles, next to horse-drawn carts carrying more Jews who had been thrown out of their homes. Sad and terrified faces, lost in the cold night, surrounded the convoy on all sides. No one knew what was in store for them; no one was sure of the future.

The truck stopped in the heart of the ghetto and the driver unloaded the belongings of the passengers on the sidewalk. Armed German soldiers passed by and uttered obscenities. A thin old man fainted in the street and the soldiers kicked him for fun. When they were fed up with their amusement, they left to hunt down more victims. Dr. Berman rushed to help the old man, but he was dead by the time the doctor reached him.

As far as the eye could see, the sidewalk was packed with desperate Jews sitting on bundles of clothes and household goods. Pale mothers took out their breasts for their hungry babies. Sick people lay helplessly in the heaps of objects and prayed for a miracle to put them back on their feet.

The doctor devoted the following hours to searching for someplace to live. The selection of apartments was meager and the prices were high. Finally, he found a one-room apartment and moved his family there.

"What will we do now?" asked his wife anxiously.

Dr. Joseph Berman tried to calm her. "I'm told there's work in the Jewish hospital. I'll try to get a job there."

. . .

There was uncertainty in the crowded apartment and oppression had drawn lines on the face of the doctor's wife. The children ate dry bread and drank tap water. There was only one bed in the room for the four souls who huddled there together.

Soon after getting a job in the hospital, Dr. Berman learned that there wasn't much he'd be able to do. Long lines of sick people waited at the building on Zavalna Street, which was too small to contain them. Stocks of medicine ran out and all the doctors could do was put cold compresses on the foreheads of the seriously ill and pray for their recovery. The number of deaths increased with every passing day.

Two weeks later, Dr. Berman stopped getting paid because there was no more money in the hospital coffers. He went on working as a volunteer, and his wife sold all her valuables one by one in order to survive. Day after day, she stood for hours in line at the bakery to buy bread. Sometimes she returned empty-handed because the bread had run out. In the small greengrocer shop, there were usually only crushed, rotten fruits and vegetables that weren't fit for human consumption.

The worst was still to come. Organized groups of Lithuanians, in collaboration with German units, continued a systematic extermination of the Jewish population. They raided the homes of Jews in the ghetto, announced that they had come to take the men for work, and drove them into the nearby forests where they murdered them in cold blood and threw them into pits. Other Jews were snatched as they walked in the street and were executed. A big reward was paid to anyone who brought information about Jews hiding outside the ghetto.

Dr. Berman, who could no longer pay the rent, moved with his family to the supply cellar of the Jewish hospital. The families of other doctors lived there with them, crowded and in bad sanitary conditions. For the time being, the Lithuanians and the Germans didn't raid the hospital. They let the patients die slowly, but they all knew it was only a matter of time until the hospital would be destroyed and the end would come for those there.

The Jews of the ghetto vacillated between hope and despair. They wanted to believe that the Germans mainly wanted to use them as a labor force and didn't intend to destroy them. That was what Jacob Gens also thought; he was a former police officer appointed by the Germans as chief of the ghetto police and later chairman of the Judenrat, the Jewish council. He wanted peace, obedience, and submission and warned against any organization designed to resist the Germans by force. But Dr. Berman and some of his friends thought otherwise. They were sure the Germans had decided to destroy the ghetto, as they had done in other occupied cities. So they established secret cells, amassed weapons, and prepared for battle. Itzik Vittenberg, a friend of the doctor, was appointed commander of the ghetto underground.

Despite the secrecy surrounding its operations, the Germans discovered the existence of the underground as a result of an informant and knew that Vittenberg was in charge. They tried to locate him, but he hid in a place known only to those loyal to him. The Germans finally called in Gens and demanded that he turn over the leader of the underground. Gens appealed to dozens of Jews, asking them to tell Vittenberg that he wanted to meet with him for important talks. He promised that if Vittenberg was arrested by the Germans during the meeting, a bribe would be paid to willing hands for his liberation, as when important Jews had been arrested in the past. Vittenberg came to the meeting in Gens's office, but had the area surrounded with his people to provide security. His fear was justified. Before Vittenberg entered Gens's office, he was attacked by two Lithuanian SS men and German agents, who tried to drag him to their car. Vittenberg's bodyguards realized that he had fallen into a trap. They assaulted the Lithuanians, got their leader away from them, and fled with him. During the incident, Vittenberg was wounded in the arm. Dr. Berman was called to bandage his wound. Vittenberg explained that he was now more certain than ever that the Germans were trying to capture him in order to weaken the underground and to prevent it from fighting. He was committed to completing preparations for the uprising.

The Germans were furious when their prey slipped out of their hands, and they told Gens they would kill hundreds of Jews if Vittenberg wasn't turned over to them. Gens issued an emotional appeal to the Jews of the ghetto to locate Vittenberg. "If he goes on hiding," he warned, "many of you will die."

In the tense atmosphere of the ghetto, where uncertainty and anxiety overflowed, those words only intensified the fear. Hundreds of Jews—men, women, and children—went searching for Vittenberg. Mothers shouted at every house, every storage room, and every cellar: "Mercy on our children and us. Turn yourself in."

The rage among the Jews grew from one hour to the next. Everyone talked about Vittenberg's stubbornness. The few who tried to take his side were vilified.

Vittenberg received constant reports about what was going on. He knew that if so many were searching for him, he would eventually be found. After long hesitations, Dr. Berman was called to the remote room where the commander of the underground was hiding. Vittenberg was as pale as a ghost.

"The Jews of the ghetto don't understand that their end is near anyway," he said in a pained voice. "But I don't want them to blame me for it when they're lead to their death. So I've decided to turn myself in. Please give me a poison capsule."

Dr. Berman tried to persuade him to give up the idea, arguing that the underground needed him now more than ever, but Vittenberg persisted. Berman consulted with his colleagues, who agreed that there was no other way out, and he had to fulfill Vittenberg's request. The doctor brought him the capsule.

The next day, Vittenberg came out of hiding and turned himself in. The Germans took him to the torture chamber where he swallowed the poison capsule and died a few minutes later.

Dr. Berman and the other members of the underground were left without a leader. They were sure the end of the ghetto was near and there was nothing they could do to prevent the disaster.

CHAPTER 8

Unexpected Savior

1.

She didn't expect to see him again. Mainly she didn't expect to see him dead.

But it was him. No doubt about it. That mane of black hair, those shiny leather boots, that evil smile on his face when he threatened them with the gun and stole Lydia's valuables.

Emil the chauffeur was lying on the sidewalk. His eyes were closed and his chest was covered with a big bloodstain. People passed by him, glancing indifferently. Dead people lying in the streets was a frequent sight, ever since the refugees had inundated the city. The sight of them didn't seem to upset anyone anymore.

Two men came out of a nearby shop, grabbed Emil's arms, and dragged him to the curb away from the door. One of them covered the blood on the sidewalk with sand.

"What happened to him?" Gertruda asked the two.

"There was a brawl here. Somebody took out a knife and stabbed him."

"Where does he live?"

The man pointed to a nearby group of buildings. "Around there," he said.

Gertruda bent over Emil's body and burrowed in his pockets. They were empty. Without a word, she straightened up and went to find out where he lived. She knocked on a few doors until she located the landlady.

"Does Emil live here?" she asked.

The landlady was a fat, ruddy-faced woman.

"Yes," she said casually. "Who are you?"

"I'm his sister."

"What do you want?"

"Emil's dead," said Gertruda.

Not a muscle moved in the woman's face. "Lucky that he paid me the rent at the beginning of the month," she growled. "You know how it is these days, people behave like animals. They rent an apartment, they don't pay, and they run away in the middle of the night."

"Can I go into his apartment?" asked Gertruda. "I have to take a few family documents from there, if you don't mind."

The landlady hesitated. "I'll come with you," she said.

They went into the dingy room. A few shirts and trousers were hanging in the closet. A half bottle of vodka stood on the table. The bed was unmade.

Gertruda made a quick search. She didn't find any of the jewels or money Emil had stolen and the landlady was beginning to lose patience. "Enough," she said. "I don't have time for this."

Gertruda begged her to let her search a while longer. She rummaged among the kitchen items in the cabinet and in the pockets of the trousers in the closet, hoping to find at least some of Lydia's jewelry and the documents from her purse. She didn't find a thing.

As she was about to leave, her eyes made out Lydia's gun at the bottom of the closet. Gertruda picked it up carefully, as the landlady looked on in horror.

"Don't leave that here," the woman called out. "Take it and get out before the Germans arrest me because of it."

Gertruda stuck the gun in her coat and left the apartment.

In the street, she felt the gun burning her skin through the pocket. She didn't know what to do with it, but it did give her a sense of confidence.

2.

Gertruda was haunted by thoughts of the fate of Dr. Berman and his family. Disturbing information constantly filtered out of the ghetto. Jews were being taken for forced labor or sent to concentration camps. Those who tried to flee from the ghetto were shot. People were starving to death and dying of terrible diseases.

She was sure the doctor's family was suffering, maybe even starving. In her pantry there was food she wanted to get to them, but all the roads to the ghetto were blocked by German soldiers. She heard that Jewish children crawled through the sewers from the ghetto to the nearby neighborhoods every night to rummage in garbage cans and collect remnants of food. She told this to Michael.

"If only I knew how to get to those sewers," he said.

"Why, Michael?"

"Because then I could bring Dr. Berman a little food."

She loved the way he thought, his daring. The hardships of life had made the five-year-old as mature as a grown-up. She thought about the Berman family starving and the great moral obligation she owed those people who had helped her in her time of need, whom she couldn't help when they were in distress.

One night, on her way home from writing a request to the military authorities for a customer, Gertruda was walking through a narrow lane and saw a sad child emerge in a shabby, oversized coat. He asked for alms and she gave him a few pennies.

"Are you from the ghetto?" she asked.

He hesitated and then nodded.

"Do you know a doctor named Berman?"

"No."

"Are you going back to the ghetto?"

"Why?"

"Berman is a friend of mine. I want to send him some food."

"You can't do it yourself."

"Why not?"

"Because there's only one sure way, through the sewers. It stinks terribly there. It's not for you. But I can take the food to the doctor. You can trust me. What's his address?"

"I have no idea."

"I'll find out. I've got connections. What's your name?"

"Gertruda."

She gave him the bag of fruit and vegetables she had just earned.

"Take a little bit for yourself, too," she said.

"Thanks, lady."

"Let's meet here tomorrow at this time," she said. "I'll bring more food."

"Great."

She watched him until he disappeared into the sewer and then returned home with a light heart.

Michael listened to her story with sparkling eyes.

"Is the Jewish child scared to come here?"

"Of course he's scared, but he has to."

"If the Germans catch him, they'll kill him, right?"

"Maybe."

"He must be very hungry. I'd do the same thing if we didn't have any food."

"I know, Michael," she said and hugged him warmly.

3.

The winter of 1941 was colder than ever. Thick snowflakes covered Vilna with a white shroud and people wrapped themselves in thick coats and long wool scarves when they went out. The child from the ghetto was shivering in his rags but hunger got the better of him. He slipped out of the ghetto again almost every evening and often found Gertruda waiting for him in the alley with food for the Berman family and for him.

One evening, the child stumbled toward her with shaking legs.

"What happened to you?" asked Gertruda in terror.

"I don't feel well," he murmured and leaned on the wall next to the opening of the secret passage to the ghetto. His hands were empty. "For a few days now I haven't been able to find food," he said.

"But I give you fruit and vegetables every day."

He dropped his eyes. "What you give to the doctor, I take to him. And what you give me, I sell," he said.

"Why?"

"To buy medicine for my aunt. I live with her."

"And where are your parents?"

"Died in the ghetto."

"When was the last time you ate?"

"Don't remember."

She opened the bag of food for Dr. Berman's family and gave him an apple.

The boy put it in his pocket.

"Eat it here, now," Gertruda insisted. He relented easily and gobbled it up.

"Come with me," she suddenly decided.

"Where?" His eyes gazed at her in wonder.

"To my home."

"Why?"

"I'll make you a hot meal," she said.

His childish face glowed. "For a hot meal, I'm willing to do anything," he said.

It was an impetuous and dangerous act. Gertruda knew that if the two of them fell into the hands of the Germans, their fate was sealed. But her heart couldn't bear his distress.

"Follow me," she said. "Keep a distance. I live close by."

The boy followed her like a shadow. She cautiously checked the staircase of the house. When she saw there wasn't anyone there, she ran upstairs to the apartment with the boy.

Michael was surprised to see the guest.

"This is the boy from the ghetto," said Gertruda. "I invited him to eat with us."

She made him soup with a piece of meat. The boy ate hungrily and color returned to his face. He told them about life in the ghetto, about the hunger and the shortages, the bodies lying in the streets, the people taken supposedly to work for the Germans and who didn't come back.

"I'll also die in the end," he said in a dry voice, as if stating a fact.

"You mustn't talk like that," said Gertruda. She thought of Michael, who was also constantly threatened by serious danger. "The war will end and life will go back to normal. You'll also go back home."

"The war won't end so fast," he said with the tone of someone who has already seen and knows everything. "We'll all be killed first. Nobody in the ghetto has a chance."

She gave him a little food for himself, handed him the bag for the Berman family, and checked the staircase again to make sure nobody would see him as he left.

From the window of the apartment, she watched the tiny figure clinging to the buildings on the way to the secret passage.

"I want him to get to the ghetto safely," said Michael.

"So do I."

4.

The snow piled up in the streets and it grew colder. Gertruda heated the fireplace with pieces of wood she got as payment from a farmer who needed her as an interpreter. The wood could run out quickly, so she was careful to ration it. When the fireplace wasn't burning, the cold was intense and bit painfully. It also brought fear. More than anything else, Gertruda worried that Michael would catch cold, would be bedridden, and would need a doctor. Any doctor, she worried, would immediately discover the secret that Michael was circumcised. If that happened, they would almost certainly be turned over to the Germans. She dreaded the thought that

Michael might be taken from her and that she would never see him again.

Michael got through the first months of winter, but in December he contracted pneumonia. He had a high fever, became delirious, and couldn't breathe properly. Gertruda did her best to take care of him with her meager means: cold compresses and constant prayers. But the child's fever rose and his breathing turned into a wheezing. She sat helplessly at his side and waited in vain for his condition to improve.

Only a doctor could help and there was only one doctor she could trust.

She was determined to get to him, whatever the risk. She told Michael she had to go out for a while and he had to stay alone for a few hours.

"Don't open the door to anyone," she warned him. "Don't answer if they talk to you outside the door."

"All right," he whispered. "Come back soon, okay?"

Gertruda put on Lydia's fur coat and slipped into the alley by the secret opening to the ghetto in hopes of finding the Jewish child there who could summon Dr. Berman. The night was dark and terrifying, and the child wasn't there. For hours she hid in the entrance to the house near the opening of the sewer. German guards passed by her but didn't see her. The cold penetrated her bones and froze her body. She thought constantly of Michael, feverish in their apartment, and the fear that his condition would worsen drove her crazy. As time passed, she knew that at dawn the chances of slipping into the ghetto and getting in touch with the doctor would vanish.

There was only one way to be sure of getting there. She bent over the opening and crept into the sewer, ignoring the danger, the stench, and the turgid liquid sloshing at her feet as she walked bent over through the puddles.

The streets of the ghetto were silent. Candlelight flickered in a few windows and dark figures slipped past. The snow-covered curbs reeked of piled-up garbage and corpses. A truck loaded with German soldiers stopped at one of the houses. The soldiers burst inside and dragged a group of frightened men, women, and children to the truck. Some of them had managed to wrap coats over their night-clothes. Those who hadn't were shivering. The children wept and the soldiers hit them with the butt of their rifles. Gertruda knelt near a pile of garbage until the truck disappeared and then continued on her way. She entered a nearby house and knocked on the doors, pleading with them to open up. After a long wait, one door was opened a narrow crack. An old woman looked at her in fear when she asked for the doctor's address. The woman said she didn't know him and slammed the door.

Only after repeated attempts in nearby houses did she manage to find out where he was. Plodding through the snow, she hurried to the cellar of the hospital where Dr. Berman and his family lived. Her feet were frozen, her teeth were chattering, and her eyes darted around to make sure the German guards weren't in the area.

Gertruda entered the dark staircase of the hospital, groped her way to the cellar, and knocked on the door. A panicky rustling of feet and a hasty whispering were heard inside, but the door didn't open.

"I'm looking for Dr. Berman," she called in Polish, in a desperate voice. "It's very urgent."

She saw the door open. The inside of the apartment was dark. A man's voice asked from the darkness, "Who are you?"

She felt a wave of joy when she heard the familiar voice. "It's me, Gertruda, Michael Stolowitzky's nanny."

"Gertruda!" The doctor didn't believe his ears. "Come in, come in, please."

"Michael's very sick, doctor." Her voice gave out and she started weeping.

"What happened to him?"

Gertruda briefly described the symptoms of the illness.

"Has a doctor examined him yet?"

"No. I was afraid to call a doctor I didn't know."

"How did you get here?"

"Through the sewer."

"Did anybody see you?"

"Nobody."

"Wait a minute. I'll get my bag and I'll come with you."

Only now, in the dim light of the kerosene lamp, did Gertruda see that the doctor looked like a walking skeleton. His face was emaciated and bore the stamp of suffering. His body had shed most of his flesh.

The doctor's wife came to them.

"First drink some tea," she said to the nanny. "You must be freezing."

"I don't have time. Michael's waiting for me."

"You can't imagine how grateful we are for your help," she added. "The food you send really saves us."

The woman's eyes were fearful as her husband packed his examination instruments in his bag. She knew he was risking his life, that there was a good chance he would be caught by the Germans, but she said only, "Please, be careful."

When they were about to leave, Dr. Berman kissed his wife's cheeks.

"Don't worry," he said. "I'll be back before dawn."

He and Gertruda went into the street. Danger, heavy and threatening, hovered in the night air. German guards constantly moved around in the ghetto, their fingers poised on the triggers of their guns. Every figure that moved at night was a target. The Germans preferred to shoot rather than to ask questions. Gertruda was glad that, despite the danger, Dr. Berman didn't hesitate to come with her.

"How are you getting along?" Gertruda asked the doctor in a soft voice as they walked in the snow.

"It could be better. There's no more food, people are dying like flies, the Germans are clearing out the ghetto systematically. Every day more and more people are sent to what they call labor camps. None of them have returned to the ghetto."

"Do you manage to work?"

"Yes. Unfortunately, there are a lot of patients. They can't pay, of course, but I try to help them as much as I can. In the awful living conditions, without heat or food, with stocks of medicines running out, and with no possibility of being hospitalized, there's not much chance for anybody who gets sick here."

"What do you live on?"

"The food you send, selling personal items, and the hope that better days will come."

The way to the sewer, as expected, was fraught with danger. They walked next to the houses and a few times they had to hide when a patrol passed by. Fortunately for them, no one was at the entrance to the sewer. The two of them crawled inside and, with trembling hearts, passed through to the other side of the city. They knew the danger hadn't passed, even after they got out to the street. If the German patrol discovered Jews sneaking out of the ghetto, they were shot on the spot.

Finally, they came to the house where Gertruda lived with

Michael. She opened the door. The fire had died down to the last embers and a kerosene lamp on the table illuminated the face of the sick child, who lay in bed covered up to his neck.

"Hello, Dr. Berman," he murmured.

"Hello, Michael, I hope that next time we meet, you'll be healthy."

Dr. Berman examined him for a long time.

"Pneumonia," he confirmed. He took some medicine out of his bag that would ease Michael's breathing. It was the only medicine in his bag and in the black market he could have sold it for a lot of money. By the time he gave Gertruda instructions for taking care of Michael, the night was coming to an end.

"I have to hurry," he said.

Gertruda thanked him with tears in her eyes, filled his bag with food, and gave him some pennies.

"Take care of yourself," she said.

The doctor slipped into the staircase and went out to the street. The snow was falling and it was still dark.

He got back to the hospital without incident as dawn was breaking, and his wife embraced him.

As Michael slowly recovered, Gertruda regularly watched the alley that led to the opening of the sewer. She continued to meet the boy who smuggled food into the ghetto and gave him fruit, vegetables, and bread for the Berman family, along with food for the boy in payment for his errand.

5.

Joachim Turner entered the offices of the bank in Zurich, talked with one of the clerks, and soon emerged with a briefcase full of banknotes. He went to the railroad station, bought a ticket to

Genoa, and from there he went to Pontrepoli, where he spent hours looking for the address Jacob Stolowitzky had sent him in a telegram. He knocked on the door and Anna stood there, looking at him inquiringly.

"My name's Turner," he said hesitantly. "Does Mr. Stolowitzky live here?"

"Yes. Please come in. I'm Anna, his wife. My husband has been expecting you for some time."

The Swiss lawyer entered. Jacob Stolowitzky came to meet him. They embraced warmly.

Joachim Turner took bundles of Swiss francs out of his case and gave them to Stolowitzky.

"If you want more money," said the attorney, "send me a telegram and I'll come again."

They drank coffee and Stolowitzky told his agent that he had married Anna after he concluded that his wife and son had been killed in the war. He wound his arm around her shoulders and she gave him a loving smile.

"We got here right after the wedding," he said in apology. "We haven't had time to arrange things properly."

"Good luck," said Turner, still surprised at the revelation that Jacob Stolowitzky had remarried.

"Anna is a wonderful woman. I was very lonely . . . she cheered me up, we fell in love," said Stolowitzky.

Turner sat down on the shabby sofa.

"Naturally, this is only a temporary home," Jacob told him. "When the war ends, we'll move to our own house. Of course, if I'm still alive then."

"Why won't you be alive?"

"If the Germans reach here, too, they'll send me to a concentration camp immediately," said the manufacturer from Warsaw.

"Are there other Jews in this town?"

"No."

"Then what do the Germans have to do here?"

"Thanks for the encouragement, Joachim. You always were a good friend. I wanted to ask you something, something extremely important."

"Please."

"I want to write a will."

"Why?"

"I have to think of every possibility, even the possibility that something bad will happen to me. I'd like you to be a witness to my will."

Joachim Turner nodded. Jacob Stolowitzky picked up a pen and began writing:

Being of sound mind and body, I thus bequeath all my property after my death to Mrs. Anna Massini, whom I married after I concluded that my wife Lydia and my son Michael were no longer alive. If it turns out that my wife and son are still alive, all my property will go to them and Anna Massini will have a grant of 10,000 Swiss francs.

He asked the guest to witness the document, and Turner complied. "We'll drink a toast when the war ends," he said before he left.

When the door closed behind him, Anna turned to her husband.

"You surprised me with the will," she said. "I hope you know that I didn't marry you for your money."

"I know, my dear."

6.

In the middle of the night, a tap was heard on the door. Gertruda woke up in a panic. She was afraid of sudden visits. Most of them meant only one thing: disaster.

Michael was sound asleep under the blanket in their double bed when Gertruda put her coat over her nightgown and went anxiously to the door.

"Who is it?" she asked through the locked door.

"Denka. Please open the door. It's worth your while."

She remembered his last visit on the stairs. Then he had tried to persuade her to spy on Dr. Berman so he could turn him over to the Russians. The neighbors told her that after the German occupation he had changed sides and now worked for the Germans, reporting people who had played roles under the Russian government. He also made a lot of money in the black market, buying jewels from refugees and giving them food in exchange. He sold the jewels to the German soldiers for cigarettes, bread, and canned goods. He was well dressed, spoke arrogantly, and was loathed by all the other tenants in his sister's apartments.

"I can't open the door now," said Gertruda in a trembling voice. "It's late."

Denka didn't give up.

"It's important," he said.

"We'll talk in the morning," she tried again.

"The morning will be too late." His voice was aggressive.

She opened the door hesitantly and he pushed himself inside, smelling of alcohol and cigarettes.

"What do you want?" she asked, her hands clutching her coat to her body.

The guest reached out and stroked her face with a coarse hand. She flinched.

"What do you want?" she repeated and demanded to know.

"Calm down," he smiled. "You know that I only want what's good for you."

He pulled two cans of sardines out of his coat pocket and put them on the table.

"That's a little present from me," he said in a hoarse voice.

"Thank you," she said reluctantly.

His eyes examined the shabby room.

"Hard for you, eh?"

"I'm not complaining."

"Is there anything I can do for you?"

"No."

"Money? Food? Cigarettes? Candy for the kid? Just ask."

"I don't need anything, Denka. Thanks for your kindness. Now, please, get out"

He didn't show any sign of leaving. Instead, he came even closer to her. She retreated, but he grabbed her. Her coat was open and his big hands invaded her nightgown and crushed her breasts.

"No," she insisted. "Please, no."

But he refused to listen to her. His hands tore her nightgown and she couldn't fight back. He was too strong for her. Only when he put her on the floor and bent over her did she shout. She expected him to be scared that the neighbors would rush to her aid, even though she knew that only a few of them would dare come out of their apartment to help her. Denka had scared them all.

He put his hand over her mouth, spread her legs, and roared like an animal. With what was left of her strength, she got her right hand out of his grip and stuck a finger into one of his eyes. Her sharp fingernails hit the lens of the eye and made him shout in pain. For a moment, he let go of her. She managed to flee to the other room and quickly pulled the gun out of its hiding place under the bed. Denka chased her, but froze when he saw the gun barrel pointing at him.

"Get out!" she growled.

For a moment, he stood still, hesitating. He then blurted out a curse and left the apartment. Gertruda locked the door and stood there a long time, shaking with cold and fear, afraid that the thug would break down the door at any minute. That didn't happen.

She went back to bed and hugged Michael, who was still sound asleep. The warmth of his body dissipated the cold that chilled her limbs and the fear that had encompassed her heart.

7.

The little smuggler from the ghetto looked around in fear, but the street was still quiet and the night looked darker than ever. No German soldier was seen in the area, no sound of military boots was heard. Gertruda gave him two bags with fruit and vegetables.

"This is the last time we'll meet," he whispered.

"Why?" she wondered.

"In the ghetto, they're planning an uprising. I may not be able to get here anymore."

The boy's words scared Gertruda. Revolts in the ghetto seemed to her to be battles lost in advance. She feared for the fate of Dr. Berman and his family.

She made her way home, deep in thought. She was willing to do whatever she could to help the handful of desperate Jews who had decided to fight against all odds, but she couldn't figure out what she could do. Not until the middle of the night did an idea pop up in her head. Yes, she could help.

The next evening, Gertruda returned to the secret passage that led to the ghetto. Even though she knew the boy wouldn't be there, she waited for him awhile. He didn't come. She entered the sewer with a firm resolve and crawled along until she reached the ghetto. There, she ran out of the sewer and hurried to the Jewish hospital. Dr. Berman greeted her with terror.

"You shouldn't have come," he said. "It's dangerous."

"I came only to give you something," she said, and pulled out an old shirt with the gun peeping out, the gun Emil had stolen from Lydia. "Take it," she said, gasping with excitement. "It might help you."

Dr. Berman grabbed the weapon and clutched it to his chest.

"You have no idea how grateful I am to you."

The ghetto was completely deserted when she started making her way back to the Christian quarter. She quickly went through the big, dark sewer, came out onto the street, and looked around, afraid of running into a Nazi patrol. In a few minutes, she'd get through the secret passage and soon after that she'd be home. Michael, she thought, must still be sleeping.

Near the sewer, her worst fear materialized: the silence was suddenly shattered by the clatter of a rifle bolt and a sharp scream in German.

"Halt at once!"

Gertruda obeyed in fear. The tread of army boots beat on the cobblestones. Two German soldiers burst out of the dark alley and aimed their weapons at her.

"Damn Jewess!" shouted one of them. "What are you doing here?"

"I'm not a Jewess," she replied.

"Liar. Did you escape from the ghetto?" they demanded.

She gave them Father Gedovsky's letter. The German examined it carefully.

"If you're not a Jewess," he said, "what were you doing in the ghetto?"

She desperately scrambled for any excuse at all that the soldiers would accept.

"I was looking for a Jew who owes me money," she said after a brief hesitation.

"Where do you live?"

"Mala Stefanska Street."

"How did you get to the ghetto?"

"Through the sewer," she said. "I was afraid I couldn't get in any other way."

"Who told you about that way?"

"Everybody knows."

The Germans gave her a long look. They were still suspicious.

"Come with us," one of the soldiers ordered her.

"Where? I left a child at home. He's waiting for me."

"Let him wait," decreed the soldier.

They led her to Gestapo headquarters. In the gloomy building, she was put into a small room on the second floor. A nervous officer wrote down her personal details.

"Tell me the truth," he raised his voice. "What were you doing in the ghetto? Did you smuggle weapons to the underground?"

She turned pale. His guess was precise.

"I went to collect a debt."

"What debt?"

"I earn a living by writing requests to the authorities," she said. "I did work for a Jew and he didn't pay me."

The German wanted details and an address. Gertruda gave a name and address she made up.

"Do you have contact with Jews?" he asked.

"I have contact only with people who want me to write letters in German for them. Some of them are Jews."

"And aside from those people?"

"I don't have contact with any Jew."

"I don't believe you."

She fixed pleading eyes on him. "Please let me go. My son is alone at home."

"First tell me the truth," the officer persisted.

"I already told you."

"It doesn't seem reasonable to me that you snuck into the ghetto only to collect a few pennies from somebody. You're hiding the truth from me."

Gertruda denied it forcefully.

He swung his hand and slapped her cheek hard.

"That's only the beginning," he said. "I suggest you talk."

Her cheek burned and she put her hand over it.

The officer punched her in the chest. A sharp pain sliced through her body. She was still silent, which made him even more furious. He kicked her and pulled her hair brutally.

She groaned in pain but remained adamantly quiet. If she told the truth about what she had done in the ghetto, that would have been the end of her and of Michael. That thought gave her new strength. She felt that no torture in the world could break her.

The Germans thought otherwise. Torture was always an effective tool to break those who were being interrogated. Gertruda's torture went on nonstop until she passed out. When she woke up, she found herself lying on a hard mattress in a detention cell. She heard the sighs and voices of her cellmates. She couldn't see a thing in the thick darkness. She was in terrible pain, but her fear for Michael's fate was even worse. Ever since the war had started, she had been able to cope with every difficulty, overcome every obstacle with her strong will, her love for the child, and her determination to keep the oath she had sworn to his mother. She hoped that all of that would keep her going this time, too.

The hours seemed like days. She had no idea what time it was, whether it was day or night, or what had happened to Michael when he woke up and didn't find her at home. Suddenly the door opened and a jailer called her name.

"Come," he said.

She heaved herself up from the mattress. Her whole body hurt. She was sure her torture was about to continue, longer, more tormenting. The jailer led her to the office, made her sign a release, and sent her home.

She rushed to the street, not believing that she had indeed been set free. Every step tortured her, but she tried to distract herself from her pain and hurried home. When she opened the door, she saw Michael sitting at the table, weeping. She spread her arms to him and he fell into her embrace.

"I was so worried about you," he cried. "What happened to you? Your whole face is full of blood."

"I had an accident. I was hit by a car."

"Lie down. I'll take care of you."

He led her to the bed, soaked a towel in water, and sponged the clotted blood.

"Rest," he said. "It will pass."

* * *

The night was peaceful. So was the next day. When evening fell, she felt vaguely uneasy. She put Michael to bed and was glad he fell asleep at once. She then went to the window and stood there for hours, watching the street without knowing exactly what she was looking for.

The window overlooked houses where well-off Jews had lived. Red and white geraniums had once stood on the windowsills of those houses and had been watered every day. Those windows had once opened to the breezes that floated the white lace curtains, to teeming streets where children once played tag, and to green parks where loving couples strolled, arm in arm.

Now there were no flowers on the windowsills or bustling servants, the children had disappeared, and so had the couples. Now the windows looked into dark rooms and apartments, like eye sockets of the dead. Many of the people who had lived in them were no longer alive. Others were now fighting a war for survival in the ghetto.

Suddenly she shuddered.

She saw a car with its headlights off slide onto the cold pavement of the deserted street and stop at the sidewalk. Four young men with short hair and wearing raincoats got out of it and walked quickly to her house.

Gertruda genuflected and said a prayer, locked the window, and turned out the kerosene lamp. From the bed in the depths of the room came Michael's soft voice asking what had happened.

"Nothing," she replied. "Try to sleep."

She tried to hear what was going on in the staircase. For a moment or two, it was silent and then, all at once, the peace was disturbed. The sound of boots climbing the stairs echoed in the air.

His eyes open, the child jumped out of bed and nestled in Gertruda's arms.

"Are they coming for us?" he whispered.

"I hope not."

"But what if they are?"

"Don't be scared. They won't do anything bad to us. Try to sleep."

She tried to encourage him, although she herself had no reason to believe what she was saying. With her heart pounding, she waited for the knock on the door. She knew it would come.

A fist landed on the door. Gertruda held Michael and gestured to him to be silent.

The door was kicked open.

"Light the lamp!" someone shouted in German.

Gertruda obeyed. Three rifle barrels were pointed at them.

The woman and the child looked in dread at all the weapons aimed at them. It was too late to escape from the trap, to seek another place of safety, to be saved. More than for herself, Gertruda's heart worried about the child who had been snatched against his will from his carefree childhood and now expected to die from a German rifle at any minute.

"Where is your gun?" roared one of the invaders.

"What gun?" Gertruda opened her mouth in artificial amazement. She guessed that Denka had told on her. He had promised her that she would be punished for her refusal to give in to him. He had kept his promise.

A shot burst out of a rifle and shattered the window. Michael sobbed silently.

"That's a first and last warning!" shouted the man.

"I don't have a gun and I never did," Gertruda insisted. In her heart, she thanked God that she had gotten rid of the weapon in time.

The men in the raincoats turned the apartment upside down.

They cut the bedclothes to shreds, threw every item of clothing and every object out of the closet, tore up the wooden floorboards, and when they didn't find anything, they cursed and left.

8.

Feverish preparations for the uprising in the Vilna Ghetto went on secretly. A few weapons and a little bit of ammunition were collected with great toil. People were mobilized for battle and trained in hidden rooms. A system of attack and defense was prepared, but all efforts ceased. The few dozen men and women of the resistance movement decided that they had to fold up since there was no chance of a successful revolt with the German mobilization all around and the enemy's enormous quantities of weapons and ammunition. Instead, they decided to sneak out of the ghetto to the forests around the city and join the partisans in ambushing the Germans.

Dr. Berman's parting from his family was difficult and painful. He announced his decision to join the partisans and promised to come back soon, but his wife and children knew they would probably never see him again.

"You must understand there is no other way," he said as he hid Gertruda's gun in his clothes. "We have to fight. If we don't strike the Germans, we'll all die."

His wife wiped her tears and kissed him. He hugged and kissed his children and then slipped out of the ghetto. On a winding path that few managed to get through alive, he reached the Botovitc Forest, where he found Jewish friends from Vilna preparing for battle.

That same night, the partisans ambushed a German weapons convoy, shooting at it as it passed by the forest. Some of the escort were killed on the spot and others fled. The weapons—rifles, guns, and mortars—fell into the hands of the partisans.

The guerrilla warfare often ended in failure, though. Many of the Jewish partisans were killed, wounded, or captured. Life in the forest was hard and dangerous. There was little food; sleep was fragmentary and tormented; they leaped from one hiding place to another because of German patrols that occasionally raked the forest. Dr. Berman, like the other partisans, couldn't stay in touch with his family back in the ghetto. He worried about their safety and at night he was tormented by nightmares of the hardships they were suffering.

One snowy winter dawn, the partisans set up an ambush on the side of the highway to Vilna. After a few ambush attacks, the Germans were now much more prepared and careful, ready for almost any surprise. The convoy of half a dozen trucks, defended by armed soldiers, drove quite fast. When the partisans opened fire, some of the soldiers were hit, but their comrades leaped out of the trucks and assaulted the attackers.

The partisans retreated, were pursued into the forest, and many of them were hit.

Dr. Joseph Berman was one of the first to be killed.

Less than a week later, Nazi soldiers entered the Jewish hospital, took out all those living in the cellar, and sent them—including Dr. Berman's wife and children—to the gas chambers.

9.

Every minute, every hour of the day and night was permeated with paralyzing fear. The boundary between silence and unavoidable disaster was usually thin and fragile. It was impossible to know what would happen in the next moment, who would knock on the door and why, who would burst in when he wasn't answered. Gertruda was living in a nightmare, staying awake whole nights listening intently to every noise in the street and on the staircase. The war was at its height. Rumors told of more German conquests. There was no sign of an end.

Gertruda spent a lot of time in the apartment with the child. When customers came to ask her to write letters for them, Michael would play in his room behind a locked door. He loved to be with Gertruda. They read books and played games. Very infrequently, when Gertruda didn't think there were any Germans around, she furtively took Michael for a walk.

One Saturday, when the street was empty, the two of them went out for a short stroll. On their way back, a jeep stopped next to them and a German patrol got out and blocked their way. There were four of them, two soldiers, a sergeant, and an officer. There was no way to escape, no way out.

"Documents," demanded the sergeant. Gertruda obeyed. The sergeant looked at Michael.

"That's my child," she said.

"How old is he?"

"Six."

"What happened to your husband?"

"He was killed in the war."

"When?"

"When you entered Poland. He was a soldier in the Polish army."

"Show me his documents."

"I don't have them." She tried to keep cool. "The documents were stolen from me when I escaped from Warsaw."

Gertruda and Michael. Vilna, 1942.

They carefully examined the certificate the priest had given her. Michael looked at the Germans in fear.

"This is your mother?" the soldier pointed at Gertruda.

The child gazed at her.

Gertruda translated the question from German to Polish and he nodded agreement.

"What's her name?"

"Mamusha."

"What was your father's name?"

"Marek," Gertruda quickly answered instead of him. She was sorry she hadn't prepared the child to endure such an interrogation.

"I didn't ask you!" shouted the German sergeant. "Come here, boy."

Gertruda took Michael's hand and led him to the soldier. In her heart she said a prayer that the encounter wouldn't end in disaster.

"Take down his pants," the German ordered her.

She froze, helpless, desperate.

"Why?" she asked, even though she knew the reason.

"We want to make sure he's not a Jew."

"Don't do that to him here in the street," she pleaded. "It will humiliate him."

People passed by and looked at them indifferently. Such sights were an everyday thing in the city.

"Shut up!" the sergeant growled at her. "Take down the boy's pants or I will!"

She looked at the German with hostility and her head was spinning. Her body landed on the ground and she blacked out.

When she came to, her face was wet with the ice-cold water the soldier had sprinkled on her from his canteen. The officer bent over her and asked her to get up. She could barely stand.

"What are you afraid of?" asked the officer.

"Nothing . . . it's just that I haven't eaten for a few days . . ."

The sergeant clasped Michael's shoulders.

"Take down your pants!" he ordered him again.

The child looked desperately at his nanny.

Gertruda was silent. She knew it was all over, that the game was up. Now it was time to pay for the lie.

Michael stood frozen.

The German was fuming and started pulling down the child's pants. Michael held on to them with all his might, hoping to prevent the sergeant from undressing him.

The officer standing nearby the whole time without intervening now approached the sergeant.

"Leave the boy alone!" he ordered him sharply.

The sergeant looked at the officer in surprise and let go of Michael's trousers.

"Is that child really your son?" the officer asked Gertruda.

"Yes."

"The two of you really aren't Jews?"

"Really."

"Fine, I believe you," said Karl Rink.

He looked at Michael affectionately and thought of the child's distress. If only they had managed to get him out of the inferno in time, as he himself had gotten his daughter out of Germany before his colleagues from the SS had arrested her. Since she was the daughter of a Jewish mother, he knew there wouldn't have been any chance for her to survive there, as this child had almost no chance to survive the war.

"Where do you live?" asked the officer.

"On the other street."

He walked her home. "Be careful," he said. "There will be a lot of other searches like that. Take my advice. If you don't want them to bother you, look for a safer place for you and the boy."

She looked at him with tears in her eyes.

"Why?" her lips moved. "Why did you do that?"

He smiled.

"Maybe someday, if we meet again, I'll tell you."

"At least tell me your name," she asked.

"Karl Rink," he said, turned around, and went back to the patrol.

10.

To save Michael, to get him away from the danger lurking for him at every moment, to guarantee that they would no longer be in danger of surprise visits at night—those were now the most important tasks. Gertruda knew that their luck wouldn't hold out for long if she didn't take immediate action.

She concluded that the church could be their only refuge. Michael remembered the first day he went there with Gertruda. In a blend of fear and embarrassment, he followed her into the big hall of the Ostra Brama Church. The cement arches supporting the ceiling, the paintings of the crucified Jesus, and the gilded altar stirred mixed feelings in him. It didn't take Gertruda long to make him understand why he had to go with her. He understood very well that, for the outside world, he was the son of a Christian mother, and the pretense he had to adopt was a pledge for his life.

Now he stroked Gertruda's hand, let her lead him to one of the statues at the front of the church, and was terrified when he saw a group of German officers near them who were kneeling and praying. Gertruda looked at them with fake calm, also knelt, and pulled Michael down, too. He moved his lips as if he were praying, even though he didn't know a single prayer.

The church was full of local residents and a group of German soldiers and officers who came to Sunday mass. The priest, Andras Gedovsky, passed among the worshippers, nodding to people he knew. Michael looked at him with curiosity, examined his kind face and his white robe as he moved like an angel hovering toward the altar and sank down in prayer.

A young officer raised his eyes to Gertruda and Michael and looked at them with a long, strange look. He stood up and came to them. Michael turned pale.

"Is that your child?" asked the officer in German. He had light blue eyes and fair hair carefully combed. He carried a vizored hat in his hand. His uniform was perfectly pressed and a gun was hanging on his leather belt.

"Yes, this is my child," she replied in German.

"What's your name, boy?" the officer asked in Polish.

"Michael," he answered softly.

The officer stroked his hair.

Don't make any unnecessary move, Michael ordered himself, don't show any sign of fear.

"He looks so much like the child I left at home," said the officer sadly to Gertruda.

"How old is your boy?" she asked, looking innocently at the officer.

"Six. And yours?"

"He's also six."

"You speak good German." The officer complimented her. "Where are you from?"

"Poland. I learned German in school."

"And your husband?"

"I'm a widow, sir."

He pulled his wallet out of his pocket, took out some money, and gave it to Michael.

"Buy yourself a present," he said.

Father Gedovsky mounted the pulpit and preached a sermon about the importance of helping your neighbor, quoting the appropriate passages from the New Testament. Afterward the children's chorus, in white robes with gold embroidery, sang Sunday songs, passed among the rows, and spread clouds of incense.

After mass, the priest stood in the door of the church, smiling, shaking hands with the worshippers, and exchanging a few polite words with everyone. Three German officers stood patiently in line to shake the priest's hand, their eyes haughty, their uniforms gleaming, their shaved faces confident. The priest spoke German with them. "We enjoyed the prayers very much," they told him. "It was like home." They wished the priest good health and got into the jeep waiting for them at the curb.

Gertruda waited until everyone had gone and then went to the priest, who looked at her affectionately. Ever since Lydia's death, Gertruda had come to church with Michael almost every Sunday.

"Father," she murmured, "can I talk with you in private?"

The priest looked at her gently. "Of course, my child."

She asked Michael to wait for her on a bench in the church, and let the priest lead her to his office. Once inside, the priest closed the door. His eyes looked at the woman's face lined with distress and anxiety. Out the window, the day turned gray and long shadows crept into the room.

Gertruda wanted to speak, but tears choked her voice. Uncontrollable weeping racked her body. The priest put his warm hand on her shoulder.

"How can I help, my child?" His voice soothed her.

"I don't know what to do, Father," she said at last. "I don't know who to turn to."

He waited patiently for her to tell him her distress. Every single day, people like her poured out their bitterness to him. They related their pain for their partner or relative who had been arrested by the Nazis, all traces of them lost. Some complained about their economic situation. Most of the time, the priest had to make do with a few words of encouragement. He knew that wasn't enough, but that was practically all the help he could give.

"It's about my child," said Gertruda.

"The sweet child with the blue eyes sitting there outside?"

"Yes."

Fear of what she was to reveal in this room nailed her to the spot. Her body was shaking, but she knew she had to go on. The priest was the only person she could pour her heart out to, the only one she could trust.

She told him the truth and he looked at her with eyes opened wide in surprise.

"I didn't realize that the child was a Jew," he said.

Gertruda wiped her eyes.

"I'm afraid the Nazis will find out the truth and take him away from me," she said. "I'd die if that happened."

"Bring him to me," he said.

She called Michael.

"Do you know who Jesus was?" asked the priest.

"The man everybody prays to," replied the child. He remembered the prayers he had heard in church.

"And what is the Holy Trinity?"

Michael frowned and repeated what Gertruda had recited to him: "The Father . . . the Son . . . the Holy Spirit."

The priest sprinkled holy water on him and said a prayer.

"From now on, you're a Christian like all of us," he said. "Tomorrow morning you'll start attending the church school."

A warm wave of happiness flooded Gertruda. That was more, much more than she had expected.

"But," she stammered, "I don't have money to pay."

Father Andras Gedovsky smiled.

"I'm not worried," he said. "God will reward me."

The priest sat Michael on his lap and stroked his hair.

"You want to hear a story?" he asked.

"Yes." .

"In chapter two of the book of Daniel, there's a story of a king of Babylon, Nebuchadnezzar, who woke up one night in panic after a horrible dream. In his dream, the king saw a statue with a head of gold. A big stone suddenly smashed the statue into slivers. The king called the sages of Babylon and asked them to interpret his dream. None of them could. When the prophet Daniel learned of this, he came to the king and interpreted. The statue, he said, is your kingdom. The stone symbolizes the kingdom of Heaven that decided to smash your kingdom to dust."

A slight smile hovered over the priest's lips.

"You know what is the kingdom of Nebuchadnezzar?" he asked.

Gertruda nodded. The comparison with the Nazis was obvious.

"I promise you," said the priest, "that the end of the wicked will be as the end of Nebuchadnezzar's statue."

She left with Michael and hurried home. The child was saved, at least for the time being, and that was what was most important. She wasn't worried about his Christian baptism. She was sure that, just as Michael was born a Jew, he would go back to being a Jew when the war was over.

11.

On the morning Michael was about to enter the school of Ostra Brama Church, Gertruda dressed him in his best clothes, packed up his belongings in a small suitcase, and went with him to Father Gedovsky's office, where they were greeted warmly.

"Leave the child here and go in peace," he said. "Here he'll be protected from every evil."

Gertruda kissed Michael's sad eyes.

"Don't worry," she said. "I'll come visit you often."

The priest went with Michael to the school building next to the church, showed him his bed in one of the dormitory rooms, and then put him in class. The children looked at him with curiosity and at recess they tried to size him up. He said what Gertruda had taught him to say: that his mother was the widow of a Polish officer and that he was her only son.

On his first night in the boarding school, Michael wept into his pillow, homesick for his adopted mother. The strange atmosphere he had wound up in, the isolation, and the fear that his real origin would be discovered weighed heavily on him. In the following days, it was hard for him to get used to the Christian holy scriptures, the prayers, and the harsh hand of the teachers, but he remembered what Gertruda had repeated to him before he left: "You've got to, Michael. The church is the only place where you can be safe. I promise you that as soon as the war is over, I'll take you out of there." She warned him not to get undressed, not to shower, and not to urinate with the other children so they wouldn't discover that he was circumcised.

Despite the strict studies and the fear that accompanied Michael day and night, life in the boarding school was rather comfortable. There was enough food, he had his own bed, and Father Gedovsky kept an eye on him. The children in the boarding school were divided, as always, into better and worse. Some wanted to be his friend. Others looked for his weak points and teased him a lot. He was glad to make friends with children he was fond of, and avoided responding to the teasing from the others.

· · ·

One of Michael's classmates, Stephen, was eleven years old and from a Polish Catholic family who had become poor in the war. Father Gedovsky responded to the pleas of his parents and put him in the church boarding school so they would have one less mouth to feed. Stephen was an evil boy, a troublemaker, tending to get caught up in lies. Michael shared with him the candy Gertruda brought him and thus won his friendship.

"Look at her. Doesn't she look like a Jew?" Stephen whispered to Michael one day. He pointed at a girl who had come to the school two days before.

"Why do you think she's a Jew?" asked Michael.

"Look at her eyes: black like Satan's. She's got a crooked Jewish nose and a twisted back. Only Jews can look like that."

"Her name's Marina. That's not a Jewish name." Michael tried to defend the girl. If she was a Jew, he knew, no one must suspect that, just as no one must know that he himself was a Jew. The rumor his friend was beginning to spread might be fateful for the girl, if indeed he was right about her origin.

"Nonsense," laughed Stephen. "Didn't you hear that Jews take names of Christians to disguise themselves?"

"I don't believe she's a Jew," Michael persisted.

"I'll tell my father. He knows a German officer. The Germans will come here and find out the truth in a few minutes."

"What will they do to her?"

Stephen shrugged. "What they do to all the Jews," and made a choking gesture.

Michael quickly snuck into Father Gedovsky's office and told him about Stephen's suspicions.

"Thank you for telling me," said the priest.

"I didn't know there were other Jewish children here," said the boy.

"There are no Jewish children here." The priest smiled mysteriously at him.

That same day, the classroom door opened in the middle of the lesson and Father Gedovsky stood in the door with a woman dressed simply. A big cross hung around her neck. "Marina's mother wants to talk with her for a few minutes," he said to the nun who was conducting the class. The little girl stood up in amazement. She had never seen that woman in her life, but she responded to the priest's request to leave the class. "I know this isn't your mother," he told her. "But we have to do it. Somebody might suspect you're a Jew and then you couldn't go on hiding here. From now on, tell everyone who asks you that your mother's name is Joanna, your father is dead, and you were born a Catholic. Clear?"

"Yes," replied the girl with a grateful look.

From then on, Stephen didn't talk about the girl's Jewish origin anymore, and Michael refrained from asking the priest who the woman was who had pretended to be her mother.

Not until after the war did Gertruda reveal the secret: the woman was Father Gedovsky's sister.

12.

In the summer of 1942, when the pears ripened in the orchards of Kibbutz Kfar Giladi, only a few people believed that the members of the kibbutz would complete the harvest. Like everywhere else in Palestine, a profound fear of an impending disaster prevailed there, too. Information from the war front said that the German army was quickly advancing to the Land of Israel. Rommel, the legendary general, burst eastward from Libya and was at the entrance to Alexandria.

The situation in the Land of Israel was terrifying. There was nowhere to run or hide, no safe refuge from the Germans. Members of the British government sent their families to Iraq and packed their bags, waiting for the order to withdraw. They feared it wouldn't be possible to withstand the German army closing in on the country.

An emergency meeting of the members was called in Kfar Giladi. Seventeen-year-old Elisheva Rink also attended. Dozens of members of the kibbutz gathered in the dining hall to hear the grim prognosis of the Haganah members. The Land of Israel, they said, might soon be under German occupation.

One of the participants suggested setting up posts at the side of the main highways and greeting the Germans with gunfire, but no one took that suggestion seriously. In the weapons caches of Kfar Giladi, as in other hiding places in Palestine, there were very few weapons hidden from the British, and the few that did exist wouldn't serve as any defense against a German army invasion. The great fear in the Land of Israel was, as in other countries the Germans occupied, that many settlements would be destroyed and burned down and thousands of people would be killed or sent to concentration camps. One of the Haganah members told about a plan called "Masada on the Carmel," where they would concentrate all the Jews in the area of the Carmel, between Athlit and Beit Oren, to set up fortresses in the foothills of the mountains and dig caves there that could hold tens of thousands of people.

Throughout the discussion, Elisheva's thoughts wandered to her father. Ever since she had come to Palestine, she had gotten only one letter from him, and she didn't know where he was. Was he wounded, captured, or killed? If he was still on active duty, she thought, there was a chance he would come here with the occupying force. What would happen then? Would he save her from death? Would he also rush to help others?

Most of all now, with the possibility of a German invasion, it was important for her to keep her father's activities secret from the members of the kibbutz. She didn't talk about him, not even to her best friends.

13.

One summer day in 1942, Karl Rink's friend, Kurt Baumer, knocked on the door of his office in Vilna. Karl was surprised to see him and the two of them went to a local restaurant popular with Nazi officers.

Baumer said he was only passing through Vilna on the way to his new job.

"Have you heard of Walter Rauf?" he asked Rink.

"Yes," said Karl. Rauf was the infamous inventor of the "death trucks," in which myriads of Jews were executed by exhaust gas from vehicles that was fed into the freight section where the victims were packed.

"I'm joining him soon," said Baumer. "Rauf ordered a special unit of twenty-four SS men to destroy the Jews of Palestine when our army invades there. He expects that, as in other countries where the method has been in operation, non-Jews in the country will also help us in the work of annihilation." He said that the Germans were already in touch with a few agents active in Palestine and were getting up-to-date reports from them to prepare the basis of the annihilation.

Karl Rink turned pale. He thought of the danger lurking for his daughter.

"When will you enter Palestine?" he asked softly.

"Right away. The German army is advancing quickly."

Karl twisted in his chair. He hesitated to admit what was bothering him, but he knew he had to. Only Baumer, he thought, could help him.

He told him about Helga.

Baumer looked at him in amazement. "I didn't know you had a daughter in Palestine," he said.

Rink wrote down the name and address of Yossi Millman of Kibbutz Dafna, who was supposed to know where the girl was.

"I want you to go to him," said Rink, "and make sure that no harm comes to her."

"Don't worry," he said. "Nobody will harm her."

"Thank you," said Karl. He asked his friend if he had heard anything about the disappearance of his wife.

Baumer felt uncomfortable. "I told you to leave that alone," he growled.

"You're hiding something from me." Karl looked straight into his eyes.

"If I had told you the truth in Berlin," said his friend, "they would have executed me."

"You're not in Berlin anymore. Tell me now."

"I repeat that there is no point to go on looking for your wife," Baumer persisted.

"They killed her, right?"

"Right."

"Who?"

Baumer writhed. "You can guess," he said.

"Schreider?"

"He gave the order. His people carried it out. I'm sorry, Karl."

"That's what I thought." Rink sighed.

They parted sadly and Baumer joined Walter Rauf on the out-skirts of Egypt. The new unit took command of a fleet of trucks and prepared to take them to Palestine.

But things didn't turn out as Rauf had planned. The Afrika Korps, commanded by General Erwin Rommel, which had ad-vanced beyond the Suez Canal in North Africa, was defeated in No-vember 1942. Kurt Baumer was killed in Egypt in an ambush of a British commando unit. The German army wasn't able to reach the Land of Israel.

14.

Nothing seemed to disturb the peace that had always enveloped the small town of Pontrepoli, an isolated nature preserve among the green hills of northern Italy. The only indication of the war taking place somewhere was the roar of airplanes that rose now and then from the Tuscan hills going out or coming back from bombing mis-sions in enemy territory. During 1943, even after Italy signed a se-cret truce with the Allies and German army units entered the areas where the Allies hadn't reached, the town continued to enjoy its undisturbed peace and its inhabitants showed little interest in what was going on in the outside world. What mattered to the local peas-ants was mostly the rise in the prices of fruits and vegetables be-cause of the war; otherwise, their situation had never been better.

But the Germans soon indicated that they wanted to demon-strate a military presence even in the pastoral area of the town. At first a German army base was established near the town and vehi-cles carrying soldiers, ammunition, and supplies passed by on the nearby roads. Then sophisticated shooting ranges were built and the sounds of rifle and gun shots disturbed the peace day and night.

Jacob Stolowitzky followed events with profound concern, fearing that sooner or later the Germans would reach him. Radio London, which he listened to in secret, reported that the Allies had already conquered Sicily and southern Italy. He believed that the war was coming to an end, but he was still cautious. He stopped taking his nightly walks around his house, closed himself inside, read a lot, helped his wife with her housework, and waited for the war to end. But this relatively tranquil life was short-lived. The Germans soon began systematically exiling the Jews of Italy to death camps and instituted searches in all settlements, cities, and remote towns to locate Jews who had been hiding from them. They didn't intend to overlook Pontrepoli.

One September morning in 1943, a downpour fell on the town, swallowing up the roar of the German vehicles arriving there for the first time. Gangs of armed soldiers passed from house to house, raking the local monasteries and barns, looking for Jews. At last, they came to the house where Stolowitzky and his wife lived and demanded their identity documents. Anna gave them her passport and their marriage license. They left her alone and started a long interrogation of her husband. When they discovered that he was from Poland, they said they had to arrest him. Anna pleaded with them to leave him at home. She claimed he was sick, that taking him out of the house was liable to worsen his condition. She offered them money to leave him be. The soldiers took the money but insisted. Jacob Stolowitzky was taken for questioning and it became clear that he was a Jew.

Anna mobilized the mayor, who went to the Germans and tried to make them release her husband. But he couldn't save him. Jacob Stolowitzky was put on a truck, where he met other frightened Jews also captured in the surrounding towns. They were taken to the railroad station and sent to Auschwitz.

Anna never saw her husband again.

15.

The order to liquidate the Vilna Ghetto was issued in mid-September 1943. Karl Rink, who was supposed to take part in rounding up the Jews from their homes, couldn't bring himself to do so. On the day the Germans were about to invade the ghetto, he pretended to be sick and stayed in bed.

Enhanced SS and armed units arrested masses of Jews. Some were taken to be executed in the nearby forests and others were sent to death camps. Only very few managed to hide in safe places and elude death.

Two days after the liquidation of the Vilna Ghetto, Karl Rink was called to his commander, Albert Shrek, who didn't waste time on small talk. He gave Rink a long look.

"What happened to you?" he asked.

"Why do you ask?"

"I heard you were sick."

"I was."

"Really sick?"

"Of course."

"I've had my eye on you for a long time now, Karl. I've noticed that you've lost your enthusiasm. You're too withdrawn, not focused, working mechanically. What happened to you?"

"I have no idea what you're talking about." He tried to duck the issue.

"Are you hiding something from me, Rink?"

"Nothing, sir."

Shrek sighed. "I hope that's true," he said. "At any rate, I've got a new job for you. Maybe it will finally excite you a little." Shrek signed a document on his desk, put it in an envelope, and gave it to Rink.

"That's a transfer," he said. "You're to leave today for Kovno. Report to Wilhelm Goecke, who's in charge of the Kovno Ghetto. He needs reinforcements."

Rink took the transfer document and left. He quickly packed his things, and on the train to Kovno he tried to guess what Shrek really knew about him. Did he suspect that Rink wasn't doing his job?

When he came to Kovno, it became clear to Rink that the German command was composed of harsh and brutal officers. And Wilhelm Goecke, a lover of classical music, literature, and philosophy, was responsible for the murders of tens of thousands of Jews and Russian prisoners in the Mauthausen Concentration Camp, where he had previously commanded. He also participated in suppressing the uprising and liquidating the Warsaw Ghetto. The orders Rink received from Berlin when he came to Kovno were unequivocal: to liquidate the ghetto, annihilate the women and children, and leave alive only the men, who could be used for the German war production.

Karl Rink was put in charge of the workshops employing thousands of Jews, including several children who wore adult clothing to remain at their jobs and avoid being sent to death camps. The Jews of the ghetto quickly figured out who Goecke was, but couldn't discover what was hidden behind Karl Rink's frozen expression. They knew only that he treated them decently, didn't seek excuses to abuse them, and often overlooked the fact that one or another worker was too weak to fill his production quota.

Moshe Segelson, the Jewish manager of the workshop, became as friendly with Rink as he possibly could. They often chatted about classical music and German literature, which they both loved, and never talked about the war. Many of those who attended a ghetto orchestra concert of works by Jewish composers were surprised to see Rink in the first row. He applauded the orchestra and expressed personal admiration for the performance after the concert.

On New Year's Day, Moshe Segelson wanted to give Rink a gift. "The present is to express our appreciation for your decent treatment of us," he told him.

"We're not allowed to take gifts," said Rink. "But even without a gift, I can promise you that my treatment of you won't change."

Karl Rink lived in a large apartment in a building inhabited by other SS officers. On the wall of his bedroom, facing his bed, were framed pictures of his wife and daughter. One morning, when he left the house on his way to the workshop, he saw three SS men who had caught a frightened young Jew and were about to shove him into a military truck. Snatching children was an everyday thing in the ghetto and the fate of those who were taken was known in advance.

Rink went to the SS men and demanded they free the child.

"I know him," he lied. "His father is collaborating with us."

The boy was released immediately.

Sometime later, in the middle of the day in the shoe shop, a Ukrainian SS man was sent to look for hiding children and came to the workshop. Segelson knew that only Rink could prevent the evil decree. He hurried to Rink's office and told him that children were indeed hiding in the attic and his daughter was one of them. Rink went to the Ukrainian and asked what he was doing.

"We got information that dozens of children are hiding in the attic," said the SS man. "We've been told that strange noises were coming from there."

"There are no children here," stated Rink and ordered him to leave.

Shortly thereafter, the Ukrainian came back with a senior SS officer.

Rink told both of them that he had already searched the attic thoroughly and hadn't found anything.

"You're sure?" asked the officer.

"Definitely."

The two of them left and Segelson, with tears in his eyes, thanked Rink for his help.

"I'll never forget what you did," he said.

That evening, Rink ordered Segelson to come with him to his apartment to check up on repairs done there by employees of the shop. They set out, but Rink didn't head his car toward his home. Instead, they drove around the streets of the ghetto for a long time in silence, and then Rink finally took Segelson back home. The next morning, Segelson discovered that while he was absent, arrests were made among the managers of the workshops. He was sure that Rink had come to his aid this time, too.

16.

The hopeful news of the Russian advance was spread by whispers in the Kovno Ghetto. Radio London was the first to report it and the broadcast was picked up on some of the secret radios in the ghetto. The Jews were afraid to show their joy to the Germans, but they were excited.

Changes were also visible on the ground. The German soldiers and their commanders looked nervous and frightened. Army units passed in the streets of Kovno on their way to the new front lines, and partisans attacked them from the forests. Soviet planes bombed the city, and at night the horizon glowed with the mortar shells attacking the German army.

In the ghetto workshops, work went on as usual. Rink still came to his office every morning, but he was restless and couldn't concentrate. Moshe Segelson understood him and left him alone. Their meetings were limited to work issues, until one day Rink called him into his office and locked the door.

"I want to talk to you not as a commander, but man to man." Rink surprised him. His voice was soft and hesitant.

Segelson listened attentively.

"The war will end soon," said Rink. "Our army is crushed and Germany is about to be defeated. I want you to know that I never hated Jews. My wife was a Jew and I smuggled my daughter out of Germany at the last minute. I did the best I could to save Jews. I avoided carrying out orders to liquidate them or send them to death camps. I did that deliberately and I'm glad I could help."

"I know," said Segelson.

Karl Rink wiped away drops of sweat on his forehead.

"I'm not sure I'll remain alive," he went on. "But you have a good chance to survive. I've got a secret and I want to tell it to you. Promise me you won't tell anyone until the war is over."

"I promise."

"I know that my daughter is on a kibbutz in Palestine, but I don't know exactly where. After this is all over, you'll probably get there. Please, look for my daughter, give her my love, and tell her about me. I'd like her to know the truth about what I did in the war."

Segelson didn't hide his amazement.

"You're sure your daughter is in Palestine?" he asked.

"I sent her there with a group of young people from Berlin just before the war. Her guide's name was Yossi Millman. From Kibbutz Dafna. He must be able to tell you where she is."

"If I'm still alive," said Segelson, "I promise to look for her."

Rink shook his hand and Segelson's heart beat with excitement. It seemed strange to him that a Nazi officer would shake the hand of a Jew, but Karl Rink had already done many unusual things.

"I'm glad to have met you," said Segelson.

"So am I," said Rink. He wrapped his coat around himself, left the workshop, and Segelson never saw him again.

17.

Gertruda's fear remained even after Michael had found a relatively safe refuge in the church. She was still afraid that something unexpected would happen and his secret would come out. She waited impatiently for the war to end, but when the bombing of Vilna intensified, she understood that the danger lurking for her and Michael was greater than staying in the city. Mortars landed at random in Vilna and wounded and killed many citizens. Those who were left feared their turn would also come. Gertruda was scared that the church would be bombed.

At the height of the bombing raids, Gertruda packed her few clothes in a suitcase, rushed to the church, and took Michael.

"Where are we going?" asked the child.

"To a safer place," she replied.

They waited until nightfall and then walked for hours on remote roads until they came to a small village. Their feet hurt and their stomachs were grumbling with hunger when they finally found shelter in the rubble of an abandoned house. They stayed until morning, and then headed to a big house on the hill above the village. Gertruda knocked on the door and an old servant opened it and looked at her inquisitively.

Gertruda introduced herself.

"Come in," said the woman. "I'll call the master."

The corridor was nice and warm and filled with smells of cooking. A young man with a beard quickly came and looked at the two of them.

"I'm glad you're finally here," he said to Gertruda. "Is this your son?"

She nodded.

"I've prepared a room for you," he said, and led them to a little room in the attic.

"I hope you'll be comfortable here," he said.

"We'll be very comfortable."

"Come, I'll introduce you to my wife."

He led her to a big room. In the middle stood an ornate fourposter bed where a pale young woman was lying. On the night stand were bottles of medicine.

"Karla," said the man gently to his wife, "this is Gertruda. She'll take care of you until you recover."

Gertruda went to the woman, who looked at her impassively, shook her soft hand, and made herself smile. "I'll help you as much as I can," she said, and the woman nodded.

The man's wife had been suffering from tuberculosis for some years. Her husband took her to Dr. Berman in his clinic in Vilna.

The doctor had started treating her and managed to stave off the development of the disease. In the clinic, her husband had met Gertruda and offered her a job nursing his wife. Gertruda said that she had a child and so, if she did accept the offer, she would bring him with her. The man agreed on the spot. He was a rich landowner and promised to pay her more than she earned with Dr. Berman. Working in the remote village delighted her, mainly because it was far from Vilna, even though she knew she was taking a big risk. Tuberculosis was a contagious disease and was rarely cured, but Gertruda understood that living in the farmer's house was likely to save Michael. She couldn't count on miracles like the SS Karl Rink saving him. Miracles, she knew, didn't happen twice, and if the Nazis arrested her and the child in the street or made a sudden raid on their apartment, they were liable to discover the truth about Michael. So she had to get as far away from there as possible. She was glad the sick woman hadn't died in the meantime.

The sick woman's husband was sorry Dr. Berman had been exiled to the ghetto and couldn't be of service anymore. He had brought other doctors from various places to try to cure his wife. They sometimes came two or three times a week, examined the woman for a long time, and prescribed new and different medicine, but even if her condition did occasionally improve to some extent, the improvement never lasted long.

Gertruda sat at the sick woman's bedside for hours, fed her, made sure she took her medicine on time, read books to her, and talked with her as long as the woman was able to. A few months after her arrival, the sick woman's condition worsened. Gertruda stayed with her almost all the time and prayed for her recovery. She knew that when the woman died, she would have to return to the war, to mortal danger.

The sick woman soon died. The war hadn't yet ended and Gertruda felt that the husband, who no longer needed her, would dismiss her and she would have to return to Vilna. But he didn't intend to do that. The man called her to his office, thanked her for her devoted care of his wife, and suggested she stay in his house.

"I like you," he said. "When the period of mourning is over, we can get married."

Gertruda looked at him in amazement. He was a rough and awkward man, but he treated her and Michael as if they were members of the family. She knew that if she refused, she would be asked to leave the house.

"I didn't expect . . . ," she mumbled. "I'll have to think about it."

The fact that she didn't immediately refuse him gave him hope.

"I'm still young," he said. "My wife and I didn't have children. Of course, I'll want children with you. Lots of children. I'm sorry to tell you, but if you agree to marry me we'll have to send your child to an institution or give him up for adoption. Michael won't have any place in my family."

She was stunned.

"I'll pay handsomely to any institution that will take him, anyone who's willing to adopt him," he added.

"I'm sorry," Gertruda replied firmly. "He's my son and he'll stay with me until the day I die."

She stood up, went to her room, packed her things, took Michael, and they left the house on the hill.

They walked fast, past the German soldiers preparing to retreat, and left the village. A little while later, they entered the forest. They were alone there and it was almost nightfall. In the dying daylight, Gertruda discovered an abandoned bunker and went in with Michael.

The boy huddled fearfully in her arms and neither slept at all that night. The thunder of explosions was heard closer than ever and the heavy smell of fires rose from the surrounding villages.

"I'm hungry," murmured Michael.

Gertruda looked at him anxiously. Michael's pleas for food broke her heart. She was sorry she had forgotten to take food and water, but she didn't dare return to the village now. At dawn, she came out of the forest and ran to the nearby fields, where she quickly gathered a few heads of cabbage and went back to the bunker. The next night, she brought more vegetables.

For more than a week, they hid in the bunker, slept on a bed of grass that Gertruda had gathered in the forest, and ate the few vegetables she picked in the fields.

One morning, footsteps were heard outside. Gertruda and Michael were careful not to utter a word. The footsteps grew louder and suddenly a man appeared at the entrance in a uniform Gertruda didn't recognize. The soldier aimed a submachine gun at them. Michael shut his eyes in terror and Gertruda shouted: "Don't shoot! We're Poles!"

The soldier lowered his weapon and smiled. He was a Russian.

18.

At German headquarters in Kovno, the atmosphere was more desperate than ever. Bleary-eyed from lack of sleep, the commanders gazed at a map spread on the table. The red lines indicating the progress of the Red Army units grew longer from one day to the next. The German defense lines shrank considerably.

The reports from the front were bad. Thousands killed, tens of thousands wounded, many prisoners, the collapse of positions, and panicky retreat characterized the crucial phase of the war. A German defeat was inevitable.

The shuddering shriek of mortar rounds sliced the air as the lights went out and mighty thunder deafened the officers at headquarters. Walls collapsed, a cloud of dust choked them, and broken shouts of the wounded were heard all around. Karl Rink was knocked out. When he opened his eyes a while later, he felt his limbs and was relieved to discover he wasn't hurt. He quickly moved among the dead and wounded bodies, and slipped out of the building a minute before a another precise hit destroyed what was left of headquarters.

There was no reason to stay in Kovno and wait for the occupying forces. A few days before that, Rink had saved thirty-seven young Jews who were hiding in a cellar in one of the buildings in the ghetto, but he didn't expect those he saved to testify for him with the occupiers. When the Russian soldiers came, he knew, they would shoot every German in the area without asking questions. Rink was afraid to stay there. As far as he was concerned, the war was over and his only goal was to return home.

In the yard of headquarters he saw a few intact motorcycles and mounted one of them. The gas tank was full and the motor turned over. Without any hesitation, he got on the road and drove like a maniac between, the columns of stooped, dejected soldiers, who wanted to get away from the enemy closing in on them. He rode a whole day, and when the gas finally ran out he left the motorcycle and walked for hours until he sneaked onto a freight train crawling to the German border. Two days later, without sleep or food, he came to a half-destroyed German village. A farm couple gave him shelter, a meager meal, and civilian clothes. They burned his SS uniform and offered him a hiding place in their barn. Rink stayed there a few days, until the thunder of Allied machine-gun fire approached the village. He left the farmers and started making his way on foot to Berlin. He wandered for weeks on side roads, living on fruits and vegetables he picked in the fields and furtive meals and a bed at night in the homes of the rural people. In time, he joined a group of German soldiers who had deserted their units and were also going home to Berlin. They walked mostly at night, ahead of the advancing Red Army units, hiding in the forests when they felt it was too dangerous to move. It wasn't until eight months after he had left Kovno that Karl Rink found himself at long last on the outskirts of Berlin. The city had been under constant attack. Most of the buildings were destroyed and only a few people were seen in the streets. Everybody knew that the Russians were approaching and that the city would be conquered in a few days.

Karl Rink looked for his house. He walked amid the rubble where buildings he knew well had once stood. When he reached the house, he found a heap of rocks and remnants of burned furniture. An old woman in torn clothes came out of the ruins and told him that most of the tenants of the destroyed houses had been killed or had fled.

From there he went to the SS headquarters. The top story of the building had been completely destroyed and frantic men were making feverish preparations on the lower floors. No one noticed him when he came in. His feet led him to Reinhard Schreider's office. He opened the door without knocking, but no one was in the room.

Karl Rink went back to the street. He walked amid the shriek of shells flying and the sound of tremendous smashing, clouds of dust, and slivers of stone from houses that had been turned into heaps of ruins all at once. Dread and fear penetrated him when he thought the enemy would reach the middle of the city at any minute. He made his way between the rubble of the houses and looked for something to eat. With his army knife he burst into dust-covered kitchen cabinets and refrigerators. He found nothing.

19.

The soldier spoke only Russian, and Gertruda spoke Polish and German, but the Russian understood that these were a woman and child in distress and he gestured to them to follow him. All around were groups of Russian soldiers, tanks, and trucks. Soldiers brought Gertruda and Michael cans of meat. As they ate, an interpreter was found who told them that Vilna had been occupied only a day before by the Red Army and that the Germans had retreated or were taken prisoner. Gertruda shouted with joy and breathed a sigh of relief. As far as she was concerned, five years of fear and suffering and a grim struggle to stay alive had come to an end. "Where do you want to go?" asked the interpreter. Gertruda didn't know what to answer. She didn't yet have any plans.

"I'll send you to Vilna in the first truck going there," he decided for her.

"Thank you," she said and hugged Michael.

The battle rations stilled their hunger. They were put on the truck and reached the center of Vilna. Now Russian soldiers filled the city instead of Germans, and they were looking for loot and women. Islands of rubble were left of the Jewish ghetto. Refugees who had survived the battles ran around the city searching for their homes and their families.

Gertruda and Michael went to meet Father Gedovsky in the Ostra Brama Church. His face lit up when they stood before him.

"Thank God, who watched over you," he said.

He hugged Michael warmly.

"What will you do now?" he asked.

Gertruda remembered her oath at Lydia Stolowitzky's deathbed.
Yes, she had to take Michael to Palestine. But there was something
else she thought she had to do first.

"Maybe we'll visit my parents in Starogard," she said. "I'm very
worried. I haven't heard from them all through the war."

"That won't be so simple, my dear." The priest shook his head.
"Poland isn't yet liberated."

Her face grew gloomy. She knew it was only a question of time
until the Germans were defeated there, too, but what would happen to her and the child in the meantime?

"Do you know where I can get work?" she asked.

"I need a cleaning person," said the priest. "I can't pay money,
but you'll get room and board, and Michael can continue to attend
our school."

That was the best deal she could expect in the destroyed city,
still licking the wounds of war.

"Thank you very much," she said. "I'll be glad to work here."

That very day they got their own room and Gertruda immediately started working. Michael went back to the church school.

"How much longer will we be here?" Michael asked Gertruda a
few days later.

"A few weeks, no more," she estimated.

But it took more than six months for the Red Army to enter
Warsaw, liberate Poland, and start the trains running again.

20.

Gertruda and Michael went to say good-bye to Father Gedovsky. She thanked him over and over for his kindness and warmth. He took a few bills out of his wallet and placed them in her hand.

"Good luck," he said to them and watched them until they disappeared, walking hand in hand to the railroad station.

The platform in the Vilna railroad station was packed with civilians and Russian soldiers. People stormed onto the freight cars of the first postwar train to Poland. Gertruda and Michael were crushed among hundreds of men and women who filled the filthy car. They waited for hours in the stifling heat until the train moved, and for whole days they went without food. They divided one bottle of water between them and had to stand up most of the time because there was no room to sit or lie down and get some rest.

The dejected passengers, with their share of hardships, including several sick people, didn't dare leave the car when the train stopped in stations on the way. Most of them were silent throughout the journey. One woman who did speak was a Jew with a worn face, a survivor of Auschwitz who was going to Warsaw to look for what was left of her family. She told Gertruda that camps had been set up in Germany for Jewish displaced persons who wanted to go to Palestine.

Early on a rainy gray morning, the train stopped in Warsaw. Gertruda looked at the ruins of the city stretching beyond the railroad station. Her heart stopped when she thought of the good years she had spent there. "Come," she said to Michael with sudden resolve, and she pulled his hand. "We'll get off here."

"Where are we going?" he asked.

"To your house."

Men and women in rags walked around aimlessly in the city that had been hit hard by the bombs. They burrowed in the smashed rocks, broken doors, and twisted water pipes scattered on the hills of ruins of destroyed houses, as if they still hoped to save something valuable from the abandoned piles. Gertruda and Michael walked on paths between heaps of rubble. No signpost remained to indicate where they were, but Gertruda walked to the nearby river. From the river, she thought, she would easily find the house.

To Gertruda's amazement, Ujazdowska Avenue wasn't damaged. The mansions stood exactly as they had on the day she had fled with Michael and his mother from the approaching Nazi army. They went to number 9. A metal board still waved above the entryway with the German eagle and swastika on it. The door was wide open. Inside, the floors were covered with shreds of documents that had been hastily burned. She saw desks, abandoned typewriters, and some of the family furniture now broken and overturned. Pictures of Hitler still hung on the walls.

Michael stood among all this, perplexed, but he remembered where his room was, went up to it, and found pieces of toys that reminded him of his childhood.

"Will we come back to live here?" he asked.

"No point. Your mother wanted me to take you to Palestine and that's what I will do," she replied.

"And who will live in the house?"

"I don't know. For the time being, it's impossible to live here, but you must remember that this house now belongs to you. Someday, you'll probably take it over."

They inspected the house for a long time. Every valuable item—

the statues, the paintings, and the ancient books—had vanished. All that remained was filth and a slight smell of smoke from the burned Nazi documents.

In the yard the trees had withered and the flower beds had disappeared. A military Mercedes convertible was abandoned in the garage, its motor exposed. A military motorcycle was lying on its side.

They went to the street on their way back to the railroad station. Even though all the houses nearby weren't damaged, they were abandoned as in a ghost town. On the sidewalk, Russian soldiers were stretched out dozing or chomping on food. On the banks of the nearby river lay batteries of German machine guns that could no longer be used and in Chopin Park the peacocks had disappeared from the lake, which itself had turned into a turgid swamp.

"Will we have a house in Palestine as in Warsaw?" asked Michael.

Gertruda stroked his head. "We'll have a house, maybe not so big, but a real house."

The train that took them traveled all night, until it stopped in the small station of Starogard. Gertruda and Michael got off and walked to her parents' house. She didn't know any of the passersby she met. Her parents' house badly needed fixing up. The flourishing flower garden around the house and the kitchen garden were deserted and full of weeds. Gertruda went inside, dreading what she would find. Her parents weren't young when the war began, and she feared they were no longer alive.

But both her parents were still there. The house was more meager and poorer than she remembered, and her father and mother had grown very old. Her mother was sick in bed with a fever, covered with a torn blanket. Her eyes filled with tears and her voice broke when she saw her daughter. "I didn't think you were alive," she said.

Gertruda's father said that her mother had fallen ill a few weeks earlier and the doctor had diagnosed pneumonia. He advised hospitalization, but the hospital was full of sick and wounded refugees.

"It's good you came," said her father. "Maybe Mother will recover for you."

Gertruda didn't plan to stay more than a few days with her parents, but her mother's condition forced her to stay longer. It was hard for her parents to support themselves, let alone a couple of unexpected guests. Her father said that during the war they had eaten only what they found in the fields, and they usually went to bed hungry. Most of the neighbors loathed them. They claimed that Gertruda had sold herself to the Jews and had run away with them.

Gertruda found work as a substitute teacher in the nearby school and was paid a meager amount, barely enough to buy food. Michael usually stayed home. The neighbors refused to let their children play with him.

Months went by. Her mother's condition improved. She got out of bed, her appetite returned, and she looked better. One Sunday when they came back from church, they gathered around the dining room table.

"Now that I'm healthy," the mother said to her daughter, "things will go back to normal. You'll find real work and I promise you, your father and I will take care of Michael with devotion and love."

Gertruda shook her head. "I don't think we'll stay here."

Her father and mother looked at her in amazement, unable to understand.

"I swore to Michael's mother that I'd take him to Palestine," she said. "And that's what I intend to do."

"But," her mother tried to protest, "you were born here, this is your home. It can also be Michael's home."

"I know," said Gertruda. "But I swore to his mother I'd raise him as a Jew."

"Then find a way to send him to Palestine by himself. You don't belong there, in a strange country, among Jews. Did you forget that you're a Catholic? They won't love you."

"They'll love Michael. That will be enough for me."

Her parents' attempts to persuade her continued day and night. They exhausted her.

Finally, she announced that she was leaving.

"Michael and I will go to one of the Jewish refugee camps and from there they'll take us to Palestine," she said firmly.

Gertruda gathered their few clothes, thanked her parents for keeping them, stuffed a few bills from her last paycheck in their

Gertruda and Michael. Displaced persons camp, Berlin, July 1947.

hands, and parted from them tearfully. They hoped they'd meet again someday, but they knew the chances of such a meeting were very slim.

Gertruda bought train tickets to Munich, and after a long trip they arrived. She rented a room in a wretched hotel near the railroad station and immediately began looking for people to show her the way to the displaced persons camp. She met some American soldiers who told her about the camp set up near the city, and immediately she and Michael headed there.

The camp was at the edge of a forest. Behind a fence stood dozens of huts, and many people were sitting beside them or walking around the area. Laundry hung on lines and children played with balls made of rags. In the director's office Gertruda was asked to fill out a routine form and was sent to one of the huts. It was very crowded. Partitions of blankets separated the beds and a heavy smell of sweat permeated the air.

"How long will we be here?" asked Michael.

"Not long, I hope."

"From here, we'll go to Palestine?"

"Yes, my son."

"And there we'll meet Father?"

"Maybe."

CHAPTER 9

The Cruise Ship

1.

While Gertruda and Michael entered the displaced persons camp in Germany and waited to be taken to the Land of Israel, a frantic search began for ships that could carry thousands of Holocaust survivors to the shores of their new homeland.

The searches were conducted by agents of Mossad le'Aliyah Bet, established by the Haganah. After several attempts, a gigantic junk heap was discovered in the port of Baltimore, Maryland. The ship was slowly rotting away at the docks of inactive ships. On the prow of the ship, through a thick layer of rust, burgeoned the original name it boasted in its glory days: the *President Warfield*.

It had cost more than a million dollars to build in 1928, as a luxurious riverboat, and provided cruises to those who could afford its high prices. The best bands played dance music every evening in its ballrooms, accompanied by the best American singers.

After World War II, the demand for cruise ships fell off and the *President Warfield* sailed several times, almost without passengers.

The ship was requisitioned by the British navy and refitted as a transport ship. Its decks were covered with thick armor, cannons were fixed to its prow, and the fine wooden cabins were destroyed to make room for vital military cargo.

Veteran sailors believe that some ships are cursed. The *President Warfield* was one of them. To ward off evil, her sailors hung a big crucifix on the prow and put three cats on the third deck with lucky amulets. Nothing helped. In the middle of the war, the ship was hit hard in a German submarine attack, and it took months for it to be repaired and transferred to the American navy, which used it to transport soldiers to the landing at Normandy. In 1946, the navy retired the ship completely and towed it to the junkyard in Baltimore harbor, where it was sold for fifty thousand dollars to the secret shipping company established by Aliyah Bet.

2.

A few tanks wallowed near Hitler's bunker in Berlin, trucks unloaded soldiers, and jeeps moved around in the big square facing Kaiser Wilhelm Memorial Church, which had been partially destroyed in the bombing raids. A strange silence prevailed. No more thunder of cannons, no shriek of mortar shells, no rumble of airplane engines. Hitler and a few of his senior aids had committed suicide. Many of the staff officers had been arrested and imprisoned. The war was over.

Barricades had been erected in the center of the city and Allied soldiers were checking the documents of passersby. Karl Rink wanted to get as far away from there as possible. Even though he was wearing civilian clothes, he was afraid of being arrested at any moment, and a quick check would discover the SS tattoo under his arm.

He slipped into side streets, tried to avoid groups of soldiers, and finally found himself on the edge of the prestigious neighborhood of Wilmersdorf, where many of the houses had been spared the bombings. No soldier or military vehicle was seen in the area, and he hoped to find a safe hiding place there. Only a few dejected people were walking in the streets. The stores were locked and the windows were shuttered. For some days, he had had nothing to eat or drink, and Karl searched in vain for remnants of food in garbage cans.

His hunger and thirst were unbearable, and he was even willing to beg for a few pennies to buy bread.

In a doorway, Karl saw an old man in a wheelchair with a checkered blanket over his legs. He approached him hesitantly.

"Excuse me," he said. "I'm hungry. Can you help me?"

The old man looked up at him inquisitively.

"Who are you?" he asked.

"I was a soldier," replied Karl.

"Do you have a family?"

"My wife is dead and my daughter is abroad."

"Come with me," said the old man. "But don't expect much."

Karl pushed the wheelchair into a spacious apartment on the first floor. The old man directed him to the kitchen. On the table was a loaf of bread and on the stove was a kettle.

"That's all there is," he said. "Make yourself some tea and take a few slices of bread."

"Thank you," said Karl gratefully.

The old man looked at him as he devoured the food.

"Where do you live?" the old man asked.

"I have no place to live."

"You can live with me for the time being," said the man in the wheelchair. "My wife died two days ago and I need help. What do you think?"

• • •

In early August 1945, Helga-Elisheva Rink received a letter from her father:

Dear Helga,

At long last, the war is over. Fortunately for me, I have remained alive and haven't been imprisoned. Apparently God has taken pity on me. A few days ago, I met an old man in a wheelchair who gave me food and shelter in exchange for taking care of him. We live in the neighborhood of Wilmersdorf, in a nice and comfortable apartment that wasn't damaged in the war. The old man manufactured stockings, and throughout the war he and his wife existed by selling valuables on the black market. Now he occasionally gives me some expensive object he has left and I sell it to buy food and medicine for him.

I have my own small room, we eat modest and simple food, and the old man occasionally gives me a little pocket money. I have to find regular work, but for now there is no chance of that. Chaos reigns here. The factories and many shops are either destroyed or closed, and others haven't yet opened. Four different armies circulate in Berlin, arresting members of the Gestapo and the SS and holding them in transit camps. I hope that doesn't happen to me.

I have a lot of time to think about you and Mother. I miss both of you, even though Mother is apparently no longer in this world. I hope you are well. I await the day I will hug you.

Yours,

Father

3.

"Stolowitzky?" asked one of the two young men in amazement, stopping at Gertruda and Michael's beds in the DP camp. Their eyes looked at the name written crudely on the suitcases at the head of Gertruda's bed.

She had seen the two of them for the first time only a few minutes before, when the director of the hut allotted them two beds. The brothers Zvi and Joseph Yakobovitch had lost their whole family in Auschwitz. Their parents were taken to the crematoria, but the two boys had miraculously been spared. Joseph was seventeen and Zvi was fifteen. They escaped from the death camp during the turmoil there when the German staff realized the Red Army was approaching. The two hid in the forest until Russian soldiers found them and took them to a military hospital, where their wounds were treated and they were fed.

"Are you Mrs. Stolowitzky?" asked Joseph.

"He's Stolowitzky," said Gertruda, and pointed to Michael who was sound asleep. "I'm his adopted mother."

"We knew a Stolowitzky in Auschwitz," added the lad. "He lived in the same hut with us."

"What was his first name?"

"Jacob. He was a charming man. He took care of us like a father until the Germans took him to the gas chambers."

The awful news made Gertruda shudder. She had still hoped that Michael's father would come through the horrors of the war safely. Now she knew that only she and Michael were left.

"Did he tell you anything about his family?" she asked.

"Only that he had had a big house in Warsaw and a factory for railroad tracks. He didn't know what had happened to his wife and son."

"Don't talk about that to the child," Gertruda pleaded with them. "Jacob Stolowitzky was his father. The child thinks he's still alive."

They promised not to tell, and she decided to tell Michael the truth only when the journey of hardships they faced on the way to the Land of Israel came to an end.

Like many of those in the camp, the brothers were still haunted by the horrors of the death camp. At night, they would sneak into the camp kitchen and steal loaves of bread, which they hid under their pillow, and during the day they hoarded every object that looked useful: empty cardboard boxes, ragged clothes and torn books thrown in the trash by the camp inmates, as well as dull knives and used bandages. Gertruda was the only person they trusted, and they poured out their heart to her. They had a faded photo of their parents in their house in Poland. They kept only that souvenir and burst into tears when they looked at it, trying to cling to those happy days when the whole family was alive. They also loved music. Zvi said he had learned to play the violin as a child. One day he found an old violin on his bed in the camp. He shouted with joy and hugged Gertruda when he discovered that she had bought the violin for pennies from one of the refugees.

Zvi played with gleaming eyes and many of the camp inmates gathered to listen to him. In time, a youth orchestra was formed consisting of an accordion, a flute, a piano, and a violin. The camp administration assigned them a corner in the dining hall for rehearsals, and they also organized concerts. At every concert, Zvi reserved front-row seats for Gertruda and Michael.

The two brothers wanted to go to a kibbutz. Zvi dreamed of establishing an orchestra there and Joseph wanted to work the fields. They were sorry their parents couldn't come. Their father, who had been a teacher, had planned to immigrate to the Land of Israel but was too late. Zvi composed a song in Yiddish in memory of him:

My father always knew everything,
Torah and math, Rashi and Talmud,
Only one thing he didn't know:
To flee in time from the land trampled by hobnailed boots . . .

4.

A week after he started taking care of the sick old man, Karl Rink had his first day off. He got up early, washed and dressed the old man, made him enough food for the whole day, left the house, and went to the eastern part of the city. Most of the houses in the neighborhood were destroyed, street signs had disappeared, and he wandered around for a long time until he was able to find where Reinhard Schreider lived. His commander's house had also been hit by bombs. One of its wings had collapsed, but the others were still inhabited.

Karl Rink remembered Schreider's apartment. He knocked on the door of the intact ground floor. No one answered. He knocked again, but in vain. He walked to the end of the corridor and knocked on the door of another apartment. A woman's voice came from inside the apartment: "Who is it?"

Karl said he was looking for Schreider and would be glad if she could give him some information about him.

"What do you want with him?" the woman asked suspiciously.

"I'm a friend of his."

The door opened. A woman of about fifty stood in the entrance and behind her shoulder, a man peeped out. His face lit up at the sight of the guest.

"Karl!" the man shouted happily. "Come in, please come in."

Karl Rink recognized him immediately. Before the war, for many months, the two of them had worked at SS headquarters in Berlin.

"There were rumors that you were killed in the war," said the man.

He insisted that Karl have a cup of tea and a simple cake his wife had baked.

"Why are you looking for Schreider?" he asked.

"No special reason . . . I just thought it would be nice to meet. After all, he was my commander and was always nice to me."

"He had bad luck," said the man sadly. "When we knew it was all over, many of us burned our uniforms, put on civilian clothes, and went into hiding at home. The Americans caught Schreider when they came to Berlin and took him to a military base for questioning."

"Is he still there?"

"Yes. It doesn't look like they'll let him go anytime soon."

5.

She walked like a ghost on the paths of the DP camp in Germany. Sixteen years old, her body skinny as a stick, her face long and her eyes sad. On her chest, under her faded shirt, was a word carved in the death camp of Treblinka: WHORE. Such tattoos were etched in the flesh of the girls and women assigned to satisfy the sexual needs of the German staff. The forced whores were given a temporary guarantee of life, a passport to the humiliating journey of survival that left an eternal scar in their heart. They would never forget the coarse, mostly drunken soldiers who behaved with them as they would never have dared behave with the women they had left at home.

Like many inmates of the DP camp, the girl's whole family had died in the gas chambers. When the Germans fled for their lives from the approaching Red Army, she was caught up in the wave of survivors who went through the open gate, scattered in the fields, and breathed the air of freedom. Her eyes were dry, her heart was sealed, her legs buckled with weakness. On her way to the DP camp, her indifferent eyes passed over German trucks burning and farmhouses whose fearful inhabitants had locked themselves inside. She didn't know what was in store for her and she didn't care what happened as long as she didn't have to go back to that hell.

At the DP camp she was given new clothes and assigned to a bed in one of the huts, but closed places terrified her. She refused to go into the hut and avoided going to the dining hall or becoming friendly with girls her own age. For whole days, she wandered around idly, and at night she stretched out on a bench on the side of one of the paths and had nightmares.

Groups of overworked psychologists worked in the DP camp with the many young people and adults who needed their care. Some were in a state that required hospitalization. The girl from Treblinka was called to a meeting with a psychologist, but fled into a grove at the edge of the camp.

The camp administration didn't know what to do. All attempts to get to her, talk with her, put her in touch with young people, had failed. Gertruda saw her sleeping on the bench one night, brought a blanket from the hut, and covered her gently. The girl woke with a start and threw off the blanket. Her eyes looked suspiciously at the stranger.

"I'm sorry," Gertruda apologized softly. "I just wanted to help."

The two of them spoke Polish.

"I don't need any help," said the sixteen-year-old.

"We all need help," said Gertruda. "All of us came here wounded and desperate. We have to help one another."

The girl was silent.

"My name's Gertruda." She sat down on the bench and very slowly talked about herself, Michael, and the hardships they had experienced.

The girl was silent.

"I live in hut 23 with Michael. There's an empty bed next to us. If you want to, you can sleep there at night. It will be more comfortable with us."

The following night, Gertruda passed the bench again. She brought Michael with her. The girl was awake, as if she had been expecting her. The blanket was laid aside, folded.

"This is Michael. I wanted you to meet him," said Gertruda.

The girl looked dully at the boy.

"Gertruda told me about you," he said. He broke a chocolate bar in two and gave her half of it. "This is for you."

She didn't budge.

"Take it, please. It's very good," he pleaded.

When she didn't hold out her hand, he put the chocolate next to her on the bench.

"Come," Gertruda repeated her offer. "The bed in our hut is still free."

The girl shook her head no.

"If you do want to come," said Gertruda, "remember we're in number 23. Goodnight."

She held Michael's hand and returned to the hut. The sounds
of deep breathing of dozens of sleeping people filled the room. Here
and there a candle was lit so people could write letters or journals
in its light.

The next day, Gertruda again passed by the bench where the girl
slept. She wasn't there, but the blanket was left there. She sensed
that something was wrong, and she reported the girl's absence to
the camp administration. A group of workers went out to search for
her in the camp but couldn't find her, so they asked for help from
the police.

Gertruda went to the nearby villages with Zvi and Jacob Yacobovitch to look for the girl. They hitchhiked, rode on farm carts
and trucks loaded with vegetables, asked passersby and shopown-
ers if they had seen the missing girl, but no one had.

When that failed, Gertruda and the boys went to Munich,
walked around for a long time among the prostitutes, money chang-
ers, and black market dealers in the alleys near the railroad station,
and described the missing girl to them. No one had seen her; no
one had heard anything about her.

Two days later, her body was pulled out of the nearby lake. She
had left no note, and when she was buried in the old Jewish cemetery
in the nearby city, the only mourners were Gertruda and Michael.

6.

Aliyah Bet offered command of the *President Warfield* to various experienced ship officers, but they all refused. They feared the ad-
venture was too dangerous, that the ship couldn't make such a long
trip, that the British would arrest them. The Haganah offered a lot
of money to tempt them, but they still refused.

At an emergency meeting in Marseille, the leaders of Aliyah Bet discussed their crisis. Somebody mentioned Isaac (Ike) Aaronovitch, who had attended school for naval officers in Richmond, England.

"He makes an excellent impression," he said. "Let's give him a chance."

The suggestion was accepted, although not enthusiastically, but there was no other option and time was of the essence. The job had to be offered to Ike.

He was only twenty-two years old and lacked real experience in sailing ships. The offer was more than likely several sizes too big for him.

"I've never commanded a ship," he said apologetically.

"That's not important," they replied. "We've been keeping an eye on you. You've got what it takes to do the job right."

"I suggest you keep looking for somebody else," said Ike. "I'll take the command only if I have to."

Isaac (Ike) Aaronovitch. At sea, July 1947.

"A waste of time, Ike. There is no other choice."

"Okay. I hope I won't disappoint you."

7.

SS officer Reinhard Schreider had been imprisoned for six weeks on the American military base. He had been interrogated for hours and consistently claimed that he had served ultimately as an administrative officer in Berlin and had not been involved in any war crimes. His interrogators hadn't been able to crack his story and they finally let him go without a trial.

Karl Rink, who went to Schreider's house every week on his day off and always found the door locked, was surprised when one day Schreider opened the door to him, in light suspenders and a white undershirt. The two of them looked at each other for a long time. Schreider looked unchanged. The same broad, bony face, the same firm expression, the same evil look in his eyes.

"You've changed, Karl," said Schreider. "Obviously you didn't have an easy time of it in the war. Lucky you're still alive."

"Yes, I was lucky," muttered Rink. "Can I talk with you a few minutes?"

"Please," said Schreider, repressing his surprise. What, he wondered, did they have to talk about?

They went into the big living room that had once been full of antique furniture. On the walls were a few faded landscapes. The windows were closed and on the table was a bottle of wine. Cigarette smoke stood thick in the air.

"How can I help you?" asked the host.

"Something's been bothering me, Schreider, for several years now."

"What?"

"You remember our conversation after my wife disappeared?"

"No." Schreider played innocent.

"I asked you then if you had any idea what had caused her disappearance."

"That was a long time ago. You don't expect me to remember every conversation I had."

"You told me you had no idea what had happened to her."

"Let's assume I said so."

"You lied."

Schreider's face flushed with anger.

"I want to know if you killed my wife," Rink demanded.

"I didn't kill her, Karl. If that's why you came, you don't have anything more to do here."

He pointed to the door.

Karl Rink felt his rage burning in him. For years he had nursed a terrible frustration and loathed himself for not daring to resign and avoid serving the people who had murdered his wife. Now he stood before the man who was responsible for Mira's murder. Schreider had avoided punishment at the hands of the Americans, thought Karl, but he won't escape my punishment. He took the switchblade out of his pocket and released the blade before Schreider's hostile eyes.

"Are you crazy?" shouted the SS officer.

"You have to pay for what you did," Karl said slowly.

"What did I do?" Schreider shouted. "I was only obeying orders. And anyway, why do you care so much about that Jew?"

"I loved her, she was my wife, and you killed her."

"She didn't deserve to be the wife of an SS officer. You should have understood that yourself."

"She wasn't hurting anybody."

Schreider looked hypnotized at the blade aimed at him.

"We wanted to allow you to devote yourself entirely to the SS. Your wife was stuck in you like a bone in your throat," he said.

"What exactly did you do to her? I want to know."

"She didn't feel a thing, Karl. It took only a few seconds."

Karl Rink attacked Schreider. He was shorter and not as strong as his former commander, but his rage gave him a superhuman force. Schreider struggled, but Rink managed to stick the blade in his throat. A burst of blood and a death rattle ended the commander's life.

Afterward, Rink didn't feel a thing. Not anger, not satisfaction. He knew only that he had settled an old account, an account that had to be closed. He turned around, went out the door and into the street. A sense of loneliness crept into him, but he comforted himself with the thought that at least he had managed to avenge his wife's death and save his only daughter in time.

8.

The DP camp was no more than a way station on a long road, a short period of time before the Holocaust survivors set out for the final destination. Almost everything they brought with them was left in well-packed suitcases and personal bundles. The inmates of the camp took out only their basic needs—essential clothing and toiletries.

Many questions, with no answers, popped up: What was in store for them there, in the new country? Would they locate family members? Would they find a place to live and a job? Would they and their children adapt to the people, the environment, the language that was strange to most of them? Would they ever forget the nightmares of the war?

They had too many idle hours and too few occupations. They listened to lectures about the Land of Israel, sang together, argued about politics. Like many other children in the camp, Michael learned Hebrew. The first sentence he could read in the new language was "I'm going to the Land of Israel."

As the days passed, the tension increased. All attention was focused on the expected sailing, almost the only topic of conversation. Strange rumors circulated and each one raised or lowered the people's mood. Once it was rumored that they would sail in a week, only to be told later that the ship needed more repairs, making it unclear when it could leave port. The camp administration did confirm the rumor that the number of applicants exceeded the number of places on the ship, and a special committee of the Haganah would decide who would go and who would stay. This information caused great fear among the old and the sick. Afraid they wouldn't board the ship, many of the elderly declared that they were younger. Sick people and pregnant women went to German doctors in nearby villages and got false medical certificates from them in exchange for canned goods and cigarettes.

No one deluded himself that the trip to the Land of Israel would be easy or that the ship could dock in Palestine. Newspapers from Israel that reached the camp told of ships of illegal immigrants stopped by British destroyers before they got to Palestine, their passengers sent to transit camps in Cyprus. Gertruda shuddered when she remembered what the fortune-teller had predicted on the train to Vilna, about what was in store for her and Michael: a difficult sailing, a succession of blood and victims. She ordered herself to forget those things, but they came back into her mind every day, reinforcing her fears.

CHAPTER 10

Attack at Sea

1.

In the big dining hall of the DP camp, Yossi Hamburger, a twenty-nine-year-old native of Jerusalem appointed to command the ship alongside Ike Aaronovitch, introduced himself to the illegal immigrants and said: "The time of departure is approaching. It may happen this week."

A roar of satisfaction went through the audience.

"You must know that it won't be a pleasurable cruise," added Hamburger. "It will be very crowded on the ship; it will be hot and stifling in the hold. Children, pregnant women, and older people will suffer especially. Diseases may also break out. But that's not all. Right now, we're not sure if we'll get to Palestine. The British will try everything to keep you out of the Land of Israel. Previously, they have exiled illegal immigrants to transit camps in Cyprus. They may want to do that again this time."

"We'll resist!" shouted someone in the audience. "They won't exile us!"

"That won't be so easy. We have to defend against them, but carefully. The British have weapons and we don't, and if they want to, they can easily take over the ship."

"So what's the point of this sailing?" asked a pregnant woman.

"First of all," said Hamburger, "we believe there is a chance to break through the British blockade and take you to the Land of Israel. There have been illegal immigrant ships that have succeeded. Moreover, we want to stir world opinion, pressure the British government to let the refugees from the Holocaust immigrate to Palestine. Never have we brought so many immigrants all at once and this has to arouse great interest in the world press and will mobilize public opinion for our struggle. Nevertheless, I must tell you now that anyone who doesn't want to sail can stay in the camp for the time being. Anyone who wants to stay here, raise your hand."

Nobody did.

"Then," he smiled, "all I can do is wish you bon voyage."

The refugees slowly scattered and Gertruda returned to her hut, thoughtful, once again remembering the words of the fortune-teller: "There's a curse on that ship. I see a lot of blood, violence, dead people." She still saw the possibility of not sailing, waiting until they could go straight and sure to the Land of Israel. But she knew she couldn't. She had been looking forward to that trip more than anything else. At long last, she had to find a real home for Michael.

The next day, the camp residents were told that all passengers had to give up most of their belongings, that they were allowed to take only twenty-two pounds of personal objects. The DP camp seethed and stormed when the order was given. No matter how worthless they were, objects were an integral part of life. People were closely bound to the things they or their loved ones had and it was hard to leave them. Many of the Holocaust survivors carried their own keepsakes and those of their families who had been killed in the camps: clothes, eating utensils, secret journals. Ever since their liberation, they had amassed more things that were dear to them. Many of them also feverishly hoarded food, afraid they would once again suffer from hunger. They protested loudly to the camp administration, pleaded and explained, but the decision stood: there was room on the ship only for passengers, not cargo.

Like the others, Gertruda also received the order with a heavy heart. She had many objects that she had collected. Michael had precious personal mementos, too. She wanted to keep kitchen utensils and other household objects she could use in the new country. She also had books she had collected over the years, but she had to abandon almost everything. Michael took his parents' photo album and the New Testament given to him as a farewell gift by Father Gedovsky.

2.

The eyes of the camp administrators were red from lack of sleep; their faces were pale from overwork. They worked day and night to finish the list of candidates for the ship and discovered that their fear had come true: there weren't enough places on the ship for all those who wanted to sail. The inevitable conclusion was that at least a few dozen refugees would have to stay behind.

Deciding who would go and who would stay was excruciating. The Israelis who had been sent to manage the camp and get its occupants to the Land of Israel were members of political movements and had clear priorities. Representatives of Ha-Shomer Ha-Tza'ir wanted to bring those who would establish the new kibbutzim; the He-Chalutz movement preferred its people, as did the other movements whose representatives now determined who could board the ship.

Passengers who might be left behind were taken off the list: single men and women, parents of newborn infants—and Gertruda, who, unlike all the other prospective passengers, wasn't Jewish. She was called for an interview and entered the room where the members of the administration were seated at a long wooden table.

They scanned her documents.

"I understand that you're not a Jew," said one of them.

"I'm Catholic."

"And the child you're with is a Jew, correct?"

"Correct."

"We've read your personal file and we, of course, are very appreciative of the fact that you protected the child during the war. We have no doubt that he is still alive because of you."

"Without me, he would have nobody in the world," she added. "His parents are dead."

"We know," said one of the members of the administration, a young man in a shabby leather jacket. "Do you have a family?"

"Yes. My parents live in Starogard."

"Why don't you go back to them?

"Because I promised Michael's dying mother to take him to the Land of Israel. She wanted him to grow up there as a Jew," she said.

"We'll take him to the Land of Israel," he said. "You can count on us."

Now she suddenly understood what he meant. He didn't want her to sail.

"I went through all the hardships of the war with that child," she said emotionally. "I saved him from certain death. I risked my life for him every day and every hour. You have no right to prevent me from keeping my promise to his mother."

They looked at her uneasily.

"Understand," said one of them, "we don't have room on the ship for all those who want to immigrate to Palestine. Many people will have to stay in Europe. We have to give priority to Jews who see their future in the Land of Israel, and so we can't, unfortunately, allow you to go. Michael can of course sail."

Her face flushed with anger and offense. "That's not acceptable," she said.

The man softened his voice. "I can understand how close you are to the child. You deserve full appreciation for your sacrifice, but you must accept that your role is in fact over."

She pierced him with her eyes.

"My role will be over when Michael doesn't want me to be with him," she declared.

"He's a little boy. He doesn't really understand what happened to him."

"That's exactly why I have to stay with him."

"Sorry," he said. "With all the sorrow I feel for you, we have no choice, madam. I suggest you prepare to part from the child. It will be for your good and his."

"It won't be for his good," she protested. "Michael will go only with me. I won't leave him."

"Our decision is final," stated the man. "We can't allow ourselves to put someone on the ship who isn't Jewish."

"My decision is also final," she said. She stood up and left the room with her head high.

3.

Gertruda stumbled back to her hut in the camp, collapsed on her bed, and buried her face in the pillow. Her body shook with weeping and Michael looked at her in amazement. In all the years they had been together, with all the hardships they had faced, she had almost never shed a tear. She always made every effort to radiate confidence and force, to strengthen the boy with the sense that she was a solid pillar of support for him. Now something had broken inside her.

Michael stroked her back until she stopped crying and turned her face to him. He asked what had happened and she told him.

"They're bad people," he said angrily.

"They're not bad, Michael. They just don't understand that I promised your mother never to leave you."

"I'll go talk to them." His firm resolve confirmed something Gertruda had been seeing in him for a long time: despite his young age, he was no longer a child. The war had given him wisdom and an adult perspective. It had taught him to be hard, to overcome difficulties, never to give in.

Gertruda lovingly kissed his forehead.

"They won't listen to you, Michael. We'll have to think of a more effective way to change their decision."

She remembered that a group of journalists was supposed to visit the camp that week to hear the hard stories of the homeless Holocaust survivors. The camp residents were told about the journalists' visit in advance and were asked to emphasize in their conversations with the correspondents their strong desire to immigrate to the Land of Israel, their only homeland. Gertruda's name was on the list of those the journalists wanted to interview.

* * *

On the morning of the visit of the media representatives, Gertruda knocked on the door of the office.

"Gentlemen," she said, "have you changed your decision about me?"

"Unfortunately, no" was the reply.

"Can I appeal?"

"No." The members of the administration were impatient and waited for her to leave, but she stood still.

"The journalists will come today," she said quietly. "You can imagine what will happen when they find out you won't let a Catholic woman take a Jewish child—who she risked her life to save—to the Land of Israel, as she promised his mother on her deathbed."

All faces turned to her with an expression of displeasure.

"We ask you not to tell that to the journalists," said one of them.

"And I ask you to reconsider your decision."

They writhed uneasily in their chairs.

"This is blackmail," they said angrily.

"Right," she answered coolly.

"Fine," said the director of the camp. "We'll bring your case up for a decision by Aliyah Bet. They're responsible for carrying out this smuggling of displaced persons and what they determine has to be accepted by you and by us."

"Bring it up with whomever you like," said Gertruda. "But take into account that there is only one decision I will accept. Tell your superiors I won't accept any decision that goes against the good of Michael."

"We'll tell them your position," they promised. "Meanwhile, don't talk with the journalists about this."

4.

As if there weren't enough obstacles preventing the sailing, Gertruda Babilinska's personal case came to disturb those in charge of the operation. On the day of the long series of meetings on how to defend the ship against British attacks, the Aliyah Bet leadership in Paris had to discuss a question that, on the face of it, appeared quite peripheral: whether to let the Catholic nanny of a Jewish child sail to the Land of Israel with him.

One of the organizers of the operation, Mordechai Rozman, a short, thin, high-strung young man, brought up the question with his four colleagues. They tried to postpone the discussion, but he persisted on the pretext that the woman was promised the subject would be discussed in this meeting. Rozman laid out the chain of events. Most participants in the meeting argued that top priority on the ship had to be given to Jews, and so Michael would have to sail alone.

Rozman thought otherwise. He argued forcefully for letting Gertruda go.

"Everyone who saves one soul," he quoted, "it's as if he saved the whole world. We can't be so strict and insensitive. That woman gave up her life so the child would live. There's no greater sacrifice than that. She deserves to sail with him."

He told them of a case he had heard about in the camp of a barren woman in Auschwitz who saved an orphan infant and was now going with him to the Land of Israel where she would raise him as her son.

"What's the difference?" he asked.

"She's a Jew and Babilinska isn't" was the answer he received.

He couldn't change their minds.

"If we offer her money to return home to Poland, will that help?" they asked him.

"No chance," said Rozman.

"We can put her on another ship in a few months," said one of those present. "It won't hurt them to wait a little."

"You know very well," replied Rozman, "that we have no idea when there will be another ship. After all the suffering they've gone through, that woman and child want to and need to live in Palestine."

"Maybe they should try to convince the child first?"

"They already talked with him. He won't give in either. He says she's like his mother."

Rozman still could not change most of their minds.

Finally, he said: "Gertruda Babilinska will be listed as one of the most outstanding figures among the Righteous Gentiles. We have no moral right to leave her behind. This entire discussion gives me an uneasy feeling."

"She threatened to complain to the press about us," said somebody, and Rozman responded: "She seems to be a very firm woman. If the war didn't break her, we won't either. She did everything to save the child in the war, and she'll do everything not to part from him. She'll tell the press, organize demonstrations. It will be very unpleasant for us."

The members of Aliyah Bet continued deliberating for a long time. They didn't want to change their minds, but they had to. Fear of Gertruda's public protests tipped the scales in her favor.

Rozman personally told her of the decision.

She wasn't surprised. She was sure there was no other way.

5.

The announcement to prepare for the journey that day spread like wildfire through the camp in the morning. Cheers of joy were heard in the huts and people hugged one another.

At nightfall, a long convoy of trucks entered the camp, some of them taken without permission from British army garages and others rented from various moving companies. The residents of the camp were packed in them and the convoy set out. At the French border the convoy was asked the purpose of the trip, transit documents were checked, and, after a generous gift of cigarettes to the border guards, the trucks were allowed to continue to the camp near Marseille, where all illegal immigrants were given Colombian visas and told to tell anyone who asked them as they boarded the ship that they were Jewish refugees immigrating to Colombia. The visas had been procured by Aliyah Bet from the Colombian consulate in Marseille for fifty dollars each and the promise that none of the visa holders would come to Colombia.

After a few days of nerve-racking delay, the passengers were taken to the port of Sette near Marseille, where the ship was waiting for them. When they got there, port officials were still gathered in the captain's cabin on the ship, filling their bellies with abundant delicacies: sausages and champagne, chocolate and fine wines, which they hadn't tasted throughout the war. Afterward, satiated and weary, the officials stood at the bottom of the gangplank, hastily checked the Colombian documents, and let the bearers board. Quite a few members of the French government suspected the ship was about to sail to the Land of Israel, but they preferred to turn a blind eye and had no legal cause to interfere: the passengers had Colombian documents and the ship had permission to sail from the Honduran government. The British also knew they had no cause to exert pressure on the French government to delay the departure, but they didn't sit idly by. As the survivors were boarding the *President Warfield,* a British patrol plane circled above photographing them and sending the pictures to British intelligence headquarters.

On the afternoon of July 11, 1947, the port administration gave official permission to sail. The Honduran flag—five blue stars on a white background—flew at the top of the mast and thousands of passengers began to pray, pleading with the Creator to bring them safely to their destination.

When all were on board and anxiously waiting to move, the breakdowns on the ship began. Ike ordered the motors turned on and the ropes connecting the ship to the dock cut, but he learned to his dismay that the propeller was entangled in the cut ropes. Bill Bernstein, Ike's first mate, dove under the ship and released the propeller. At long last, they believed, the *President Warfield* was on its way, but the problems continued. Before it was able to leave the bay, the ship got stuck on a sandbank. Sweaty and nervous, Ike decided not to call for help. He ordered the motors turned on full and breathed a sigh of relief when the ship moved successfully.

The passengers were thrilled when, at long last, they saw the expanse of blue water and the white wake behind the ship. The *President Warfield* sailed fast. The monotonous roar of the motors signaled that the engine room was working properly. Ike opened a bottle of wine, poured everyone in the pilot's cabin a glass, and made a toast.

The good mood spread through the ship. The passengers on deck started singing the national anthem, "Ha-Tikvah."

"Why are they so happy?" asked Bill Bernstein, and pointed west, where the British destroyer, the *Mermaid,* was clinging to the wake of the *President Warfield.* The *Mermaid* was one of the fleet of destroyers that was supposed to prevent the illegal immigrant ship from reaching the shores of Palestine.

6.

Thousands of displaced persons, old and young, children and pregnant women, looked at the British destroyer following them and prayed to Heaven for deliverance. Even the greatest optimists among them now understood that the journey wouldn't be easy.

A group of men climbed up to the top deck and hung a gigantic sign with the new name of the ship in Hebrew and English: HA-GANAH SHIP EXODUS, 1947. The Honduran flag gave way to the blue-and-white flag of the Jewish nation. A sense of historic mission was in the air.

The first Sabbath on the deck of the ship revived old and painful memories for Gertruda. She remembered the Sabbath eve in the grand dining room of the house on Ujazdowska Avenue, Lydia's insistence that she join them, even though she wasn't Jewish. Gertruda knew all the blessings and songs by heart.

Because there were so many passengers, the meal was divided among several halls, and in each the atmosphere was excited. Thousands of them crowded around the tables, sitting and standing. Women blessed the Sabbath candles, and Gertruda's lips whispered along with them.

After dinner, they burst into Sabbath and Israeli songs, and started dancing on the deck to the music of accordions and violins. Gertruda and Michael were swept up into the circles of dancers. Outside the circle stood the minister John Grauel, who had volun-

The President Warfield *(Exodus). Haifa Harbor, Israel, 1949.*

teered to go with the ship and wondered whether to join everyone. "Come on!" called Gertruda. "It's not so complicated." He took her hand and imitated her steps. "You see, it's not hard," she laughed.

When the dancing ended, Gertruda sat down with Michael on the pile of bundles at the edge of the deck and the minister approached them.

"My name's Gertruda and this is Michael," she said.

"Gertruda, if I'm not mistaken, is a popular Jewish name." He spoke German with an American accent.

She laughed. "It's not a Jewish name at all. I'm a Catholic."

"Interesting," he said. "Tell me what you're doing here."

At length she told her story.

"You're an amazing woman." Grauel was impressed. "All of you on this ship are amazing people. I'm proud I was given the opportunity to help you."

Gertruda furtively admired his height, his solid body, his expressive face, and an old, almost forgotten feeling, which had grown dull over the years, revived in her heart: she liked him.

She asked him to tell her about his life. Grauel said that he had been born in Germany and had wanted to be a minister at an early age. He had moved to the United States with his parents as a child and, after studying theology, at the age of twenty-eight, he was appointed a minister in a Protestant church in a small American provincial town.

"Do you intend to return to the church when the trip is over?"

"Maybe," he answered.

"Do you have other plans?"

"Not right now."

In the following days, Gertruda noticed that Grauel spent a lot of time with her. They ate together in the dining room and got into long conversations on deck when the day's heat subsided and the sun began to set. Michael noticed that since she had first met Grauel, Gertruda paid more attention to her appearance, and even put on lipstick. Grauel was affectionate to the child. He found a fishing pole and they tried to pull fish out of the sea. They loved to fish together, even though they didn't get even one bite.

In the cool evening, the deck was packed with passengers who came out of the hold to breathe some fresh air. Some of them lay on the hard wooden boards, babies cried, and children vainly sought a place to play. Zvi Yacobovitch played the violin. Despite the crowding, Grauel, Gertruda, and Michael found their own corner.

Father John Grauel, 1984.

Grauel talked about his childhood; Gertruda translated for Michael. The child listened, wide-eyed. One of those stories stayed etched in Michael's brain even many years later.

"My father," said Grauel in his deep voice, "came from Germany to America in the early 1920s and found work as a simple laborer in a metal plant. He worked there devotedly and lovingly for years. He didn't make much, but he made enough to support my mother, me, and my little brother, until the Depression of 1929. My father was fired, and we had to wander around the United States looking for work for him. I remember we went to Washington. The city was flooded with thousands of unemployed living in a gigantic tent camp in the middle of the city. My father was depressed. Every day he sat for hours on a bench in a public park and pitied himself. He thought he had no chance of getting work. The little bit of money we had quickly ran out and we knew that within a few days we wouldn't have any food to eat.

"I couldn't watch my father sink more and more into his depression. I decided to do something a bit crazy. I went to the White House where the president lived and slipped inside without the guards seeing me. I walked around the corridors and looked for a door that said PRESIDENT. Finally, someone in a tailored suit stopped me and asked what I was doing there. I said I had come to ask the president to give my father work or we would all starve to death. The man smiled at me and said: 'I like your daring and originality.' He went and brought me a cheese sandwich and a bottle of soda and asked me to send my father to him the next morning.

"I went home and told my father. He hugged me in his strong arms and was so excited, he couldn't sleep all night. In the morning he went to the White House, met with the man, and was sent to work on a building the government was constructing in the city. We were saved."

Grauel stroked Michael's head.

"You loved your father very much, didn't you?" asked the child in Polish, and Gertruda translated.

"Very much."

"So did I. It's been a long time since I saw my father."

Gertruda's new friendship with the minister stirred feelings in her that grew stronger. The pleasant man won her heart and she wanted to believe that he felt the same way about her. One night, on deck, they got into a long conversation. She said that she intended to accompany the boy to the Land of Israel, guarantee that he was accepted there, and, if possible, stay with him until her dying day.

"I'm also considering staying in Palestine," said Grauel.

"Have you ever thought of settling down with a woman you'd love?" she asked cautiously.

"No," he mumbled.

"If you like . . . I'd be willing to convert to Protestantism for you . . . I'd be glad if . . . " She blushed.

He patted her hand. "You're a charming woman," he said. "You deserve somebody better than me."

He wanted her to understand: "I'm not attracted to women," he said softly. "That's why I haven't gotten married until now."

She understood and her heart fell. All the dreams she had spun about life with him vanished.

"You don't feel well?" asked Grauel when he saw her pale face.

"I'll recover," she said, and averted her face so he couldn't see her tears.

7.

The fleet of British destroyers following the *Exodus* grew in number almost every day. By the fourth day out, six of them were seen. The destroyer *Ajax,* which had shot a mortal hit to the German flagship *Graf Spee* in the war, approached the ship and the question came from its loudspeaker: "Are you taking illegal immigrants to Palestine?" The *Exodus* didn't answer. The British voice called again: "We know exactly who you are and where you want to go. You will never get there. You won't pass because our navy is invincible. Don't endanger women and children in vain. In the name of humanity, we ask you to prevent the attempts of your leaders to break through our blockade. Change your course while it's not too late."

In reply, the *Exodus* turned its loudspeakers to the British ships and broadcast Hebrew songs.

All the British destroyers were now in very close range to the survivors' ship. They sailed beside her, demonstrably maneuvering their batteries of guns. Armed commandos stood on the decks wearing gas masks.

The crowding in the holds and on the decks of the *Exodus,* the heat that oppressed and choked the thousands of immigrants, the lack of any privacy, the lack of any possibility of finding a quiet corner, and primarily the tension and fear sown in them by the British destroyers—all that turned life on the ship into an almost impossible endurance test. Many of the forty-five hundred men, women, and children who bore on their bodies—and mainly their souls—wounds that hadn't yet healed had brought customs from the camps that were hard to get rid of. Here, too, on the ship, harsh scenes of brutality appeared. People pushed each other in lines for food and water, burst into the clinic to get treatment before everyone else, horded food despite the abundance, and tried to get to the bunks near the windows and the openings. Organized groups almost always got what they wanted at the expense of those who weren't pushy. Fistfights broke out almost every day.

Alone, too tired to fight, Gertruda had to get up early in the morning to stand in lines before dawn, to get food and water when the morning distribution began. She often found that many people had preceded her in line. Sometimes, the long wait was near pointless and when she got to the distribution point, almost nothing was left for her and Michael. She was no stranger to frustration and disappointment. She had experienced them intensely during the war and knew how to overcome them without complaining.

Michael often insisted on standing in line with her. For hours he stood there looking helplessly at the people who got what they wanted through force. As during the war, his heart hurt now when he saw Gertruda's sad face.

One day, when Michael and Gertruda had returned empty-handed, he went to the commander of the ship, Yossi Hamburger, and demanded that the crew establish order, but all the commander's efforts to ensure that everyone got his portion met with failure. The laws of the jungle were stronger than he was.

The minister Grauel often offered to share his food with Gertruda and Michael. They refused to take food from him, but he pleaded until they gave in. The three of them usually ate together.

"You can't blame those people," he said. "They survived hell because they fought for every piece of bread. They'll go on fighting out of habit. It will take time for them to return to themselves."

8.

Even though the *Exodus* was clumsy and heavy, she did have some advantages over the British destroyers assigned to prevent her from getting to the shores of the Promised Land. She was higher than they were, surrounded by layers of steel, and thus better defended than other illegal immigrants ships. The British calculated that only their command bridges, in the top section of the destroyers, were parallel in height to the decks of the *Exodus*. That was the only place, even if not the most convenient, from which the illegal immigrant ship could be stormed. British naval engineers had learned of this in time and secretly built elevated scaffolds on every destroyer to make it easy for the soldiers to assault when they came alongside the *Exodus*. To hide those scaffolds, the destroyers took care to sail behind the *Exodus* at an angle to conceal the new towers.

On Friday night, July 18, 1947, the passengers of the *Exodus* had a modest meal. They were heavyhearted and frightened. The ship was sailing at full steam to the shores of Palestine, now only fifteen miles away, and eight British ships, their lights out, were chasing them like stubborn hounds. Both the British soldiers and the survivors understood that the inevitable clash would occur in only a matter of hours.

At that time, under cover of dark, two Palmach units were hiding on the shore of Tel Aviv to get the immigrants off the ship quickly when they arrived. About twenty fishing boats and barges, secretly mobilized, waited in the port of Tel Aviv for orders to go to the ship and start transferring the immigrants to shore. The assumption was that if the operation were carried out quickly, many of the ship's passengers could slip into Tel Aviv before the British could block the area. But all plans and hopes vanished that night.

Preparations for the British attack on the *Exodus* began in the evening. A state of high alert was declared on the British ships. The soldiers ate a hasty meal and were ordered to put on battle gear, load their weapons, and stand by for orders. When the operation started, the destroyers were supposed to accelerate. Two of them would attach their sides to the *Exodus*. The scaffolds would be thrown onto the deck of the illegal immigrant ship so the soldiers could swoop onto the deck, stop the progress of the ship, and take control of it. At the same time, the other ships would sail close by, ready to send reinforcements if needed and prevent the illegal immigrants from fleeing to shore in the lifeboats.

The mood aboard the *Exodus* was tense. The ship made its way silently, most of its lights dowsed. Even though none of the passengers knew what the British were liable to do, they were sure they wouldn't let illegal immigrants ashore. Most of them lay in bed, but couldn't sleep. Only the children slept. The roar of the motors rose from the belly of the ship, dull and monotonous. A dreary moon sailed in the cloudless sky and a warm wind scattered the smoke rising from the smokestack.

At 1:52 A.M., the order was given to attack. The British sailors were ordered to increase speed and the destroyers shrank the distance. Bright spotlights were trained on the decks of the *Exodus* and flooded the ship in a blinding light. The loudspeakers split the air and drowned out the roar of the waves.

"Stop at once!" echoed the warning in English. "You have illegally entered the territorial waters of Palestine."

At these words, Ike Aaronovitch's face turned red with anger.

"Dammit!" he shouted. "They're lying. We're still in international waters. They have no right to stop us here!" Every seaman knows that stopping a boat outside of territorial waters is an international crime. The British didn't care. They were determined to stop the *Exodus* no matter what.

Ike stood in the pilot's cabin, his hands angrily gripping the wheel. Yossi Hamburger was standing next to him, just as furious. He was certain the British would do anything to stop them, even if international law didn't allow it.

"If you won't stop," the loudspeakers went on thundering, "we shall be forced to come up on your deck, to arrest all of you and take the ship to Haifa."

Hamburger rushed to the radio cabin and ordered the radio operator to broadcast an answer to Commander Gregson, in charge of the British operation:

> *On the deck of this ship,* Exodus 47, *are more than 4,500 men, women, and children whose only crime, apparently, is that they are Jews. We are ascending to our Land on our own and not by the grace of anyone. We have nothing against your sailors and officers, but unfortunately, those people have been chosen to carry out a policy that doesn't concern them. Never will we recognize the law that*

prevents Jews from ascending to their homeland. We are the last ones who want to shed blood, but you must understand that we will not go willingly to a concentration camp, even a British one. I warn you that you will be personally responsible for every incident of firing into a crowd of defenseless and unarmed people or children.

Commander Gregson's reply was brief:

We are acting on orders we received. A commando unit is about to board the ship. Let them tow you to Haifa. Do not resist, I repeat: for your own good, do not resist.

Ike spun the wheel and turned the prow of the ship back to the open sea, to remove any doubt that the *Exodus* was sailing in international waters. Minister John Grauel turned on the siren and dejection spread among the thousands of passengers.

The siren shook Gertruda's body. She sat up straight in bed and looked anxiously at Michael who was sound asleep. The passengers began streaming onto the deck and she hesitated to leave the child and hurry there with all the others. A woman with a baby in the next bed said: "I'll watch him. You can go."

"Thank you," said Gertruda, and she rushed to the deck.

With a deafening wail of sirens, two destroyers approached the *Exodus*. By the light of tracers shot incessantly by the British, the pale faces of the soldiers could be seen as they prepared to assault. At the front stood the commandos in green uniforms, wearing white hats and gas masks, leather gloves and life vests. Submachine guns were hanging on their chests, guns and bayonets in their belts. Behind them were soldiers in khaki, wearing helmets and also armed with submachine guns.

Hundreds of survivors streamed onto the deck, determined to repel the attacks. They threw canned goods, bottles, and pieces of metal at the soldiers. The English responded with ice-cold jets of water.

And then, unexpectedly, the destroyers began to retreat. For a few moments, it seemed that the resistance had worked and the expected attack had been restrained. Victory cheers resounded on the deck of the *Exodus,* but they were premature. Withdrawing the destroyers had been calculated in advance. They increased the distance between them and the *Exodus* only to gather speed and ram her harder. With groans of panic, the passengers of the *Exodus* watched the big metal monsters gallop toward them. In a wink, the steel prows of the destroyers shook the body of the *Exodus* and hundreds of people on deck fell from the force of the blows. The shattering of wood and metal filled the air. Through the few breaches, seawater began entering the belly of the ship.

Simultaneously, British soldiers tried to lay nets on the deck of the illegal immigrant ship to attack it. Four attempts were repelled by the passengers, who managed to put the nets in the water with dozens of soldiers on them. Among the waves, flashlights of distress of the British began to burgeon, fluttering in the water until they were picked up by the lifeboats.

One of the destroyers stretched a gangplank to the deck of the *Exodus* and a few commandos leaped on board. Two more destroyers tried to hook on to the ship. One failed. The other did succeed, but only two hours later. Over the scaffolds, British soldiers tossed smoke grenades and tear-gas bombs to the decks teeming with passengers. Submachine guns were shot into the air.

On orders from Aliyah Bet on the eve of the ship's departure, no weapons were brought on deck. The resistance of the immigrants was supposed to be unarmed, but no one could guarantee that the British wouldn't open fire. And so, Molotov cocktails and smoke bombs had been prepared in secret places on the *Exodus* and hopes were riding on the effectiveness of the hose to spray boiling hot steam on the British soldiers.

When the soldiers began lobbing smoke grenades and tear-gas bombs, the passengers were furious and counterattacked, tossing the Molotov cocktails and smoke bombs at the British. They tried to spray boiling steam, but the hose didn't work. Instead, they brought pots full of boiling oil to spray at the decks of the destroyers clinging to the ship, but the wind blew the oil back to the *Exodus* and her decks became slippery. Many people slipped and fell on the surface that turned black with the filthy oil. Gertruda stumbled a few times, but finally managed to get to her position. Two passengers stood there with iron poles. One of them handed her a pole.

Close to forty British soldiers were already on the deck of the *Exodus*. Ike accelerated and the ship sailed in a twisted path to get away from the destroyers and make it hard for the others to get on board.

A platoon of soldiers hurried to the engine room to stop the ship, but the iron grates and the locked doors kept them out. Four commandos made their way among the masses of immigrants to the wheel and bludgeoned anyone who tried to stand in their way. Some passengers were struck. One of the commandos screamed, "Move or I'll shoot!" When three of them finally broke into the pilot's cabin, they beat Ike's first mate, Bill Bernstein, until he was bloody. Ike dragged him out to get first aid. The rest of the crew also slipped out of the cabin, locked the door, and imprisoned the three commandos. On the deck, beaten and injured, despairing of the possibility of taking control of the ship, the British opened their safety catches and started shooting in every direction. Fifteen-year-old Zvi Yacobovitch was wounded in the head by a submachine gun salvo when he waved a blue-and-white flag. He lost consciousness and his blood stained the flag. Dozens of wounded collapsed after him on the deck.

The destroyers continued their ramming, and in the hold on the lower deck, children fell out of their beds when the destroyer banged the side of the ship. Water began spraying inside and panicky shrieks were heard on every side. The engine room was flooding with seawater and dozens of passengers were called there to empty the water using buckets.

The resistance of the immigrants was bolder than the British had expected. When the Molotov cocktails and smoke bombs ran out, they attacked nonstop with a hail of metal trash, pegs, screws, nails, bottles, canned goods, and potatoes. They chased the soldiers and tried to take their weapons. Gertruda took an active part in the resistance. She blocked the way to the lifeboats where a group of soldiers was hurrying to take control of the deck. One of them pushed her coarsely. Gertruda stumbled and hurt her ankle. She swallowed a groan of pain and looked helplessly at the blood flowing from the wound. Medics were taking care of those who were wounded more seriously than she, and she didn't dare call for help. Suddenly somebody came toward her. She lifted her eyes. "Don't worry," said Minister Grauel. "I'll take care of you." Before she could respond, he tore a strip of cloth from the bottom of his shirt and bandaged her ankle. The battle raged all around, the soldiers were making their way with rifle blows, the healthy immigrants kept lobbing objects and scraps of food at them, and the wounded were wailing in pain.

"I've got to help the other wounded." Grauel stood up. "Be careful. I'll check in on you later on."

Four British soldiers finally managed to get onto the lifeboats. One of them began shooting in every direction. One of the survivors hurried there and cut the ropes that held the boats to their cranes. The boats dropped onto a group of soldiers who had just landed on the deck. Six of them were wounded and yelled for help.

Meanwhile, furious passengers who surrounded the pilot's cabin demanded a lynching of the soldiers imprisoned there. Minister Grauel hurried to the cabin with an American flag wound around his body. The group, which respected him, let him in. Grauel brought the three commandos out of the cabin, threw their weapons into the sea, and asked them to leave the ship.

In the hold where the women and children were huddled, there was panic. The thunder of the banging, the shattering of the shots, and the shrill shouts of the wounded stirred great fear there. Hysterical women yelled at the sight of the wounded and some even tried to hoist a white flag in surrender.

Michael ran to the deck to look for Gertruda. One of the passengers saw him and forced him back to the cabin. He curled up on his bed, frightened, and prayed for the battle to end and Gertruda to come back to him safe and sound.

A few hours after the battle began, before dawn, all the commanders of the operation gathered in the headquarters of the British navy. On information from the field, the British realized they had failed. Very few soldiers had managed to get to the illegal immigrant ship; some were captured by the raging mob, and some were captured and imprisoned in isolated cabins and had no contact with their commanders. The assault gangplanks placed by the British destroyers were damaged during the action, and the possibility of landing more soldiers on the deck of the surrounded ship was very slim.

What the British weren't aware of was that on the other side of the barricade, on the deck of the *Exodus,* many thought that the British, at least at that hour, had won a victory. The ship was in terrible shape. British soldiers who had taken over the pilot's cabin, the map room, and the navigational equipment prevented any possibility of steering the ship. There was also a fear that the punctures in the flanks of the boat would sink it. Ike moved to the back pilot's cabin and ordered an acceleration. The ship increased speed and Ike hurled it in a zigzag pattern to prevent the British destroyers from approaching.

Conditions on the *Exodus* deteriorated further. After the long and exhausting battle, hundreds of passengers were lying on the deck helpless, some of them wounded and bleeding. Only about thirty of them were still upright. The condition of the wounded grew worse and some of them needed urgent blood transfusions to save their lives. Dr. Joshua Cohen, a young doctor from Scotland who had volunteered to join the crew, took care of them indefatigably with a team of nurses recruited from among the immigrants. When he realized how serious their condition was, he hurried to the commander of the ship, Yossi Hamburger, who was with Ike in the back pilot's cabin. In the distance, the lights of the settlements of the coastal plain were sparkling. The Promised Land was within reach.

Dr. Cohen wiped sweat from his brow and said in a gloomy voice: "One of those badly wounded is a boy named Zvi Yacobovitch. He's an orphan who survived the Holocaust and was wounded while repelling the British soldiers. His older brother is standing next to his bed screaming hysterically. The wounded boy is the only one he has left in the world. If Zvi isn't taken care of immediately in a hospital, he'll die here on the deck."

Those in the cabin knew what that meant. Sending the wounded to the hospital could be done only by the British. If the commander of the *Exodus* was forced to request the evacuation of the wounded by the British, it would be a sign of surrender, the end of the resistance.

"How many mortally wounded do you have?" Yossi Hamburger asked the doctor.

"At least three."

Hamburger glanced at Ike. The captain's face was pale. He shrugged helplessly.

"Those people didn't survive the Holocaust to die here," said Hamburger gloomily. "I'll contact the British."

No one appealed his decision.

At dawn, the communications officer on the deck of the *Charity* handed the commander of the British destroyers a wire from the illegal immigrant ship. Commander Gregson was dejected; he knew it would be hard for him to explain to his superiors the meaning of the failed attack he had conducted. But as he scanned Yossi Hamburger's wire, he knew that the tide had turned. For the first time since the attack had begun, the British commander breathed a sigh of relief. At long last, the *Exodus* surrendered.

Gregson sent a reply demanding that the illegal immigrant ship stop. With tears in his eyes, Ike shut down the motors. At five-fifteen A.M., a British boat came alongside the ship, and a medical team climbed the rope ladder. The British were stunned at the sight that met their eyes: strewn over the deck were large quantities of canned goods and food that had rained down on the soldiers only a few hours before. Some of the members of the medical team hurried to gather up as many canned goods as they could carry. There was strict rationing in Britain at that time, and they intended to send the food home.

Dr. Cohen led them to the wing set aside for the wounded. There were three mortally wounded there, and 270 more with varying degrees of serious injuries. The British doctor called for more physicians and two boats brought medical teams to the *Exodus*. Twenty British soldiers also boarded the ship to make sure the battle wouldn't start again.

On orders from the commander of the fleet, the ship began making its way to Haifa. At nightfall, the ship sent a wire to UNSCOP, the international committee investigating the problem of the Land of Israel, whose members were in Palestine at that time:

Dear Sirs,

We appeal to you with a request to come take testimony from the 4,500 refugees on the ship the Exodus. *Please see with your own eyes our ship, our suffering and our efforts to reach the shores of our homeland. See with your own eyes the ruthlessness of the British who try to banish us from the shores of Palestine to put us in concentration camps with barbed wire that remind us constantly of the concentration camps we were imprisoned in under the Nazis in Europe.*

At seven-thirty in the morning, after a sleepless night filled with sadness and weeping, the ship sent to the Hebrew *Yishuv* in the Land of Israel the following announcement:

As a result of the losses, we are forced to sail at full speed to Haifa to take off the dying and the seriously wounded. The

second reason for our sailing to Haifa: the ship is damaged
and water is penetrating it. We are forced to stop sailing in
our desired direction. The ship is in danger of sinking along
with the 4,500 passengers on it.

Close to four in the afternoon, on July 19, 1947, the immigrant ship crept toward Haifa accompanied by eight British warships. At the railing, weeping bitterly in despair and disappointment, stood Gertruda, waving the flag stained with the blood of Zvi Yacobovitch.

9.

Like a beached whale, the *Exodus* slowly approached the port. British war ships and patrol boats didn't release it even after it passed the breakwater. By command of the British army, the passengers of the ship were to stay in the hold and not go up on deck before receiving a specific order. Dozens of commandos on the ship tried to make sure the order would be carried out. They blocked the hatches, threatened with weapons, but there were too few of them facing many who streamed onto the decks, waving blue-and-white flags, and singing "Ha-Tikvah" in loud voices. Many of the immigrants wept bitterly.

Facing them, on the slopes of the Carmel, the white houses of Haifa shone in the summer sun. The survivors looked longingly at the city. This should have been the gate of their entrance to Palestine, but they knew they would only see it from a distance. On the roofs of the houses and the tops of the mountain, thousands of residents watched excitedly as the *Exodus* limped to port. Many of them had friends and relatives on the ship. The hope of soon reuniting with them vanished. Here and there, a poster condemning the British was seen; shouts of protest were heard. There, too, among the big crowd on land, were quite a few who sobbed bitterly.

The tugboats of the port were tied to the *Exodus* and pulled her to the dock. Not far away, on the left, the gloomy fleet of illegal immigrant ships that had previously been captured by the British were anchored, their smokestacks cold, their windows dusty, the ropes of their anchors slack. When the *Exodus* was emptied of its passengers, she too would be moved there.

At four-thirty in the afternoon the *Exodus* was tied to the main dock of the port. Next to her were anchored three British ships of evacuation, the *Empire Rival,* the *Runnymede Park,* and the *Ocean Vigour,* which were to take the immigrants. Between the dock and the port stretched coils of barbed wire. Units of guards and soldiers of the Transjordan Legion were posted there to prevent escape. Hundreds of "anemones"—British paratroopers wearing red berets, elite airborne fighters who had fought heroically behind the German lines in the war—boarded the ship, blocked the passages, and locked the latrines. Flyers in four languages distributed to the passengers of the *Exodus* demanded that they disembark without resistance:

> We are about to take you to Cyprus. Your baggage will be taken
> by the soldiers and will be returned to you when we get there.
> Your cameras can stay with you, but all film will be examined.
> If you have letters to your friends and relatives in Palestine, you
> can give them to the soldiers and we promise they will get to
> their address.

The mood was despondent. The faces of the passengers fell, couples hugged each other, parents clutched their children to their bosoms, and Gertruda calmed the furious Michael: "Don't worry; Cyprus is only a way station to the Land of Israel. A little patience and we'll get to Tel Aviv."

First the murdered were taken off, including fifteen-year-old Zvi Yakobovitch, who did not survive his injury, and Bill Bernstein, Ike's first mate. They were taken on stretchers, only half covered to give the impression that they were merely wounded, so as not to attract the attention of the press photographers who were taking pictures of the evacuation of the *Exodus*. But the refugees weren't fooled. Protests rose among the thousands of passengers on the ship. "There are murdered men here!" they shouted to the journalists. "Don't let them hide them!" The British quickly covered the bodies.

After the murdered men, in stretchers or leaning on doctors and nurses of the ship's crew and the British army, the wounded and the sick were taken to the military hospitals in Haifa and the internment camp in Athlit. Then, by order of the British officers in stiff uniforms, carrying polished wood sticks under their arms, the operation of disembarking the rest of the refugees began. Most of them resisted and the British used force to evacuate them. The sturdy soldiers had no trouble evacuating the exhausted Holocaust survivors.

A shudder of emotion went through the bodies of the immigrants when their feet landed on the dock, on the soil of the desired Land. Many knelt and kissed the ground.

On the ship itself, behind locked doors in the storerooms of the lower deck, Yossi Hamburger and Ike Aaronovitch remained along with the other Haganah members who had played vital roles on the *Exodus*. They were hiding from the British for fear they would be arrested as soon as they got off the ship. Soldiers carefully combed the ship, but didn't discover them.

Deep in the water under the ship, dull explosions were suddenly heard. From the decks of the British guard boats sailing around the ship, sailors were placing sea grenades into the water of the port to keep Palmach divers from trying to sabotage the evacuation ships and prevent them from sailing.

Long lines of immigrants wound around the entrances of big tents. They were brought inside in groups of ten. In one of the tents, there was a strict body search for concealed weapons. In the other tent, they were sprayed with DDT. They were then hustled off to the evacuation ships. When one was filled, the other began boarding on the gangplank.

The sun set in the sea, evening fell, and big searchlights illuminated the dock. Minister Grauel stood next to Gertruda and Michael, in the line at the tent. A British soldier examined Gertruda's documents and looked at her sternly.

"You're not a Jew," he said. "What are you doing here?"

The officer demanded an explanation and she told him.

"You can stay in Palestine," he said.

"And Michael?"

"He'll be evacuated to Cyprus like the rest of the Jews. Don't worry. We'll take proper care of him."

She shook her head no. "I won't leave him alone," she declared. "I'll stay with him."

The officer shrugged. "As you like," he said indifferently.

Now it was Minister Grauel's turn. The British leafed through his American passport and asked why he was on the ship.

"I volunteered to help them," said the minister.

"What you did is a crime," claimed the officer.

"Helping poor people isn't against the law."

"But the attempt to break through into our territorial waters without permission is definitely a crime. I'll have to arrest you."

Minister Grauel parted from Gertruda emotionally and hugged Michael affectionately. "I'll never forget you," he said.

Two guards were called to the examination tent. They confiscated Grauel's documents and informed him that he would be interned in a hotel in Haifa until a decision was made to try him or deport him.

They got into a jeep, passed through the military barricades, and left the port. The jeep climbed the road up the mountain and stopped at the entrance to Hotel Savoy. Grauel was sent to the reception desk, where the two guards didn't take their eyes off him.

The reception clerk gave Grauel a registration form. At the line for address, the minister wrote "The *Exodus*." The clerk looked at him with interest.

"You're from the ship?" he whispered.

"Yes."

"The hotel bar is full of foreign journalists. They came to write about the *Exodus* and the British won't let them get near the ship. They'd love to talk with you."

Grauel got a key. "I'll be in my room," he said to his guards.

"Okay. Don't you dare leave the hotel. We've got orders to stay here as long as you're in the hotel."

"I'm tired," said the minister. "I'm going to sleep."

He turned to the staircase, but instead of going up, he went down to the bar, where a group of journalists was sitting. Grauel went to them. "I'm from the *Exodus*," he said and they stormed him. Cameras flashed and notebooks were pulled out. Grauel learned that the group represented all the major newspapers in the world. He told them about the ship's journey of hardships, the blockade in the middle of the sea, the bold resistance, the killed and wounded. They feverishly wrote his words. This was precisely the material they had been seeking.

Two American journalists told him: "You've got to tell all this to the UN commission." The commission, composed of representatives of eleven countries and set up to check the situation in the Land of Israel and to suggest possible solutions to the UN, was staying at the Eden Hotel in Jerusalem. Grauel said that he was in fact interned and that his guards were in the hotel lobby. He doubted if he could go to Jerusalem; but the American journalists, smelling a good story, said they would find a way to sneak him out. The three of them slipped him out the back door of the hotel and into a car. On the way to Jerusalem, the British stopped them at roadblocks, but the Americans waved their journalistic credentials and the soldiers let them go on.

After sixty hours with no sleep, Grauel was exhausted and could barely stand on his feet. Nevertheless, he knew he couldn't rest now. Every minute was precious. All the information he could give the members of the commission was vital. They were surprised to see him. They ordered dinner for him, and for the next three hours they questioned him about all the details of the wretched journey of the ship. At the end, they told him he had made quite an impression on them.

CHAPTER 11

A Promise Kept

1.

Battered and abandoned, the *Exodus* remained at the dock and, with British permission, a cleaning crew boarded to clean the filth and clear away the wreckage. The Haganah members hiding there asked the cleaning crew to smuggle them out of the port. A few of the cleaning crew left the boat and went down to the company offices. They came back with Ogen company work clothes and the Haganah members put them on and hurried off the ship, one at a time, before the eyes of the British guards, carrying piles of garbage like the rest of the cleaning workers. Shortly after that, there was no one left at port.

The three evacuation ships—the *Empire Rival, Ocean Vigour,* and *Runnymede Park*—were packed with passengers from the *Exodus* and sailed to the open sea. Thousands of desperate evacuees crowded on their decks and gazed at the shore of Haifa as it grew distant. They turned to their British escort and asked for information about conditions in the transit camps in Cyprus.

"You'll be very comfortable there" was the answer they received.

"How long will we be there?"

"A few weeks, no more."

The ships made their way on the sea. The weather was fine and the sea was calm. For a few hours the evacuation ships sailed north to Cyprus, and then an unexpected order came over the radio:

Change course. Go to France, not Cyprus.

The pilots of the evacuation ships immediately changed course and turned left.

A few days earlier, the British had decided in absolute secrecy to return the illegal immigrants to where they had come from. By returning the refugees to France, they wanted to set an important precedent for future illegal immigrant ships: no longer internment in Cyprus, but return to the port of departure.

The three evacuation ships kept to their new course. Conditions on these ships were hard for the passengers. Difficult but bearable living conditions had prevailed on the *Exodus:* these conditions were much worse. The refugees had to sleep on the iron floor, each of them was given only one blanket, and they had only the clothes on their backs—they had been forced to leave all their belongings at the port of Haifa. Given only meager food, one ship protested with a hunger strike.

2.

As the evacuation ships approached Porte-de-Boque, on the French coast, thousands of Jews, members of organizations and youth movements, began streaming to the town, waving posters in Hebrew and Yiddish at the ship: DON'T DISEMBARK! There were also posters in French aimed at the lenses of the journalists' cameras.

The immigrants on the decks of the three British ships, who heard that the French had tried to tempt them to disembark and stay in France, also prepared gigantic posters and waved them as they approached the port: FRANCE, THANK YOU, BUT WE WANT THE LAND OF ISRAEL.

Hundreds of journalists packed the docks of the small town. Big groups of Jewish youth movement members danced folk dances and sang in the central square. From all over the region, onlookers came to the town to see the immigrants of the *Exodus* with their own eyes. The cafés and restaurants overlooking the port were filled.

Officials of the French government boarded the three ships and offered permits for unlimited stay in France to everyone who would agree to disembark, promising a fast track to French citizenship for those who did. A representative of the survivors said, "If you want to help us, send medicine and food." He rejected the offer to disembark.

Time passed slowly in Port-de-Boque in the heavy summer heat. The French government's efforts to persuade the passengers to get off the ships failed miserably. Ultimately, only 130 passengers, some of them sick, decided to disembark and stay in France.

The British knew they couldn't leave the evacuation ships in France forever. They considered their options and decided to transfer the immigrants to a camp in the British-occupied area of Germany, ignoring the sensibilities of those refugees returning to the country that had murdered so many of their families.

The order to sail to Germany was given on Friday evening, July 28. The immigrants could only protest and sing "Ha-Tikvah." The British weren't moved.

3.

In Germany, the evacuees were concentrated in camps Pependorf and Amstau near Lübeck and greeted by local residents with open hostility. As if no time had passed since the Nazis were in power, hatred of the Jews flourished again in full force and displeased the inmates of the camp. Every single day, the survivors encountered rejection and insult. In the cafés and restaurants of the towns near the camps, they were refused service and brawls with anti-Semitic innuendos constantly broke out. In the spa city of Reichenhall, the employees of one hotel wrote a song that began: "Too bad we didn't kill enough Jews."

In mid-March 1948, two months before the British army left the Land of Israel, the borders were still closed to illegal immigrants. The evacuees of the *Exodus* finally lost patience. They detested the camps in Germany and found it hard to bear the difficult memories they felt there. They demanded that the Haganah agents do everything they could to get them to Palestine. To ease their oppression a little, the Haganah decided to launch an operation to guarantee that at least some of the immigrants would get there. About one thousand of them, including Gertruda and Michael, were chosen to trick the British and slip into Palestine without being arrested. They were outfitted with colorful summer clothing, cameras, and lots of chewing gum, taught a few useful sentences in English, and given forged travel documents. At the port of Hamburg, they boarded the grand ship *Transylvania* for a Mediterranean cruise and were ordered to behave like tourists. None of the other passengers already on the ship realized that not a single member of the big noisy group of tourists was actually an American citizen. After four days at sea, the ship anchored in the port of Haifa where buses waited to take the disguised immigrants on a day tour to the holy sites. On the docks stood British soldiers, glancing at them indifferently. Among them, Gertruda recognized some of the officers who had conducted the evacuation of the passengers of the *Exodus* only a few months earlier. None of them recognized her.

Instead of going to the holy sites, the buses turned to the Carmel and the passengers were scattered in various hotels. The *Transylvania* waited a few hours past sailing time, and finally sailed without them.

4.

Isaac Trubovitch, a relative of Michael Stolowitzky, had tears in his eyes when Gertruda told him on the phone that Michael had come to Palestine. He went to the hotel in Haifa where they were staying, hugged both of them warmly, and took them to Tel Aviv in his Ford.

Trubovitch was a well-to-do businessman, owner of a cooking oil factory. He owned the house at Weisel Street 6 in north Tel Aviv and gave the roof apartment to the nanny and the now eleven-year-old child. At long last, after years of hardships and wandering, the two of them had found a home: a big apartment, clean bedsheets, lavish meals, and warmth.

On their second evening in the Land of Israel, Gertruda told Michael about the death of his father. The boy burst into tears, hugged his nanny, and said, "Don't ever leave me."

"I promise," she said, and also burst into tears.

The next day, Gertruda and Michael went wandering around Tel Aviv. They walked hand in hand along the boardwalk on the sea, ate falafel in the Yemenite neighborhood, and enjoyed ice cream in Café Whitman on Allenby Street. Michael was interested in what was going on around him and hugged Gertruda every chance he got. She was glad to see the fear gone from his eyes for the first time.

In the evening, Michael sat down at the table and wrote the following letter:

April 1948

My Mamusha,

My heart is full of love for you and great gratitude for everything you've done for me. I know you needed a lot of strength and faith to go through the dreadful war with me. You taught me things that will stay with me all my life. You taught me that if you believe, there is hope. You were a mother and a friend to me and a guardian angel, and I hope we'll always be together and you'll always stay with me as you have.

I don't know if I can reward you for everything you've done, but I hope I can. Now it's my turn to watch over you, to make sure you'll always be happy, in spite of all the difficulties in store for us.

I'll never forget.

Love,
Your Michael

A week had passed since Gertruda and Michael came to Palestine. One morning, Sonya, Michael's uncle's wife, called Gertruda for a private conversation. The two women went to Sonya's room and closed the door.

"You know how grateful we are that you saved Michael," said Sonya. "From now on this is his home. What are your plans?"

"I want Michael to go to school, learn to speak Hebrew. I want him to have friends, to be like one of the Israeli children."

"And what about you?"

"I'll be with him, of course," said Gertruda.

"Are you sure you'll feel comfortable here? After all, you're not a Jew and everybody here is. Aside from that, Michael now has a family; he'll grow up and won't need you anymore."

"I don't understand," said Gertruda.

"What I want to offer," said Sonya, "is that maybe you should think about returning home, to your parents. We'll give you money, of course, for the ticket, and for your arrangements when you arrive. That will be better for you."

Gertruda looked at her a long time, trying to digest what she had said.

"I'm not sure that Michael will want me to disappear from his life suddenly," she said.

"He's a child; he doesn't know yet exactly what he wants."

Gertruda stood up.

"Thank you, Mrs. Trubovitch," she said. "But there's one thing you might not have taken into account. Ever since Michael's mother died, I've been his mother. I never left him and I won't leave him now."

She had absolutely no doubt that, to her dying day, she wouldn't desert her child.

5.

There was something Gertruda thought she had to do. She wanted to locate SS officer Karl Rink and send him a letter of thanks for saving their lives. For months she met with survivors of Vilna and Kovno ghettoes and heard testimony from them about Karl Rink's various rescue acts. From one of them, Moshe Segelson, she learned to her surprise that Rink had been married to a Jew and that his daughter lived in a kibbutz in the Galilee.

Trying to locate Elisheva-Helga Rink, Gertruda went to the diplomatic representatives of the United States, France, Britain, and the Soviet Union in Israel, with the same letter:

Greetings,

I, Gertruda Babilinska, Weisel Street 6 in Tel Aviv, testify that, during the world war, I took care of the Jewish child Michael Stolowitzky of Warsaw, and managed to save him from hell and bring him to the Land of Israel. Only by a miracle were the two of us saved from death by the Germans after Mr. Karl Rink, a senior SS officer in Vilna, prevented the Germans from revealing Michael's Judaism and arresting us. I have no doubt that he risked his own life with that act.

I understand that Mr. Rink was married to a Jew and has a daughter in the Land of Israel.

I don't know where Mr. Rink is now, but I feel obligated to inform you of the facts in the hope that you will forward them to the proper address and perhaps they might mitigate his punishment as an SS man during the war.

Sincerely,
Gertruda Babilinska

6.

One morning in the summer of 1949, after months of trying to locate her, Gertruda and Michael took a bus to Kfar Giladi to meet with the daughter of SS officer Karl Rink. Elisheva Rink was a charming twenty-four-year-old woman married to Mendel Bernson, a Palmach fighter from Kibbutz Ashdot Ya'akov. A young mother herself, she worked as a nurse in the kibbutz children's house and none of the members of Kfar Giladi knew about her parents. She never talked about them. The wounds of the war were still fresh and she feared that it would be hard for the kibbutz to accept the fact that her father had served in the SS. So she received Gertruda and Michael without telling anyone about it.

Gertruda and Michael sat in her room after she finished working. A cool wind brought fragrances of flowers, and children were heard shouting with joy in the distance. Elisheva told them that correspondence with her father had stopped at the beginning of the war and had resumed only recently. She read them a letter from her father sent through Switzerland just before the end of the war, in February 1944.

The last weeks have been very hard for us. The enemy force has grown incessantly and we experience one defeat after another. If things go on like this, the war will end in a few months and the victory won't be ours. I found myself in a brutal war that turned us into human beasts. I'm often ashamed of what my comrades have done. Recently, I have joined searches for Jews who haven't yet been caught. I did that deliberately although, in fact, I didn't have to participate in those raids. My

purpose was to save as many Jews as possible from the cruel fate
in store for them in the concentration camps and I was glad I
managed to do that now and then.

Elisheva talked at length about her father, his pleasant nature, and his devotion to his family. She talked about the disappearance of her mother and her own travels until she reached the kibbutz.

After the war was over, she said, her father began writing to her regularly. Karl Rink managed to avoid being arrested and tried. He found work in a dye factory in Berlin and lived alone in an old one-room apartment.

As he wrote his daughter in one of his last letters:

If there's one thing that fills all my thoughts, it's the hope that
someday we can see each other again. I have framed the picture
of your little family that you sent me. I hung it over my bed
along with the picture of your mother and I dream about you
almost every night. I would be willing to visit you in the kibbutz,
but I'm afraid I would be put on trial because of my role in the
SS. If there are Jews who would be willing to testify that I saved
them and your government would promise not to arrest me,
I would gladly come.

Gertruda gave Elisheva a copy of the letter she had sent to the diplomatic representatives in Israel. "I'm willing to testify for him," she said emotionally. "I very much want your father to come here so that Michael and I can thank him in person."

"I'll write him about that," said Elisheva. "He'll be very happy."

7.

Gertruda wasn't content to simply send letters about Karl Rink to the embassies. She went to the Ministry of Justice in Jerusalem to make sure in person that the visit of former SS Rink would take place without any glitches. The officials listened to her story in amazement, wrote down her testimony, and told her explicitly that she could tell Karl Rink he would be a welcome guest in Israel and that he could come and go in peace as long as he liked.

Elisheva wrote to her father and soon got a letter from him:

My dear daughter,
   Thanks for the encouraging news. Reading the details of your letter, I remembered Mrs. Gertruda Babilinska and the boy who was with her. I'm glad she worked to clear away the obstacles in the way of my visit to Israel. I do plan to visit your kibbutz on the first vacation I get from my job, apparently next Christmas.

Gertruda was very excited to hear from Elisheva about her father's expected visit. She promised to bake a cake and come with Michael the day after Karl Rink arrived.

Elisheva hoped that when her father came to the kibbutz, the members could hear from him about what he had done during the war, especially about saving Jews. For the time being, except for her husband, she didn't tell anyone about the expected visit.

In another letter Karl Rink wrote his daughter, on November 4, he said that he had already ordered plane tickets to Israel and would come on December 24. "You can, of course, imagine how excited I am to see you," he wrote. "I'm counting the hours to my flight to Israel."

She wrote him that she would meet him at the airport and that her husband and little daughter would also come.

On December 20, Elisheva Rink received a telegram from Germany:

> *We regret to inform you that Mr. Karl Rink died in the hospital in Berlin from a heart attack and was buried in the cemetery Friedhof Schonberg. Please accept our sincere condolences.*
>
>
>
> *Sincerely,*
> *Johan Reichtat, secretary*
> *Berlin City Hall*
>
>

8.

Life in the Trubovitch house was comfortable, but Gertruda wanted to live independently, find her own apartment, and pay her own and Michael's way. In time, she and the child moved to a small apartment in Jaffa. She worked cleaning houses all day long to support herself and to pay his tuition. After a while, she sent him to a boarding school in the youth village of Ben Shemen. He was the only light in her life. Every Saturday, she went to visit him and bring him the chocolate he loved; she would sit next to him and listen eagerly to his stories of school. In the youth village, where they called him Mike, the principal and the teachers treated her as his mother, called her to parents' meetings, and reported to her on his academic progress. She didn't miss a single class

Gertruda and Michael. Ben Shemen,
Israel, 1949.

party or graduation and Michael's friends were sure she was his
mother.

Every Sunday, she went to church in Jaffa and met for coffee
with the new friends she had met in Israel. Like her, they spoke
German or Polish, and to the end of her life she didn't learn Hebrew. She had a widower suitor her friend introduced her to, a poor
clerk, educated and well-mannered. Gertruda enjoyed his company,
but when he proposed marriage, she turned him down. She had
gotten used to being single and didn't want to bring anyone into her
life except the child she had saved from death.

But Gertruda worried about Michael's future. It seemed to her
that as time passed, it would be more difficult for her to work so
hard, her income would decrease, and her ability to support the boy
would diminish. She was haunted by the idea that, in Poland and
Switzerland, there was a large fortune waiting for Michael, big sums

left by his father. She wanted to appeal to a lawyer to restore Michael's rights, but she didn't have money to pay him. Finally, she recalled the diamond merchant Isaac Geller, the neighbor of the Stolowitzky family in Warsaw. She hoped he was still alive, and she wrote him at his home address in Warsaw, Ujazdowska Avenue 15.

A month later, she got an answer. Geller wrote that he had escaped from Vilna to Siberia and back to Warsaw after the war ended. His wife had died from a serious illness and his children were living with him. Because of the economic distress he had encountered under the Communist regime in Poland, he would apparently be forced to leave his house soon and move to a modest apartment.

He wrote:

I shall try to locate the wealth of the Stolowitzky family and will let you know soon.

Gertruda waited impatiently for Geller's updated report. And indeed, after a long time, another letter came:

Unfortunately, I don't have good news. It turns out that the Stolowitzky family house on Ujazdowska Avenue was confiscated by the Polish government for its offices there. All the wealth and bank accounts of Jews missing from the state have also been confiscated. Under these circumstances, I don't think Michael can get a single zloty.

Gertruda was shocked. She read the letter over and over and decided to hide the contents from Michael so as not to cause him more pain.

CHAPTER 12

Following the Money

1.

After his discharge from the Israeli army, Michael worked at various jobs to save money and locate his father's wealth. For that purpose, he traveled to Zurich, arrived there in mid-June 1958, and went straight to the posh offices of the Credit Bank, where an elderly official greeted Michael with a generous smile and asked him to take a seat.

"How can I help you?"

"My father had an account at this bank," said Michael.

"I'm glad to hear that."

"He died in the war and I'm his heir."

Michael took out an order of inheritance issued by a court in Israel after Jacob Stolowitzky's name was found in a list of those killed in Auschwitz and after Gertruda presented Lydia's death certificate. The official read the order carefully and looked at the visitor.

"You said your father, Jacob Stolowitzky, has an account in our bank? Do you have a document confirming that?"

"No," said Michael. "I only know that my mother said my father had an account here."

"Let me check," said the official.

He left the room and returned a short time later.

"I'm sorry," he said. "I checked everywhere and we don't have any account in your father's name. Maybe he deposited the money in another bank."

Michael looked at him in amazement.

"He did deposit money in other banks, too," he said. "But my mother remembered only your bank. She said Father deposited a lot of money with you before the war . . . before he died in a concentration camp."

The official's face remained frozen. The young man facing him wasn't the only one who had searched for inheritances of family members killed in the war. War orphans and bereaved spouses frequently came to the bank, sure they would leave there very rich. They were usually aided by batteries of lawyers, but few of them located the accounts their relatives had opened before the war.

"One of the possibilities, of course, is that before his death, your father closed the account and took the money," said the official.

Michael sat still. It couldn't be, he thought; there must be some mistake. His mother did tell Gertruda explicitly that the money was in this bank. She was fully aware at the time and left no doubt that she knew exactly what she was talking about. If his father did indeed close the account and take out the money, he must have had a good reason for it. How could it be that his mother didn't know that the account was closed? And if the money was taken out without her knowing it, who was it transferred to? Who did he enrich and why?

The official looked at him sympathetically.

"Mr. Stolowitzky," he said, "as I told you, we have no listing of an account in your father's name. But I really want to believe you that the money was deposited with us. If your father didn't take out the money and close the account, the only possibility is that your father had a secret numbered account with us."

"Meaning?"

"Many people deposited their money in unnamed accounts and used some number, sometimes a series of letters that meant something only to the depositor. Money can be withdrawn from the account only by someone who knows the secret number. Do you know your father's code number?"

Of course he didn't. His mother probably didn't know it either when she told Gertruda on her deathbed about that bank.

"What should I do?" Michael asked with increasing despair.

"Your father was apparently a rich man. Many rich people who deposited their money here hired a local lawyer or accountant to take care of their affairs. Your father may also have had somebody like that. Try to find him and get the information from him."

A spark of hope was kindled in Michael's eyes.

"How can I find that man?" he asked.

"Unfortunately, I can't help you with that."

"So, what should I do?"

"Try to get proof," the official advised him. "That's the only thing you can do. Without proof of the existence of the account, we can't help you."

2.

Michael stumbled out of the bank. He sat down on a bench in the street and felt like a little boy who had lost his way and was wandering in a thick forest, not knowing where to turn. If he had the

money, he might have hired a lawyer to fight for him. In his situation, with his little bit of money running out, he could rely only on
himself.

His task seemed complicated, almost impossible. Where would
he get proof of the existence of the account? Who would know
about that account except for his father and mother, who were no
longer alive? Nevertheless, he was determined to do whatever he
could to get the money, and he didn't intend to return to Israel
empty-handed.

At last he came up with an idea that didn't seem promising, but
was his only option. He went to the Polish consulate in Zurich, presented his birth certificate, and requested a visa.

The clerk who distributed visas asked the purpose of his trip to
Poland.

"I'm looking for details to help me retrieve my father's inheritance," he said.

"Do you know anybody in Poland?" asked the clerk.

"My father had a lot of friends there—businessmen he worked
with, people who worked for him. Maybe one of them will help me."

"There's almost no chance you'll succeed," said the clerk. "Many
of them are probably dead."

He gave Michael a visa for a week. "Good luck," he said.

Michael arrived at the railroad station in Warsaw after an exhausting trip and looked around in surprise. Instead of the bustling
city teeming with life, shops, and cafés, he saw dull gray houses,
meager display windows of dark shops, few vehicles, and enormous
pictures of Lenin on street corners. Warsaw was dreary and unwel-
coming.

In the railroad station lavatory, he washed his face and shaved.
He asked for the address of the synagogue, where he hoped to find
a Jew who would rent him a room.

A handful of elderly Jews were praying in the synagogue on Tlo-mackie Street. Michael waited patiently until they finished their prayers and asked if he could rent a room from one of them. One of the old men asked where he came from. His reply sparked much interest. Only rarely did Israelis get permission to enter Poland, and the worshippers of the synagogue took advantage of the opportunity to ask a lot of questions about Israel. He asked them if they knew his father's name. The synagogue treasurer replied excitedly: "Of course. Jacob Stolowitzky paid for the repairs to our synagogue in 1938." Michael asked to meet with the people who had worked with his father and the treasurer promised to find out for him. He also offered Michael a room in his home for free.

The modest apartment was near the synagogue. The treasurer's wife gave the guest their own bedroom and she and her husband moved to the living room, which also served as a dining room. At the meager dinner, Michael told them he intended to explore his rights to the family mansion.

"Don't get your hopes up," said the treasurer sadly. "The house has probably been confiscated by the government, like other aban-doned Jewish houses. The Poles claim that every government office was blown up in the war and documents of ownership of many buildings were lost. If you don't have a document to prove your rights, you have almost no chance of getting the house or money for it."

This was another obstacle on the way to realizing his father's legacy, another reason to give up. Michael's heart was filled with deep grief when he thought that the pursuit of his father's money was getting away from him.

The next morning, he took the trolley to Ujazdowska Avenue 9. The mansion surrounded by the river hadn't changed very much, except for the Polish flag in the doorway and the pair of armed guards standing there. Through the windows, people could be seen bent over desks. Michael asked one of the guards what the building was used for. "That's the Ministry of Agriculture," the guard replied indifferently.

There was no point going in. Michael wandered around the building, peeped into nearby Chopin Park, and roamed the streets until he returned to the home of the synagogue treasurer.

The man's wife tried to comfort him. "My husband went to look for people who knew your father," she said. "He'll be back this evening." A few hours later, the treasurer did come home with an elderly man. He introduced Michael to him and the man hugged him emotionally.

"I remember you when you were little," he exclaimed. He said that he had survived Auschwitz and returned to Warsaw alone after his whole family had been killed there. He looked sad when he heard the bitter fate of Jacob Stolowitzky and his wife. "I was a clerk for your father's accountant," he told Michael.

"Father deposited enormous sums of money in banks in Switzerland. I was at one of them. They say they don't have any account in the name of Jacob Stolowitzky."

"The money has to be there," said the man. "I remember that every month money was transferred to your father's representative in Zurich who was supposed to deposit it in the bank."

"Do you remember who my father's representative was?" asked Michael hopefully.

The old man's eyes lit up.

"Of course," he said. "His name was Turner, Wolfgang Joachim Turner."

"Do you happen to know his address?"

"Unfortunately, no," replied the man.

The next day, Michael took the train back to Zurich.

3.

Finding his father's Swiss representative was easier than Michael had imagined. In the Zurich telephone book, there was only one Wolfgang Joachim Turner, with his profession—attorney—listed next to his name. Michael excitedly copied the address, in the heart of the city's business district.

He had no trouble finding the office building. A sign in the vestibule indicated that the office of attorney Turner was on the third floor. Michael took the elevator up and knocked on the door with Turner's name. There was no answer. For a long time he wandered around aimlessly in the empty corridor. He imagined that the attorney was away from the office at some legal discussion or meeting. He had nothing else to do, so he went on waiting.

The day passed and the attorney didn't appear. Michael wandered around the city aimlessly, went to bed early, and the next day he returned to the office of the lawyer who had represented his father.

The door was closed this time, too. Michael waited patiently.

In the afternoon, someone came out of the next room and looked at him inquisitively.

"Can I help you?" he asked.

"I'm looking for attorney Turner."

"I'm sorry," said the man. "Mr. Turner died a week ago."

Michael turned pale. He hadn't considered that possibility.

"On the fourth floor is an attorney who is taking care of Mr. Turner's cases," said the man. "You can go to him."

Michael knocked on the attorney's door. He told him briefly the reason that he had come to Zurich and asked if Turner had passed on his father's file to him.

"I have no idea," replied the attorney. "I suggest you talk to Turner's widow. Maybe she can help you."

4.

The big house with tiled roofs was on top of a hill overlooking the town of Thalwil on the western side of Lake Zurich. Sunbeams flooded the leaves of the apple trees in the yard, the cultivated flower beds, and the shining paved path leading to the door. The name Turner was on the door and Michael rang the bell.

An older woman, standing straight, her hair pulled back, opened the door. She wore a black dress and looked at him in wonder.

"Mrs. Turner?" asked Michael.

"That's me. Who are you?"

He told her and she stood still in the door for a long minute, stunned and speechless.

"Forgive me," she said when she caught her breath. "I thought you were . . ."

"No, I'm not dead." He read her mind.

"Thank God," she smiled. "Come in."

He followed her into the elegant living room. She sat him in a deep armchair and sat down next to him.

"We knew that your father was sent to Auschwitz and died there," she said. "We thought you had also been killed in the war."

Michael gave her a brief account of his life since they had fled from Warsaw. She nodded in sympathy.

"I knew your parents," she said. "They visited us a few times, two charming and wonderful people. Your father never talked about his money even though he was very rich. My husband wasn't only your father's attorney. He was also one of his good friends."

Michael told her about his attempt to get his inheritance and the difficulties involved.

"I know my husband handled your father's money," she said. "He transferred money to him whenever he needed it. Only your father and my husband knew the secret numbers of the bank accounts. I'll try to find out if my husband wrote them down somewhere."

She left the room and returned soon after with an overflowing file of documents labeled STOLOWITZKY.

"Everything should be here," she said.

She leafed through the documents slowly and carefully. Soon after, she pulled a notebook out of the file and showed it to her visitor.

"Here, in my husband's handwriting, are the sums your father deposited and the money my husband withdrew for him."

Michael looked at the writing. The numbers of the bank accounts weren't indicated in the notebook, but there was a precise list of the balance of cash and gold bullion with a net worth of twenty-four million dollars. In the values of the 1930s, when the money and the gold was deposited, that was considered a major fortune. In current exchange values and after the price of gold increased, the sum was much higher.

"Maybe there's an official bank document here that confirms the existence of the account?" he asked.

She searched but didn't find anything.

"I have to know the secret number," he said hopefully.

The woman leafed through the file again.

"Unfortunately, there's no trace of the numbers you're looking for," she said. "My husband was a very discreet man. He probably kept the numbers in his head."

"Did your husband leave more documents connected with my father's money?"

"Unfortunately, that's the only file. No files were left in the office either. I took everything home."

Michael wrung his hands nervously. "Did your husband mention the names of the bank officials who took care of the account?"

"Never."

"What shall I do?" Michael wondered.

She patted his head sympathetically.

"I don't think you can do anything. Maybe it's just better for you to forget the money."

5.

Michael was restless. He wandered around aimlessly all day and tossed and turned all night. He hoped his fears wouldn't come true and that instead, when he returned to the bank, the official would have good news for him. Maybe, by some miracle, a way would be found to transfer his father's money to him.

With much hesitation, Michael returned to Credit Bank. He still had no proof of his father's account. All his information was based on his mother's words on her deathbed and the testimony of the widow of his father's Swiss representative. He feared that neither of them would change the bank's firm position.

And it didn't.

The bank official looked uncomfortable when he saw Michael.

"You must understand that under these circumstances, I can't do much for you," he said.

"I understand. I thought I'd go to an attorney who would take this case."

He stood up and shook the bank official's hand. "Thank you anyway," he said.

The official looked at him sympathetically.

"I shouldn't be saying this," he whispered. "But I will tell you something that might help you."

Michael sat down again.

"You said you're Mr. Stolowitzky's only heir," said the official.

"Correct."

"Could your father have left other heirs?"

"To the best of my knowledge, all members of my father's family are dead."

"So," said the official, "something strange is happening here. We received another appeal about your father's legacy."

"I don't understand," muttered Michael, who was stunned.

"Just recently, a Swiss lawyer sent us a request to find out details about your father's account for a client of his. Since then, I've met with him a few times."

"Who is this man?"

"It's not a man, it's a woman, who claims that she deserves the legacy."

"Can't be . . ."

"Mr. Stolowitzky," said the official patiently. "All I can do for you is give you the address of the attorney who's representing that woman. If he's willing to give you details about his client, you can soon learn who she is."

6.

Michael rode the whole night on the crowded train from Zurich to Paris, racking his brain in a vain attempt to figure out who the woman could be. Her attorney did give him her address after getting her permission to do so, but added no details about her. Michael thought of all the relatives he knew and who might demand the money for themselves. He hadn't heard a thing about them since the war began and had every reason to assume that they were no longer alive. Nevertheless, a woman had popped up demanding his father's money for herself. He was curious to meet her and harbored a dull fear that, in the race for the money, she'd get there first and the whole thing would fall into her hands.

He walked from the railroad station to the address in the Sixteenth Arrondissement, filled with public parks. When he got there, he looked at the rich houses of the neighborhood, the liveried chauffeurs waiting at the entrances of the houses of well-to-do businessmen, the handsome women in silk suits seen through the big windows and balconies eating breakfast served by maids in white aprons. He imagined that, when he knocked on the door of the house of the woman he was looking for, a uniformed servant would open it and ask him to wait until he informed his mistress why the guest had come.

The house he came to was one of the most magnificent in the neighborhood. On the door was an unfamiliar name. He looked at the note on which the lawyer had written the address of the woman he was looking for. No. There was no mistake. This was the house.

He rang the bell and a servant dressed in black opened the door.

"I'm looking for Madame Anna Massini."

"Who are you?"

"I was sent by her attorney."

"Follow me," said the servant.

He led Michael to a small shed in the yard.

"Wait here," he said. "I'll get her."

Michael waited impatiently. He soon saw the servant walking

toward him with a thin woman in her mid-forties, wearing a white apron.

She looked inquisitively at Michael.

"I'm Anna Massini," she said. "How can I help you?"

"I'm the son of Jacob Stolowitzky," he said by way of introduction.

She looked at him a long time.

"My attorney told me you'd come, but I couldn't believe it. Your father was sure you had been killed in the war."

He gave her a brief account of what had happened to him.

"Come inside. This is where I live. We'll sit and talk."

She opened the door of the little shed and the two of them went inside.

"You must be hungry," she said. "I'll make you something to eat."

She went to the kitchen and returned with two cheese sandwiches. He ate them hungrily while she rummaged through the clothes closet, took out a worn envelope and a piece of paper from it.

"This is your father's will," she said.

Michael read the writing. The will said explicitly that if he was still alive, he would inherit his father's money and Anna Massini would get a monetary grant.

She smiled sadly at him.

"Your father talked about you a lot," she said. "He loved to tell about your life in Warsaw. When he concluded that your mother and you were dead, he mourned for a long time. Then, when the Germans were approaching France, we decided to get married and moved to my mother's house in Italy. I thought he would be safer there, but it didn't help. In the end, the Germans arrested him, and after that I didn't hear anything from him."

"I was a child when we parted, and I've missed him ever since."

She nodded.

"After the war," she continued, "I tried to search for your father. Months later, I finally found out his fate. Since I couldn't find work in Italy, I came back to Paris. Fortunately, I found work as a cook in the house of a rich businessman, where you find me now."

"In recent weeks," said Michael, "I've tried to collect my father's legacy but haven't been able to."

Michael stood up to go.

"Wait a moment." She pulled his hand to make him sit down. "We haven't finished yet."

He sat down and looked at her inquisitively.

"It's true that you should get your father's will," she said. "So I don't think it's decent for me to demand the inheritance for myself."

She suggested that Michael ask her lawyer to represent him from now on. "He's done a lot of work already," she said. "I hope he can help you."

Michael heard her words with excitement, amazed at her generosity.

"I can't agree," he said. "You spent a long time with my father. You helped him in his hardest hours. He loved you and I think you should get part of the inheritance."

"You're a stubborn kid," she laughed. "Go get the money. Then decide yourself if I deserve anything."

7.

Not until August 1964, six years after Michael Stolowitzky had started his struggle for his father's inheritance, did his lawyer manage to acquire a first sum. Only $148,000 for the factories in Poland and a factory confiscated by the Nazis in Germany. The mansion on

Ujazdowska Avenue was still owned by the Polish government, since all the documents of ownership had been burned when the Soviet Union bombed Warsaw. All attempts to realize the lion's share of the inheritance in various Swiss banks came to nothing.

The money went into Michael's bank account and he consulted with Gertruda about how to use it.

"It's your money," she said. "Do whatever you want with it."

He sent half the sum to Anna Massini in Paris and the next day Gertruda found the rest of the money in an envelope on her bed.

"What's this supposed to be?" she asked in amazement.

"You told me to do what I want with the money," he replied. "I want you to be able to spoil yourself a little, to buy whatever you want and couldn't allow yourself before, to take a trip, to work less."

She wept with emotion and that same day she announced that she had decided to give the money to her parents. Michael went with her to their house in Starogard. They found the old couple living in greater poverty than he had remembered. The two carried on with much difficulty, the mother in a wheelchair and the father leaning on a cane. Their condition grew worse from one day to the next. Their house needed many repairs. The roof leaked, the walls were peeling, and the plumbing was rotten. They were shocked when Gertruda gave them the money.

"My life is fine and I'm happy," their daughter told them. "I don't need this money."

Two days later, she returned to Israel with Michael.

"I've got a feeling I won't see my parents again in this world," she said.

From then to her dying day, she didn't leave Israel.

8.

When Gertruda and Michael returned to Israel, a letter from Paris was waiting for Michael:

Dear Michael,

I was very surprised to get the money. Thank you from the bottom of my heart for your beautiful gesture. I'm sorry you didn't get the whole inheritance, but who better than I knows there is no justice in this world. At the end of the month, I'll be forced to leave my job for health reasons and the money will help me take care of myself and live honorably. Your late father always treated me with decency and love and gave me encouragement. Now I've got a feeling that God sent you to me to prove to me that the apple doesn't fall far from the tree.

Yours in eternal friendship,
Anna

Life returned to normal. Michael found work in a big travel agency in Tel Aviv and rented a nicer and bigger apartment for him and Gertruda. She furnished it modestly and happily followed Michael's progress at work.

9.

In 1962, Yad Vashem granted Gertruda Babilinska the title of Righteous Gentile and after Michael married, she moved to Beit Lokner, a home for Righteous Gentiles in Nahariya.

"I'm an Israeli," she would say proudly. "This is my home. I don't have anything outside of Israel."

As an expert in tourism for pilgrims, Michael Stolowitzky had to move to the United States, but he came once a month to visit Gertruda. On those visits, it was he who brought her the chocolate she loved.

On March 1, 1995, when she was ninety-three years old, Gertruda fell ill and told Michael that she felt that her death was near. He sat at her bed in the hospital in Nahariya day and night. Her last words were: "Take care of yourself, my son. We'll see each other up there, in Heaven." She died with Lydia Stolowizky's wedding ring on her finger.

On Thursday, March 5, an elaborate funeral was prepared in the plot for the Righteous Gentiles in the cemetery at Kiryat Shaul. Representatives of Yad Vashem prepared speeches and Michael also asked to say a few words at the grave of the woman who had become his mother.

But the body was late. Embarrassed and tense, Michael phoned the ambulance driver who was supposed to bring it from the hospital and asked nervously: "Where's the body?" The driver was surprised at the question. "As far as I know, they already buried her," he replied.

Stunned, Michael phoned the hospital and discovered, after a brief explanation, that a family from Carmiel had come to the hospital the night before and identified Gertruda as their deceased relative. The body had been taken to the cemetery in Carmiel and buried during the night.

The chief rabbi of Carmiel refused to disinter the body, but after the family from Carmiel returned to the hospital and identified the correct body of their relative, he gave his permission. Gertruda's body was taken out of the grave and transported in a helicopter to the cemetery in Kiryat Shaul. The eulogy was delivered by Father Daniel Rufeisen, who was born in Poland as a Jew, hid in a monastery during the war, converted to Christianity, and settled in Israel. He said: "God wanted Gertruda Babilinska to be buried twice, once in a Jewish grave and once in a Christian grave. No other event could be more symbolic. Gertruda was both a devout Catholic and also a Jew. May her memory be blessed."

Gertruda was laid to rest a few minutes before sundown on the Sabbath.

10.

On Holocaust Memorial Day, 2004, Etti Bernson, the daughter-in-law of Elisheva, Karl Rink's daughter, took the stage. Elisheva, confined to a wheelchair, sat in the front of the auditorium and listened to the piece read by Etti from the book *In the Heart of Darkness*, which had recently been published by Yad Vashem. The book was written by Aryeh Segelson, a retired judge, who told of his uncle Moshe Segelson:

The German officer wanted to talk in his apartment, in Kovno. Something was clearly bothering him. "Mr. Segelson," he said, "ultimately, the war will end in a defeat for Germany. But we have no way back. We go on fighting to the end. You, Segelson, still have some chance to remain alive. I, unlike you, have no chance to be saved from this war. I won't surrender to the enemy and will continue fighting him on the battlefield until I die. And you, if you

remain alive, you must go to Palestine. My daughter is
there. Tell her everything you know about me, about my
decency to you and the other Jews in Kovno. Believe me
that I didn't harm the body of a Jew, not here and not in
other places. And who knows better than you that I even
saved Jews in hiding. Of course, as an SS man, I carried out
all the orders given to me and executed the policies toward
the Jews. But I personally didn't do anything bad to any Jew.
My opinion about the Jews is completely different from the
opinion of the Nazi party. I never saw the Jews as the
enemies of my homeland Germany. Tell all this to my
daughter. I want her to know that her father wasn't a
murderer and that she should remember him as a decent
man, even if he served in the SS.

A slight rustle went through the auditorium. The audience didn't understand why she had chosen to read that passage on the evening of the Memorial Day. Elisheva looked at her daughter-in-law with tears in her eyes.

"You must be wondering why I chose to read that passage," said Etti. "This passage had a deep meaning for the woman sitting here with us, Elisheva. Today, with her permission, I can reveal at long last that the SS officer mentioned here is Karl Rink, her father."

Michael (Mike) Stolowitzky, an energetic bon vivant, lives in New York and stays in close touch with hundreds of friends in Israel. He is married to Beatrice and has a son. Mike is active in world travel and was a recipient of the prestigious World Tourism Award in London in 2007. In the plot for Righteous Gentiles in the Kiryat Shaul cemetery, he erected an impressive monument designed by an architect, and a few times a year he visits Gertruda's grave. On his visits, he tends to sit at the grave and tell her all that is happening in his life.

Elisheva (Helga) Rink, who lived in Kfar Giladi until her death, had two sons and twin daughters. Moshe Segelson moved to Israel in 1946 and soon visited her. She was moved to tears when she heard his stories about her father. Elisheva died in September 2006 and left her body to science.

Pastor John Grauel returned to the United States and settled in a small town in New Jersey. He often visited Israel. He died in 2003 and was buried in Jerusalem.

Captain Isaac (Ike) Aaronovitch established a shipping company. He is retired and lives in Zikhron Ya'akov.

Yossi Hamburger (Harel), commander of the *Exodus,* went into private worldwide business in 1950. He lived in Tel Aviv and died in 2008 at the age of ninety.

The *Exodus* was towed to an abandoned pier in Haifa by the British. After the establishment of the State, preparations were begun to turn the ship into a museum, but an electrical short set fire to the ship, which was destroyed within a few hours.

BIBLIOGRAPHY

Arad, Yitzhak. *Jewish Vilna in Struggle and Destruction* (Vilna HaYehudit BeMa'abak Vebehilion). Tel Aviv: Yad Vashem Publications, Tel Aviv University, Sifriyat Hapoalim, 1976.

Drujie, Jack. *Exodus in New Light* (Parashat Exodus Be'Or Hadash). Tel Aviv: Am Oved, 1971.

Gruel, John Stanley. *Gruel*. New Jersey: Ivory House, 1983.

Halamish, Aviva. *Exodus*. Tel Aviv: Am Oved, 1990.

Kalmanovitch, Zalman. *Diary in the Vilna Ghetto* (Yoman BeGhetto Vilna). Tel Aviv: Sifriyat Hapoalim, 1977.

Kaniuk, Yoram. *Exodus: Captain's Odyssey* (Exodus: Odesia Shel Mefaked). Tel Aviv: Publication of Kibbutz Hameochad and Daniella Dee-Nur, 1999.

Keren, Nili, editor. *Looking for a Person* (Lehapes Ben Adam). Masuot Publications, 2004.

Lezer, Chayim. *Destruction and Uprising,* (Hurban VeMered). Masuot Publications, 1950.

Lonski, Chaykel. *From the Vilna Ghetto—Characters and Images* (Mehaghetto Havilnai—Tipusim VeTslilim). Published by the Society of Jewish Writers and Hebrew Journalists in Vilna, 1921.

Reindjenski, Alexander. *Destruction of Vilna* (Hurban Vilna). Tel Aviv: Publication of Beyt Lohamei Hagetaot and Kibbutz Hameuchad, 1987.

Rudashevski, Yitzhak. *Diary of a Young Man from Vilna* (Yomano Shel Na'ar MeVilna). Tel Aviv: Publication of Beyt Lohamei Hagetaot and Kibbutz Hameuchad, 1969.

Segelson, Aryeh. *In the Heart of the Darkness* (BeLev HaOphel). Jerusalem: Yad Vashem Publications, 2002.

Tayler, Alan. *Cheerful and Contented.* Sussex, England: The Book Guild, 2000.

Trubovitch, Yitzhak. *The Story of My Life* (Toldot Hayai). Private publication, 1987.